Skills in
PERSON-CENTRED
Counselling & Psychotherapy

Series Editor
Francesca Inskipp

Skills in Counselling & Psychotherapy is a series of practical guides for trainees and practitioners. Each book takes one of the main approaches to therapeutic work and describes the core skills and techniques used within that approach.

Topics covered include

- how to establish and develop the therapeutic relationship
- how to help the client change
- how to assess the suitability of the approach for the client.

This is the first series of books to look at skills specific to the different theoretical approaches, making it ideal for use on a range of courses which prepare the trainees to work directly with clients.

Books in the series:

Skills in Transactional Analysis Counselling & Psychotherapy
Christine Lister-Ford

Skills in Person-Centred Counselling & Psychotherapy
Janet Tolan

Skills in Cognitive-Behavioural Counselling & Psychotherapy
Frank Wills

Skills in Rational Emotive Behaviour Counselling & Psychotherapy
Windy Dryden

Skills in Psychodynamic Counselling & Psychotherapy
Susan Howard

Skills in Gestalt Counselling & Psychotherapy, Second Edition
Phil Joyce & Charlotte Sills

Skills in Existential Counselling & Psychotherapy
Emmy van Deurzen & Martin Adams

Skills in Solution Focused Brief Counselling & Psychotherapy
Paul Hanton

Skills *in*

PERSON–CENTRED
Counselling & Psychotherapy

Second Edition

Janet Tolan

Los Angeles | London | New Delhi
Singapore | Washington DC

First edition published 2003. Reprinted 2003, 2004, 2005, 2006,
2007 (twice), 2009, 2010 (twice)
This second edition published 2012
Reprinted 2012

SAGE Publications Ltd
1 Oliver's Yard
55 City Road
London EC1Y 1SP

SAGE Publications Inc.
2455 Teller Road
Thousand Oaks, California 91320

SAGE Publications India Pvt Ltd
B 1/I 1 Mohan Cooperative Industrial Area
Mathura Road
New Delhi 110 044

SAGE Publications Asia-Pacific Pte Ltd
3 Church Street
#10-04 Samsung Hub
Singapore 049483

Library of Congress Control Number: 2011930193

British Library Cataloguing in Publication data

A catalogue record for this book is available from the British Library

ISBN 978-1-84860-094-2
ISBN 978-1-84860-095-9 (pbk)

Typeset by C&M Digitals (P) Ltd, Chennai, India
Printed and bound in Great Britain by the MPG Books Group
Printed on paper from sustainable resources

CONTENTS

LIST OF FIGURES AND TABLES

FIGURES

TABLES

ABOUT THE AUTHOR

Janet Tolan has worked in counselling and psychotherapy since 1979, as a volunteer, as a full time counsellor, as leader of Counselling courses at City College, Manchester and as head of the Masters Programme at Liverpool John Moores University. She has also worked in Management Development and Team Development for organisations as diverse as Manchester Airport and Salford Social Services. She now has a small private practice, working with individuals, couples, groups and teams – and also enjoys dancing salsa and singing jazz.

PREFACE TO THE FIRST EDITION

It may seem rather anomalous that a book about person-centred therapy, which is so founded upon relationships, should have 'skills' in the title. I hope that it will quickly become clear to the reader that this book is not a collection of 'techniques', but one which tries to illustrate the liveliness and immediacy of person-centred practice. The intention is not to be prescriptive, but to exemplify some of the possibilities. I can show my brush strokes, but I cannot create anyone else's work of art!

There are many excellent books on person-centred counselling, and useful examples of practice are given in such texts to illustrate the theory. My aim in this book is rather the other way around. I have tried first and foremost to show the practice – to bring person-centred therapy to life. My hope is that I have captured something of the 'flavour' of the person-centred approach for readers coming new to this orientation and for those studying it. I also hope that more experienced counsellors will find material which will be of interest to them in extending their practice.

I am delighted to include contributions from Rose Cameron, who has been in the vanguard of work on psychological contact, and Alan Brice, whose account of his work with a client who lied to him is both moving and inspiring. There are, of course, many other authors and practitioners who have influenced me over the past 20 years. I have assimilated and incorporated their teachings to the extent that I am not always aware of what I have gleaned from whom. The same is true of students, who have sometimes come up with a wonderfully effective phrase or description. I know that I have 'borrowed' these at times, but I no longer remember their origins. So I wish to apologise to anyone whom I have not credited properly.

I have used the terms 'counselling' and 'psychotherapy' interchangeably because I can see no meaningful distinction between them. I have also used 'he' and 'she' somewhat randomly when talking about people in general, but have tended to use 'she' for the counsellor role and 'he' for clients and supervisors.

It seems almost a cliché to acknowledge my debt to clients, students and colleagues, past and present. Nevertheless the debt is real and my thanks are heartfelt, especially to those who encouraged me in writing this book, read my drafts and made helpful suggestions. In particular, the 'Thursday group' encouraged me to believe that I could write this book in the first place and several members of the

CCTPCA network gave me positive feedback on an early chapter. Francesca Inskipp and Alison Poyner, the series and Sage editors respectively, have been endlessly patient with me. Dave Mearns's suggestions re-energised me and Jill Jones has been a constant source of support.

PREFACE TO THE SECOND EDITION

It has given me great pleasure – and some wonderment – that so many people have found this book useful. I do not find writing easy and I marvel at colleagues who can say 'I will write for three hours tomorrow' – and then do! When Francesca Inskipp asked me to produce a proposal for the book showing the structure and chapter headings, I was slightly panicked. I protested that it was like being pregnant – I knew that there was a book inside me, but I had no idea what it would look like when it came out. Thanks to the patience of Francesca and the support of many, many other colleagues, students and friends, come out it did.

And here is the second edition! The basic text remains, with some updating and revised references. There are also two new chapters, 'Debates and Developments in Practice' by Rose Cameron and the other, 'Edgy and Ethical Issues', a collaboration between the two of us. Rose's overview is an amazingly comprehensive and readable account of the whole person-centred and experiential field. Our joint chapter looks at some of the ethical and edgy issues that all therapists will encounter at some point in their professional lives. I hope that you will find this new edition a worthwhile and informative read.

1

THE THEORETICAL FRAMEWORK

THE IMPORTANCE OF THEORY

Person-centred theory is simple, elegant and universal. Just as an appreciation of atoms gives rise to an understanding of the whole of the physical world, so can an appreciation of person-centred theory give rise to an understanding of the complexity and richness of human experience.

People can come to counselling in extremes of psychological pain or experiencing strange thoughts and behaviours. If we are not to be frightened or overwhelmed, we need to have an understanding of *why* they are in such a state and *what we can do* to be of use. When we listen to the sheer awfulness of another person's life, it is human to feel inadequate. 'How can I, in one session a week, hope to make a difference in the face of such suffering?' One possible response is to remove ourselves a little – to disguise those feelings of inadequacy behind an elaborate analysis of the causes of the pain rather than allow ourselves to hear the suffering. Another is to rush into 'helping' – offering suggestions and solving problems in an attempt to make the other person's life easier. Both of these responses help us to cope with the person, and with our own inadequacy, while distancing ourselves from his misery.

And yet ... What is the *point* of someone expressing such agony? Won't it do more harm than good? Surely it's better to help a person to get on with his life rather than wallow in misery? He's feeling worse now than when he first came to see me. Person-centred therapy isn't working – I'd better try something else.

Without theory, how can we have any confidence in our way of working? Unless we have a hypothesis about what is happening and why, we will tend to fall into our own insecurities when the going gets tough. Theory is the map which guides us through territory which is alien and can feel dangerous. It helps us to stick to the path, however rocky, instead of panicking and running into the woods.

WHAT IS THEORY?

For us to work effectively with others, we need a set of assumptions or hypotheses which answer the following questions:

1 What do we mean by 'person' and 'personality'?

2 How do we understand the way people develop?

3 What do we consider to be 'normal', 'healthy' or 'adjusted'?

4 What do we consider to be 'abnormal', 'unhealthy' or 'maladjusted' and how do these states arise?

5 How can people move from 4 to 3?

6 How can others best assist in this process?

The person-centred hypotheses are as follows:

WHAT DO WE MEAN BY 'PERSON' AND 'PERSONALITY'?

An individual's personality has two components: *experience* and *self-structure*. An individual's experience is the information which comes through her five senses and from internal feelings (visceral experiences). The self-structure grows as the child learns to name and organise her experience – to symbolise it in awareness. It becomes her way of understanding the world and it enables her to 'fit in' to family, society and culture in order to be valued and loved.

Person-centred theory gives us a model in which the person is always striving to integrate her own organismic experience of the world with her own self-structure. When the two are at odds with each other, the person experiences uncomfortable, or even painful, emotions and it is this discomfort or pain which might bring someone into counselling.

HOW DO WE UNDERSTAND THE WAY PEOPLE DEVELOP?

Self-experiencing, sometimes called organismic experiencing, is simply that: the capacity of the organism to experience. We see, we hear, we touch, we smell, we taste, we sense our own inner sadness or happiness, anger or calm. This experiencing is essentially neutral – neither healthy nor unhealthy, neither good nor bad. It simply *is*. Without the self-structure, we would not be able to construe any of this experience or give it meaning.

In order to recognise and then name something, we need a framework and familiarity. With everyday objects, colours and so on, adults are likely to name them for the young

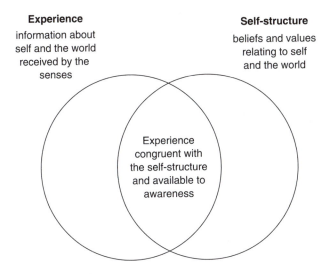

Experience

information about
self and the world
received by the
senses

Self-structure

beliefs and values
relating to self
and the world

Experience
congruent with
the self-structure
and available to
awareness

FIGURE 1.1   The Total Personality

child without distortion and without judgement. It seems natural to most parents to engage in repetition and emphasis with babies: 'Mummy', 'nose', 'spoon', 'cup', 'red', 'doggy' …

Along with some words will come other, underlying, meanings in which emotions are communicated, for example, 'No' (disapproval), 'Dirty' (disgust), 'Clever' (delight). Thereafter 'dirty' might be something to avoid. The self-experience of revelling in the oozy coolness of mud will be distorted. 'Clever' might always be a matter of pride or envy. The sense of superiority which sometimes goes along with it might not be recognised.

The self-structure is everything that a person holds about herself and about the world. Some beliefs are built through her own experiences. Others are based on the prior beliefs of her family. (Family in this sense meaning the group, or groups, of people concerned with her upbringing.)

It is as though parts of the self-structure are 'handed down' within families and cultures. *If you don't subscribe to this view of the world, you're not one of us!* The more we have to strive to be accepted, the more we cling to these 'handed down' views, even when our own experience tells us something different. Take, for example, a member of a social grouping which holds a prejudice in common: 'black people are …'. 'But', an outsider says in surprise, 'what about your friend Quibilah?' 'Oh', replies the group member, 'she's *different* – she's such-and-such, is Quibilah, not like the rest at all!'

How much experience of black people would it take to revise this person's self-structure? The answer is that experience alone will never suffice. That person's *acceptability*, often at some deep level, depends upon his believing that black people are … . If he were to move into another grouping which held a contrary view, he might, in time, amend his self-structure in order to become acceptable in the new group. But only when he felt himself to be accepted *despite* his opinions and prejudices would he truly be able to evaluate his experiences for himself and change his self-structure accordingly.

The self-structure is initially formed according to the values and injunctions of parents and other carers. *Conditions of worth* are transmitted to the child, who learns that s/he is acceptable or lovable if s/he behaves, thinks and feels in certain ways. The development of the self-structure usually entails building in such ideas about self and about the world as though they were absolute truths rather than opinions or points of view. These are known as *introjected values*.

EXAMPLES

- I'm no good at maths.
- Men don't cry.
- Gay men are effeminate.
- I'm a high achiever.

The need to be valued and loved is overriding, so the development and maintenance of the self-structure is important. Experience that conflicts with the self-structure will be distorted or denied.

EXAMPLES

- Experience: I do a sum correctly;
  Distortion: It must be a fluke. (I'm no good at maths.)
- Experience: I'm upset and I'm getting choked up;
  Distortion: It's getting stuffy in here. (Men don't cry.)
- Experience: I didn't realise Winston was gay. He seems normal;
  Distortion: He's different from the rest. (Gay men are effeminate.)
- Experience: I'm not getting this right;
  Distortion: They haven't given me enough information. (I'm a high achiever.)

WHAT DO WE CONSIDER TO BE 'NORMAL', 'HEALTHY', 'ADJUSTED' OR 'MATURE'?

The self-structure does a valuable job in a number of respects, particularly in that it enables us to make predictions. Although it is not in our awareness, we can usually anticipate correctly that the ground beneath our feet will be solid and that water will move about. We can also predict how the people around us will react if we talk or behave in certain ways.

As individuals, we are flexible where there is no conflict between our experiences and self-structure. We can predict or recognise what is acceptable to us and to others and make choices without distorting or denying our experience. We can change our judgements and values according to *our own* experience.

Also, the more someone is able to integrate her own experiences into her self-structure – in other words, the more self-accepting she becomes – the more she is able to understand and accept others.

WHAT DO WE CONSIDER TO BE 'ABNORMAL', 'UNHEALTHY' OR 'MALADJUSTED' AND HOW DO THESE STATES ARISE?

We all need a degree of predictability. The world is only a safe place when we can be reasonably sure of 'what will happen if . . .'. The self-structure gives us that safety – but at a price. The price is that we shut out experiences which do not 'fit'. None of us can hold the totality of our experience, past and present, in awareness and we are all prone to distort or deny aspects of experience. I have argued elsewhere (Tolan, 2002) that one of the purposes of the self-structure is to keep out of awareness experience which does not have a bearing on our ability to function well in our own society and culture. But some of our out-of-awareness experiences can come to hinder our ability to make choices and to fulfil our potentialities.

If we are not aware of important areas of our own experience, we cannot make flexible choices based upon balancing our own and others' needs. People often judge themselves according to whether others find them acceptable or wanting. Their *locus of evaluation* is outside of themselves. Even when someone is making her own judgements, these can be based on a system of values built into the self-structure which are not influenced by experience (*introjected values*).

EXERCISE

In the second part of each of the examples below, what might be the introjected values which are leading to denial or distortion of experience?

I'm so happy, I want to sing and dance. But since I'm in church and it would be seen as disrespectful for me to give way to my impulse, I'll wait.
One should concentrate on prayer when one is in church.

What an unfair thing to say in front of other people! I think I'm going to cry. But I don't want to get a reputation for weakness. I'll go out of the room now and then tackle it with him later, when there's just the two of us.
Remarks like that are beneath me. Sticks and stones ...

(Continued)

(Continued)

I still miss my mother. This morning, when I saw the first snowdrops, I just sat for a while and thought of her and cried.

I've always been a strong person with plenty of interests. I find that keeping active stops you from dwelling on the past.

I'm dissatisfied with my job. My parents will be very distressed and angry when I tell them, but I'm going to retrain as an artist.

I'd love to get away for a proper holiday this year. But my patients need me to be there for them. I can't afford to get depressed. Anyway, what do I have to be depressed about? I earn three times as much as my Dad. And Mum's so proud of me being a doctor ...

HOW CAN PEOPLE CHANGE?

There is a drive within every individual towards accepting important experiences into the self-structure, and therefore into awareness, which is called the *actualising tendency*. Where the rigidity of the self-structure prevents this, a person will experience uncomfortable feelings and emotions. As with physical discomfort and pain, the purpose is to alert the individual that something needs attention. It is for this reason that feelings are important in person-centred therapy.

The self-structure, however, is there for a good reason. For example, it may have been crucial to the child to be quiet and compliant in order for her to receive love or acceptance. So it would be threatening for her to acknowledge her own experiences of rebelliousness. If she does distort or deny her rebellious feelings to maintain her self-structure, she will become anxious.

However, the individual's environment changes. The *I am a quiet, compliant person* part of her self-structure may now be preventing her from achieving her full potential. It may even be preventing her from receiving the love and valuing from others that at one time it ensured from her parents.

So the actualising tendency is now working through her uncomfortable, dissatisfied feelings – prompting her to acknowledge the rebelliousness of her self-experience, urging her to change the status quo and become more assertive.

But losing the love and valuing which has previously been conditional upon her being quiet and compliant is a frightening prospect. The self-structure may be so rigid that, to begin with, it distorts the uncomfortable feelings which are prompting change. *I need to get a new job/move house/get married ... then I will be happy.*

The actualising tendency is not so easily sidelined though, and the feelings will become stronger and stronger. This can give rise to considerable emotional pain, coupled with the anxiety of a self-structure under threat.

How can such a tension be resolved? If the self-structure is threatened from outside, it will simply become more rigid.

EXERCISE (GROUPS OF THREE OR FOUR)

Each member of the group thinks of one of their own conditions of worth. One member tells the others about this aspect of themselves and the others try to convince her/him to change it. S/he may stop the exercise as soon as s/he wishes. Repeat for all members of the group.

Notice how open you are to the others' arguments or how defensive you become. In particular, notice your feelings in both roles and discuss them at the end of the exercise.

If you found yourself growing tense, feeling uncomfortable, anxious or attacked, consider the fact that you were sufficiently aware of your condition of worth *knowingly* to have chosen it. The strongest conditions of worth are those which are not available to such awareness. They are experienced as reality or truth. Others who do not perceive the truth are misguided or obstinate. Such 'truths' are defended with passion because they are part of the self-structure. They are not amenable to logic.

HOW CAN OTHERS BEST ASSIST IN THE PROCESS OF CHANGE?

So is the actualising tendency fighting a losing battle against the self-structure? If such were the case, no one would ever change. What enables one person to adapt their self-structure where another clings to it?

Remember that a central purpose of the self-structure is to enable the individual to 'fit in' and receive acceptance, love and respect. If that individual is accepted and valued by others around her, the self-structure is doing its job. But conditions of worth may still be in force. A workplace, for example, has its own culture and values which can either reinforce or challenge the self-structure. New conditions of worth can be imposed. *We value people who . . . work long hours, vote right-wing, go to the pub at lunchtime* and so on.

There are, clearly, degrees of acceptance. The more someone is accepted for their whole self and not just if they fit another person's ideas of what is appropriate, the less threatened will be their self-structure. If the self-structure is not under threat, experience is less likely to be distorted or denied.

So the task of the person-centred therapist is to provide an environment characterised by a lack of threat to the self-structure. In such an environment, a client will be able, gradually, to recognise and name experiences which they have denied to awareness and their self-structure will change accordingly.

MORE ABOUT THE SELF-STRUCTURE

Carl Rogers writes that there is 'no sharp limit between the experience of the self and of the outside world' (Rogers, 1951: 497). In this book, I am using the term self-structure to encompass both the self-concept and a person's beliefs about the world and other people in general. So the self-structure includes the individual's unique *map of the world* (including assumptions and expectations of others) as well as their self-concept.

There is, of course, a connection between the self-structure as the whole and the self-concept as a part of the whole. The general belief, *There is a God,* is usually allied with, *I believe in God.* The general belief, *Homosexuality is unnatural,* is usually allied with, *I am a heterosexual.* But such beliefs have a bearing not only upon the self-concept, but upon the individual's view of other people. Strongly held convictions can be perceived as self-evident 'truth'. The person who *knows* that there is a God will see non-believers as misguided or deluded or even wicked. This kind of construing of reality seems to go beyond the individual's view of self and the term *self-concept.* It is, however, an important aspect of personality.

Similarly, a woman who holds the view that *men should not cry* is likely to feel uncomfortable and embarrassed in the presence of a tearful man. Such a belief will probably also affect the way she brings up her children. And yet it is not a belief directly about herself, so it makes more everyday sense to describe it as a component of her self-structure rather than her self-concept.

That an individual's *world view* is a part of her self-structure is borne out by how threatened she can become if this is challenged, and how she is able to distort and deny information which conflicts with it. Someone whose belief in racial superiority is based upon introjected values will defend that view in the face of mountainous evidence to the contrary. Employing logic or reason will be ineffectual since any challenge is a threat to the self-structure and will give rise to an emotional reaction.

It is for these reasons that the term *self-concept* is used in this book only when referring to the person's beliefs about himself. *Self-structure* is used to encompass people's world view as well as their view of themselves as an individual.

NECESSARY AND SUFFICIENT

In 1957, Rogers wrote about the conditions which he and his colleagues had identified as providing the non-threatening climate in which people could begin to acknowledge and integrate those experiences which had been held out of awareness. This was a radical departure from traditional psychotherapeutic practice in that it placed more emphasis on the *qualities* or *attitudes* of the counsellor rather than specifying what the counsellor must do. In 1959, he presented the following as necessary and sufficient conditions for therapeutic change:

1 Two persons are in contact.

2 The first person, whom we shall term the client, is in a state of incongruence, being vulnerable or anxious.

3 The second person, whom we shall term the therapist, is congruent in the relationship.

4 The therapist is experiencing unconditional positive regard for the client.

5 The therapist is experiencing an empathic understanding of the client's internal frame of reference.

6 The client perceives at least to a minimal degree conditions 4 and 5, the unconditional positive regard of the therapist for him and the empathic understanding of the therapist. (Rogers, 1959)

THE THERAPEUTIC CONDITIONS

The importance of the therapeutic conditions cannot be understood without an understanding of the person-centred model of development and change. Although practitioners of many other counselling schools now believe that empathy, congruence and acceptance are important, they are often unaware that there are six conditions, not solely three (the so-called 'core' conditions), and do not believe them to be *sufficient* to bring about change. Why do we?

The simple answer is the *actualising tendency*. If your hypothesis is that people have such an inbuilt motivation to change, then your task is to help it to do its work. If your basic assumption is different, then you begin to diagnose what is 'wrong' and formulate plans to teach or show a client how to achieve change.

Person-centred theorists often use the analogy of a plant to describe their concept of growth and change. No one can *make* a plant grow. But if someone provides the right conditions — soil, nutrients, light, water — it will become the best plant it can be. No one can alter the genetic material of the plant, so no amount of effort will change a rose into a poppy. All you can do is surround it by what it needs and watch it bloom.

The actualising tendency strives to achieve harmony between experiencing and self-structure so that we can both be ourselves *and* live in the world. When the two are out of balance, we experience distress, pain, discomfort, anger — the organismic 'voices' which motivate us to change.

In person-centred therapy, we seek to create a climate in which the actualising tendency can work more effectively to achieve that harmony. We are not in the business of changing or jettisoning someone else's self-structure. They still have to live in *their* world, not in ours. We listen to the self-experiencing 'voices', but we also listen to the voice of the self-structure. We hear and respond to the struggle of someone who wants to find a more satisfying way of living, but is afraid of alienating and losing friends and family. That fear is a real fear, although we cannot know whether it is based upon a true or a false prediction.

> **EXAMPLE**
>
> People don't like me.
>
> This belief probably has two components. One is the introjected values of parents or other childhood care-givers. The other is the accurate experience of the organismic self.
>
> The baby has no expectation of being liked or loved, but learns from his care-givers lessons like *I am a nuisance, I am naughty, I can't do things right,* and so on, which become introjects. When he encounters others, he shrinks from contact, having learned not to expect that he will be accepted. They, too, find him 'difficult' – a closed, surly child. At this point, his accurate, organismic experiencing is added to the introjects. By the time he reaches adulthood, the *people don't like me* element of his self-structure is based upon both introjected values *and* experience.

Person-centred theory tells us that any attempt on the part of the counsellor actively to change a client's self-structure, whether through reasoning or persuasion, subtly or overtly (*Oh, but you're a really nice person* ... or *If only you would let people get to know you* ... or *Why don't you try* ...), will be threatening to the self-structure and will cause anxiety. However well-intentioned, such attempts only add to a client's sense of not being good enough. The self-structure has two basic ways of dealing with the threat. One is to refuse to comply – *That wouldn't work because* ... *I tried that and* ... *This counselling isn't working* ... *You are a bad counsellor* ... . The other is to comply and fail – *I did what you said but* ... *When it came down to it, I couldn't* ... *I tried my best, but* ... *I'm just a hopeless case, you're wasting your time with me* ... .

Encountering the world in a new way is a real risk. Person-centred counsellors know this and they accept *the whole person*. When a client is expressing a desperate wish or longing to change, the counsellor is also accepting of the client's (perhaps unspoken) need for the safety of staying with what he knows. When a client is bewailing the terrible relationship he is in, the counsellor is also accepting of his (perhaps unspoken) reasons for staying in that relationship.

It is all too easy, when a client is continually saying that he wants to change his job, or leave an unsatisfactory relationship, or take up playing a musical instrument, to find yourself getting impatient and mentally shrieking, '*Well, why don't you get on with it!*' The question is a good one. Take away the impatience and substitute unconditional positive regard and the mental question becomes more like, '*I wonder what your good reasons are for not making the change yet?*

Personality change is a slow process. It is not usually a single substantial moment of discovery or enlightenment, but is a series of small adjustments – minor ripples which spread gradually to affect a person's way of being. The counsellor's task is not one of actively making, or even suggesting, changes for a client, but one of creating a climate in which a client can come to know and accept himself:

> I (as a counsellor) am here as another, flawed, human being, willing to encounter you with honesty and openness (psychological contact and congruence). I understand that you are unhappy and want to change the way you are (empathy). I also believe that, fundamentally, you are okay, that you have understandable reasons for the way you are and that you will make changes when you are ready to take that risk (unconditional positive regard).

SYMBOLISATION IN AWARENESS

When something is accurately symbolised in our awareness, we know it fully. We can see it in our mind's eye and name it in words. It is not a vague and shadowy thing, associated with feelings of dread or fear. Nor is it a chocolate-box picture, false and bright.

If we experience something that is not accurately symbolised in awareness, it seems to linger somewhere in us, awaiting a time when we are ready to re-experience it and integrate it properly into our self-structure. In the process of re-experiencing and re-symbolising, our self-structure alters to accommodate the now-accurate symbolisation. This is something that happens over time if the core conditions are present.

The changes which occur through counselling are usually subtle and gradual as the self-structure loosens to accommodate experience which was previously denied or distorted. As this loosening takes place, the experience becomes more accurately available to awareness. The example below shows how, over several weeks, the process might happen.

EXAMPLE

My childhood was a happy one. My parents loved me and wanted the best for me.

I remember being forced to do homework for long hours when my friends were playing in the sunshine.

Of course. They were right, weren't they? I did well in my exams and now I have a good job.

They never listened to what *I* wanted. I have a picture of myself pleading to be allowed to go to the youth club with all the others.

They did it because they wanted me to do well. The youth club was unimportant.

But at the time, it was crucial. I sobbed in my room for hours. I told my friends that I had to do my homework, but I could see they thought me a swot. I was always an outsider, wearing the wrong things because I could never get my mother to buy me proper clothes for a teenager. I looked too young and I didn't have the same experiences as the others. As I'm telling you this, I'm feeling the loneliness and exclusion – of not fitting in.

I have had a lot of advantages, though. I earn much more than I could have done if I had frittered away my teenage years on discos and cinemas. I'm very well respected in my field.

I'm still an outsider. Colleagues chat and laugh with each other and I feel excluded – on the edges of the comradeship. They think I'm too uptight.

I do my job well. I don't see why I can't get promotion just because I didn't watch what everyone else watched on telly last night. It's rubbish, that programme, anyway.

I don't understand what they're laughing about. I wish I knew how to be accepted. I've never felt really accepted.

Mother and father loved me. They're proud of me.

They didn't understand me. They didn't accept me. They didn't want to know how much it hurt me not to have real friends. Friends I could invite into the house, like other kids did.

I know they were right, in one sense. They wanted the best for me

I still ache inside when I think of the other kids going off to the youth club without me. I was so pleased when they asked me to go with them. So excited.

My parents knew that the key to financial security was exams and University. They never had that. They scrimped and saved all their lives for us. They still give me things now even though I'm far better off than they'll ever be.

There's still something missing from my life. I don't know how to make friends. I feel awkward with other people – always on my guard, in case I say the wrong thing. I put on a good show, but inside I'm always miserable.

My parents did their best for me. but they didn't realise how lonely I was. I'm just beginning to understand it myself.

It is as though an important experience that is not symbolised accurately gets locked somewhere in ourselves, awaiting the moment when it can be freed. Like a caged bird under a cloth, it can be ignored for long periods of time, but from time to time it flutters and squawks in protest. It cannot fly away until the cover is lifted, and this involves seeing, touching, hearing it once more. What was dismissed as a dove, may in reality be an albatross. What was once seen as a vulture may turn out to be a wren. The important thing is that the bird is acknowledged for what it actually is.

Sometimes, a person will have no concept or framework within which to place their experiences. The cry 'I don't know what's happening to me' often occurs when there is no means to symbolise the experience.

EXAMPLE

I am a college student working in my holidays. My boss, a man in his for-ties, seems to take every opportunity to get physically close to me. He makes flattering and very specific comments about my body.

I am uneasy but I do not acknowledge this. My self-structure bids me to be polite to my elders and deferential to people in authority.

I do not recognise my unease for what it is. Instead I experience a feeling of nervousness and embarrassment: I feel silly because I do not know the correct way to behave.

I have no known framework for this situation. I am trying hard to fit it into the patterns of older people complimenting me on my looks or my ability; It does not fit into my known experience of flirting (at which I am not very skilled anyway) because the man is not in the right age range.

I cannot name what is happening. It is easier to act as though it has not happened and put it down to my own inadequacy. I don't tell anyone else because I am afraid of looking foolish.

I read an article in a magazine about sexual harassment. I am overjoyed. My discomfort has been validated and I now feel able to trust it and to explain what is happening to me. I have words and a concept that empower me.

A similar thing happens in therapy when the counsellor accepts and tries to find words for the client's experience. Naming it through empathy is very empowering: *This* did *happen to me. I did feel distressed. It* was *frightening.*

Some experiences are never named in some families, for example, a family which does not accept angry feelings might say to the child: *Don't be naughty, You're over-tired* or *You're not yourself at the moment, dear – go and lie down.* A client whose experience has never been named might describe himself as having 'this awful feeling inside of me'. When the counsellor, in empathy, names it as 'anger' – or 'sadness' or 'loneliness' – the client can begin to symbolise it more accurately in his awareness.

ACCEPTANCE OF OTHERS

Person-centred counselling has often been criticised for its 'unrealistic' belief that people are essentially 'good'. This is a misunderstanding of the theory.

People undoubtedly do harmful things to themselves and others. We would see this kind of behaviour as arising from distortion and denial of self-experiencing. It is an attempt on the part of the individual to meet his own, very real, needs. But because he is not able to experience his needs accurately, the person cannot attempt to meet them in a straightforward way.

Our hypothesis suggests that the more congruent a person is, the more accepting of others he can be. Why should this be?

Congruence is the capacity to admit organismic experiencing fully into awareness, without the need for distortion or denial. Experiencing involves taking in information through the five senses and also being aware of internal, or visceral, information. What we then make of the information depends upon our self-structure.

The information available to us is the whole of our world, known as our phenomenal field. It includes all the other people with whom we have contact, whether brief or prolonged. We have seen how we can distort and deny experiences to preserve the self-structure. How does this apply to our experiences of other people?

CASE EXAMPLE: DARAIUS

Daraius grew up in a household whose membership was ever-changing. His father and, later, his brothers were often away working on construction sites, his mother periodically in residential mental health care. His elder siblings resented having to look after him.

A strong element of Daraius's self-structure is a distortion of distress, in himself and in others. In his world, showing distress is weakness and causing or prolonging distress in others is pleasurable because it attracts respect, albeit in the form of fear. This is the only form of acceptance and status which Daraius had in his young life, and the only form he now recognises.

Daraius is now an adult. He sneers at distress in others and enjoys the sense of power that other people's fear gives him. His organism's yearning for close and intimate relationships is denied to his awareness and his need for acceptance is distorted so that frightened respect will, in part and fleetingly, satisfy it.

Daraius threatens serious harm to another person. If he were to experience her with the congruent part of himself, he would be fully aware of her terror, her pain and her distress. All of this would be received by Daraius, through his senses, as his experiencing of the woman he threatens to harm.

Discussion

The question, therefore, is: *Could he harm her?* Is it possible for a congruent human being to cause needless pain to another? Or must that human being deny or distort his organismic experiencing – be less aware or unaware of the true feelings of the other – in order to do harm?

The drive towards symbolisation seems to be a strong one. Experiences which affect us greatly almost struggle of their own volition to bring themselves into our awareness. It is as though our organismic selves are saying to our self-structures: *I'm not going to let you ignore me. This did happen (or this is happening). It is important. Pay attention.*

There are a number of ways in which the struggle for symbolisation can become apparent, including recurrent dreams, flashbacks, voices and visions.

One example is of a woman who felt unaccountably insecure in herself. She puzzled over this for a number of years, but reason and logic did not provide any answers. Her parents had been loving and concerned for her welfare. Of course, they sometimes ignored her needs or thwarted her wishes, but no more than other parents. So why was she gripped on occasion by anxiety and distress? One counsellor, psychodynamic in approach, told her that she must have had a traumatic childhood, but this she rejected angrily.

A second counsellor listened to her feelings of distress and abandonment. Into the woman's awareness came a recurring dream she had had in her childhood. She was on one side of a road, on a broad pavement. There were houses on either side. On the other side, walking down the opposite pavement, were her parents. No matter how hard she tried, she could not attract their attention. Throughout the dream and on awaking she experienced intense feelings of distress, panic and abandonment.

This awareness led to another. She had always known that when she was six months old her parents had left her for three months with her grandmother and aunts so that they could find work and a new home in another part of the country. Her mother's mother and siblings often referred with great affection to the time when they looked after her. She was 'theirs' in a way that her younger sisters and brothers were not.

She was then able to connect the dream and the event. Even though she had no actual memory of being left behind by her parents, her organism was symbolising the power of the event in the best way it could: through a dream. Her self-structure 'knew' that she was loved and well cared for. But organismically, she also 'knew' that she had been abandoned.

Once she had expressed the pain of this abandonment, her self-doubt and anxiety became much reduced.

The first counsellor was, in fact, correct in her surmise – there was a 'trauma' in the woman's childhood. But the woman herself was not aware of this and the counsellor's words were too far removed from her self-perception to be accepted by her self-structure. The first counsellor was in her own frame of reference rather than the client's and the client rejected her expertise.

Flashbacks are another common way in which important experiences which cannot be easily integrated into the self-structure are brought (sometimes again and again) to the fore.

EXERCISE

Norman goes regularly to a night club. It is a place where he knows most of the regulars, at least by sight, and he is known to the door and bar staff. He feels at home there. One evening, late on, he is enjoying himself with friends. Everyone has been drinking and dancing – not to excess, but so that the

(Continued)

(Continued)

atmosphere is relaxed and convivial. The fire alarm sounds, and everyone makes jokes, waiting for it to be turned off. Then, within a surprisingly short time, there is a smell of burning and pandemonium breaks out. Norman gets himself out of the building. He remembers little of those few minutes, except that at some level he knows that he had to kick, punch and trample to get to fresh air. Seventy-three people died in the fire.

Norman's self-structure is his way of *making sense of the world*. Are there aspects of the above event which he might be inclined to distort or deny because they conflict with his understanding of how the world is?

His self-structure also tells him how he *should be* in the world. Which of his own feelings or behaviours might he want to put from his mind?

However much someone might wish to put a terrible event from his mind, it is part of his history – part of who he is. Flashbacks are one mechanism for nudging him to pay attention to the event – and counselling can give him the acceptance that he cannot yet give himself.

CONCLUSION

It is important for a counsellor or therapist to have a sound theoretical base for a number of reasons. Perhaps the most important is to give us an anchor when the going gets tough. Counselling can be a lonely business at times, particularly when we are travelling with clients through their most painful experiences. They may be feeling deeply hopeless, worthless, abandoned, alone. And they may continue feeling that pain for an almost unbearable length of time.

As therapists, we would not be human if we did not wonder at such times whether we were being as helpful as we could be. A thorough understanding of how and why psychological pain arises, of how we can help and why our means of helping works, enables us to continue to stay in psychological contact with our clients. Without such clarity, there is a great temptation to 'try something else' in order to bring relief to our clients (and, of course, ourselves).

NOTE

The basis of person-centred theory can be found in the XIX Propositions which Carl Rogers outlined in *Client-Centered Therapy* (Rogers, 1951: Chapter 11). These Propositions deal with two main areas: the theory of personality and the theory of how to facilitate change. Rogers (1959) further expanded aspects of the theory in, 'A theory of therapy, personality and interpersonal relations as developed in the client-centered framework', in S. Koch (ed.), *Psychology: A Study of Science. Vol. III.* New York: McGraw-Hill. pp. 184–256.

FURTHER READING

Barrett-Lennard, G.T. (1998) *Carl Rogers' Helping System: Journey and Substance*. London: Sage.

Bozarth, J. (1998) *Person-Centred Therapy: A Revolutionary Paradigm*. Ross-on-Wye: PCCS Books.

Brodley, B. (1999) 'The actualizing tendency concept in client-centered theory', *Person-Centered Journal*, 6(2): 108–20.

Cooper, M., O'Hara, M., Schmid, P. and Wyatt, G. (eds) (2007) *The Handbook of Person-Centred Psychotherapy and Counselling*. Basingstoke: Palgrave Macmillan.

Haugh, S. and Paul, S. (2008) *The Therapeutic Relationship*. Ross-on-Wye: PCCS Books.

Kirschenbaum, H. (2007) *The Biography of Carl Rogers*. Ross-on-Wye: PCCS Books.

Mearns, D. and Cooper, M. (2005) *Working at Relational Depth in Counselling and Psychotherapy*. London: Sage.

Mearns, D. and Thorne, B. (2000) 'The nature of configurations within self', in D. Mearns and B. Thorne (eds), *Person-Centred Therapy Today*. London: Sage.

Mearns, D. and Thorne, B. (2007) *Person-Centred Counselling in Action* (3rd edn). London: Sage. (This edition is completely revised and expanded.)

Merry, T. (1999) *Learning and Being in Person-Centred Counselling*. Ross-on-Wye: PCCS Books. (Chapters 2 and 3.)

Sanders, P. (2006) *The Person-Centred Counselling Primer*. Ross-on-Wye: PCCS Books.

WEBSITES

There are a number of useful papers available on the Internet. Two person-centred websites which have good links to other sites are:

The World Association for Person-Centered and Experiential Psychotherapy and Counseling at www.pce-world.org;

The British Association for the Person-Centred Approach at www.bapca.org.uk.

2

EMPATHY

At its most basic, empathy is a simple restatement of someone else's words, to show that they are heard and understood. But at its richest, it involves a fearless exploration of another's inner world, a sensing of meanings unspoken, a compassionate naming of pain, suffering and humiliation, and of mischievousness and joy. The fullest empathy does not censor or discriminate. It sees the whole world as the other person sees it and is wholly accepting of that world.

This is not to say that the empathic counsellor loses *herself* in the world of the client. However deeply she is affected by the hopelessness of her client, she is aware of her own hope. When she hurts inside for her client in pain, she is aware that it is not her own hurt. When she hears her client's hatred of an abusive parent, she does not herself hate the abuser, but is open to hearing the client's love as well.

There is no formula for empathy, no easy or magic route to 'getting it right'. It is always a focused intention to understand how another person sees himself and the world around him. Above all, it is a two-way communication, with the therapist always implicitly asking 'Have I understood you correctly?' and the client responding either 'Yes' or 'Well, it's more like this' or 'Yes in part, but also ...' or 'No, that's not what I meant at all'.

PERCEPTION

Empathy involves two things: perception and communication. Perception by itself is not facilitative. You can hear, understand and feel very deeply *for* a client, but if that perception is locked inside your wooden and unresponsive exterior, it is not available for the client to use. In everyday life, it is common for people on hearing of a devastating event from a colleague or neighbour, say, to be tongue-tied – not because they are unaffected by the news but because they *don't know what to say*. They perceive the distress but are not able to respond to the news-teller. He might have a sense that he has been 'heard', but the silence discourages him from talking further about the event.

Equally, communication without perception is unhelpful. The person who rushes in with questions or platitudes does not hear the full import of the news. She is, perhaps, nervous about what has been said or what *might* be said. She protects herself from further anxiety through blocking off the other person's communication with her own words. In her own mind, she has heard the news and is responding as best she can. The news-teller, however, knows that he has not been fully heard and understood.

The first step in developing empathic responding is to develop your perception. In person-centred counselling, this involves listening not only to the story or narrative, but also to the feelings and emotions. If you are able, you will find it useful when expanding your range of perception to work with others. They will perceive things that you miss, and vice versa.

You may also become aware over time that you are more 'tuned in' to some feelings than to others. If six people listen to a client speaking, each might put a slightly different emphasis upon what they hear. One might hear how hurt the client is feeling, another might pick up on his anger and a third might hear his loneliness more strongly.

LEARNING TO EMPATHISE

During the first stages of learning about empathic communication, the listener is focusing on the fundamental skill of *staying in the speaker's frame of reference*. (We use the term 'frame of reference' for all of a person's perceptions, feelings, values and experience. It is their world *as they perceive it* and not as anyone else sees it.) The listener is also developing the habit of *voicing* what she hears from the speaker. In everyday communication, we often bypass this stage, moving straight to a question or a suggestion.

Speaker: My daughter starts school next week and she's quite a shy little girl. I wish I knew how to help her to settle in.
Listener: Have you thought of ... ?
Listener: Has your daughter been to playgroup or nursery?
Listener: Why don't you ... ?

In this kind of communication, the speaker turns quickly into a listener, evaluating the other person's suggestions and ideas. With the person-centred approach, the speaker is encouraged to listen not to the other person, but to himself.

These first stages of learning often begin with simple *Statement A – Response A* type communications:

Speaker: My daughter starts school next week and she's quite a shy little girl. I wish I knew how to help her to settle in.
Listener: You want her to settle in well.

The next stage of skills development involves listening for feeling as well as content.

> *Speaker:*   My daughter starts school next week and she's quite a shy little
>   girl. I wish I knew how to help her to settle in.
> *Listener:*   You sound a bit worried about her.

The listener is building upon the skills of staying within the speaker's frame of reference and voicing what she is hearing. She is also adding the skill of listening for unspoken feelings and emotions and developing a vocabulary to express them.

Staying within another person's frame of reference in this way is not, for most people, an easy thing to do. At first, it is a struggle to verbalise even the most superficial understanding. Sustaining this for 10 or 15 minutes at a time requires tremendous concentration. If someone is attending a class once a week for about three hours and practising each week, we can expect her to develop the skill of remaining in the speaker's frame of reference and verbalising her perceptions within about a year. Alongside the skills development, of course, will be taught theory, ethics and so on, so the whole time will not be spent on skills. And some course members will struggle more than others to break the habits of questioning, problem-solving, advising and so on.

However, it is important to be clear about the nature of skills development. Inevitably, it is a slow process and one that involves practice. Those of you who have learned to drive a car will know this. The simple matter of pressing three levers with your feet, moving another lever with your hand and turning a wheel – all of which most people can do with consummate ease one at a time when the car is stationary – becomes a different matter when you first try to get the car moving.

This is why you cannot learn counselling from a book or from lectures. Just as you cannot call yourself a driver while you are still thinking about which pedal to move when, you cannot begin to become a counsellor until you stop having to think about:

a   staying in your client's frame of reference; and

b   voicing your perceptions as empathic responses.

This is the point at which you move from using counselling skills into the process of becoming a counsellor. You can begin to leave behind the simple *Statement A –Response A* type communication for communication which might look more like:

Statement A – Response A

Statement B – Response B

Statement C – Response C

Statement D – Response Z

Instead of hearing each statement and responding to it in isolation, you have begun to listen to the whole communication from the whole person.

Speaker:	My daughter starts school next week and she's quite a shy little girl. I wish I knew how to help her to settle in.
Listener:	You sound a bit worried about her.
Speaker:	Yes. It's such a big step, going from playgroup to school. When she started playgroup, I could stay with her until she was OK. To start with, she just held on to my hand and watched the others. It was weeks before I could leave her on her own.
Listener:	It took her a long time to feel safe.
Speaker:	I was beginning to think she would never join in with the others. But one day, she just went over to the sand table and started to play.
Listener:	Such a relief for you.
Speaker:	Oh yes! You can't imagine.
Listener:	And now you're facing all that anxiety over again.
Speaker:	The thing is, I won't be able to stay with her this time. Parents are only allowed in on the first day.
Listener:	And it will seem like you're . . . abandoning her?

The listener thinks she may have 'heard' something which the speaker has not voiced, but which he has nevertheless (possibly) communicated. She names it tentatively, giving the speaker the opportunity to confirm, deny or amend the listener's perception.

Speaker:	The thing is, I won't be able to stay with her this time. Parents are only allowed in on the first day.
Listener:	And it will seem like you're . . . abandoning her?
Speaker:	. . . Yes, I suppose it does.

Speaker:	The thing is, I won't be able to stay with her this time. Parents are only allowed in on the first day.
Listener:	And it will seem like you're . . . abandoning her?
Speaker:	Not really. After all, the teacher is a very nice woman. I know she'll be well looked after.
Listener:	You know the reality is that she'll be ok.

Speaker:	The thing is, I won't be able to stay with her this time. Parents are only allowed in on the first day.
Listener:	And it will seem like you're . . . abandoning her?
Speaker:	Not quite that. [*Tries to find the right words*] Wanting her to be all right.
Listener:	Wanting her to have someone to turn to if she needs it?
Speaker:	Well, I know the teacher is there, but Ayinka is very shy. . .
Listener:	So you don't think she would be able to tell the teacher if she wanted something. . .
Speaker:	Probably not.
Listener:	And you're worried that she'll just suffer in silence.
Speaker:	Yes.
[*Pause*]	
Speaker:	When I first went to school, I didn't say a word for weeks.

The listener continues to follow the speaker's lead. On each occasion that the speaker amends the listener's understanding, she checks that she has correctly understood him.

Whenever she offers her perception of what the speaker is saying, the listener is open to his accepting or rejecting it. She is making a genuine attempt to understand the speaker's world *as he experiences it*. She is not seeking to establish an 'objective' view, or to impose her own view upon him. This has several consequences.

The first is that the listener's response is unpredictable, particularly when the relationship is a new one. The speaker may be taken aback by the way the listener reacts to her innocently intentioned attempt at empathy.

> *Listener:* You were really angry when he said that.
>
> *Speaker:* I certainly was not! I'm not an angry person. I don't believe in getting angry, it doesn't help the situation.

The user of counselling skills will probably retrench at this point, perhaps apologising to the speaker for having misunderstood him. Her contract with him does not allow her to go into matters which are concerned with the speaker's personality. The counselling skills user – whether she is a nurse, a teacher or an advisory worker – has a different primary task.

For the therapist, on the other hand, such a response allows her to 'hear' something of the client's personality. She has perceived angry feelings in him, but either he is not angry (she has misperceived), or he cannot accept anger in himself. He has told her that the latter is true – that in his self-structure, anger is frowned upon.

If she chooses to make an empathic response, the counsellor will show that she has 'heard' this:

> *Counsellor:* You were really angry when he said that.
>
> *Client:* I certainly was not! I'm not an angry person. I don't believe in getting angry, it doesn't help the situation.
>
> *Counsellor:* So getting angry would be quite a … weak thing to do?

The counsellor is not concerned with whether or not she is 'right'. Her perception of her client being angry might persist, but she will not try to force her perception upon him. Nor will she collude in maintaining his self-concept by avoiding his angry feelings if she hears them again. She is likely, though, to choose words which are closer to his own awareness – for example, 'irritated', 'cross', 'miffed', 'uptight'.

The important effect of the counsellor's empathic understanding is that the client can explore his own reactions *for himself.* Such exploration does not begin and end within the counselling session. In fact, the session itself often serves as a nudge to a process in which much of the reflection and insight happens between sessions. It is not uncommon for a client to acknowledge, weeks or even months after the event, that the counsellor's perception was indeed accurate, even though the client was at the time unaware of it and rejected it fiercely.

VOCABULARY

It you are to communicate your perceptions to someone else, the main medium is likely to be words. Counselling is different from everyday interactions in that the focus for the counsellor is on how a client experiences his own world. As you become more perceptive, you will pick up more and more that the client is not actually stating but is communicating to you in other ways.

Empathy is not about parroting the client's words. When you simply repeat what the client has said, you are staying on the surface of what he has *communicated*. It is important to listen to (or note, if you are communicating in sign language) his tone, his hesitations and garrulousness. If you are sighted and working face-to-face, you will have additional information from his facial expressions and posture. All of this conveys *meaning* beyond the surface meaning of the words alone. Even if you stay with the obvious, using your own words rather than his will show a slightly deeper level of understanding.

Speaker: They got rid of me, the bastards.
Listener: They got rid of you. [*This shows only that you have heard*]
Listener: So, you're out of a job. [*This shows that you have heard and have (minimally) understood*]

The words themselves, although expressive, give only part of the meaning. Depending upon *how* they are said, an underlying meaning will have been expressed, and the counsellor can respond to this:

Speaker: They got rid of me, the bastards.
Listener (1):   And you really want to get your own back.
Listener (2):   You sound quite flat. As if you were half expecting it.
Listener (3):   You're getting quite choked up, just thinking about it.

The counsellor also communicates with more than words. Your own tone of voice and facial expression tell their tale. You are trying to *understand*. You are always checking out that your understanding chimes with what your client is trying to say to you. Is it *how he sees his world?* The crucial aspect of empathy is staying within the client's frame of reference. In person-centred counselling, objective truth is not a useful concept.

Your empathic reflection is always open to correction by the client. Often, there will be a tentativeness in your voice – an implied question: *Have I heard this right?*

Speaker: They got rid of me, the bastards.
Listener: And you really want to get your own back.

If you are relatively sure of what you have heard, this can be said with warmth and understanding. If you are not sure, with a question in your voice. It would *not* be empathic to say it with disapproval!

Of course once the relationship is established, you will be hearing such words in a context and responding to them with more knowledge of your client and his world. In the following examples, the listener is drawing on this prior knowledge:

Speaker:	They got rid of me, the bastards.
Listener (1):	So you were right to be worried.
Listener (2):	That must really hurt, after all the work you put in.
Listener (3):	So you're on the 'scrap heap' again.

Empathy at its most effective communicates that you have perceived the client's whole experience, including his feelings and emotions. To begin with, you may have some difficulty in *expressing* what you have perceived. You have a strong sense of a client's distress or pain. You can almost *feel* it somewhere in your gut. But the words are not there. You struggle to communicate what you are picking up.

The following exercise may help you to bring the words to the forefront of your mind.

EXERCISE

When reflecting feelings and emotions, it is useful not only to identify the feeling, but also the right amount of the feeling. Taking anger as an example, it would not be very empathic to say 'You're irritated' to someone who experienced himself as furious. On a large sheet of paper, write down all the words and expressions you can think of to describe every possible degree of the following. (Use one sheet for each.) If you are working with others, keep passing the sheets of paper around until you have finished. If you are working by yourself, pin up the sheets and add to them as you think of new words and expressions (the workroom, kitchen or toilet are good places!). Do not limit yourself to 'polite' expressions. 'You're really pissed off', 'It's doing your head in' or 'You lost your bottle' might well be appropriate for some clients. And local words like miffed, mardy, gobsmacked and so on can be wonderfully expressive.

Angry	Excited
Happy	Anxious
Sad	Confused
Frightened	Surprised
Tired	Hurt

There is no one way, let alone a 'best' way, of saying something. There are always alternatives. For example, you notice that your client is getting tearful as he speaks. There are numerous ways of voicing this perception:

- You're getting choked up telling me about it.

- You're filling up as you're speaking to me.

- I can see that just talking about it brings the tears.

The important thing is that you find your own individual way of communicating. To begin with, you are likely to 'borrow' words and phrases from your tutors, but what sounds natural for one person to say can sound false on the lips of another. And any phrase, if over-used, can become jargon.

- Thank you for sharing that with me.
- How do you feel about that?
- I hear what you're saying.

Phrases like this must at one time have been spontaneous and meaningful, but it is hard now to use or hear them without cringing.

VOICING PERCEPTIONS AND AWARENESS

The more practice you have, first in using counselling skills and then in becoming a counsellor, the more attuned you become within the relationship. The first struggle is to stay consistently within another person's frame of reference. When you have reached the stage where you do not have to think too hard about doing this, you can begin to become aware of a range of other information.

There is a wealth of information within a counselling relationship upon which it is possible to draw:

- the client's words
- the client's emotion
- the client's tone of voice
- the client's facial expression
- the client's posture
- previous information given by the client
- the client's attitude towards you
- the client's reactions to your words
- sensed meaning – 'underneath' the client's words
- your own thoughts
- your own feelings
- your own imagination
- awareness of your own physical self
- your theoretical understanding of what is 'happening' in the client
- your own emotions
- your reactions to the client's words
- your attitude towards the client

It is not surprising that, in everyday interactions, we filter a lot of this out. But in counselling we strive, first, to become more aware of it and, secondly, to voice it. In this way, we try to become *transparent* to the client. We do not come to conclusions or make decisions which are hidden from the client.

This is often not a matter of intention but of our own lack of awareness or lack of skill in knowing how to say out loud what is in our minds.

EXAMPLE

The listener is hearing someone talking about his mother's sudden death. These are an unskilled listener's reactions, but much of it is out of her awareness:

'I can see how near to tears you are. There's a great lump in my own chest and I'm feeling tearful too. I'm overwhelmed by the dreadfulness of your story. I don't know what to say or do. I'm feeling paralysed and helpless. I want to relieve your awful suffering and I don't know how. I'm terrified of saying the wrong thing, but if I don't say something soon, you'll think I don't care.'

What she *says* is: 'Shall I make you a cup of tea?'

EXAMPLE

A counsellor is listening to her client talking about his father. In the counsellor's awareness is:

'As you tell me about your father, your voice is whining and your eyes are looking up at me although your head is bowed. I think you want me to say that he is *wrong* – that he is a *bad man*. I am a little irritated by your being such a *victim*. I'm struggling to keep in contact with your frame of reference. Ah! I'm realising that you are a bit scared as you tell me this. Your experience might be that you will be punished if you tell. Now I am also sensing your feelings of powerlessness and a deep hurt – and rage?'

In the second example, the counsellor noticed her own irritation and did not dismiss it as inappropriate. She knew that her irritation was a valid response – something happening between herself and the client (see Chapters 4 and 5 on congruence). But she also recognised that it was by no means unconditionally accepting, so she did not voice it.

She managed to understand that the client was *expecting* her to punish him and that her *'Stop whingeing and grow up'* reaction would have beautifully confirmed his self-structure.

Now she can, unconditionally, offer either empathy, *You feel so powerless*, or a congruent communication, *I'm getting the feeling that you're a bit afraid of my reaction. Are you used to being blamed – or punished – when you complain about your father?*

When I am interacting with another person, I bring my own organismic experiencing and self-structure to the relationship. I am at my most facilitative when the congruent part of myself is engaged: that overlap where my experience and self-structure are in harmony, where I can be totally flexible and open to my client's experience and to my own experience of my client. This is essential in my ability to empathise fully.

If my own value system gets in the way, I will struggle to hear accurately anything of my client's which conflicts with what I think he should do or should believe. I may not go so far as to foist my beliefs upon him, but I might well be silent rather than acknowledge something with which I disagree. And my response is unlikely to be empathic.

Similarly, I might worry about how my client may react to my words and not voice something in case he doesn't like it. But is it because my client won't like it or because I wouldn't like it if it were said to me? Is it because my own self-structure says it is wrong – and therefore unacceptable – rather than my client's? Or perhaps it is because I sense my own disapproval and do not want to communicate this to my client. Whatever the reason, it limits my empathy. For example, I may hesitate to speak of my client's envy, because I see this as wrong and am worried that my client will hear it as an accusation. But what if envious describes exactly what my client is feeling? I will be withholding my empathic response.

What if envious describes his feeling but his own self-structure sees it as wrong? Then he will deny it. He may even be cross with me for suggesting it. But if I am congruent, I do not need to be apologetic or defensive. I have offered my perception and it is for my client to accept or reject my offering.

Beginning counsellors often worry about getting it wrong, by which they mean that they might misunderstand or mishear what a client is saying. They wait until they are totally sure before giving voice. Further, they are afraid that a client might react against what they are saying or reject them entirely. This is, of course, a possibility – and a scary one. But it usually takes an awful lot of mishearing for this to happen. More usually, clients sense and appreciate our attempts to understand what they are going through and are more than willing to correct us if we are not sufficiently accurate in our empathy.

As a counsellor, I am one person in a relationship. I bring my own perceptions and awareness, however inaccurate or limited, to that relationship and my job is to communicate them as well as I am able. In that sense I cannot get it wrong. If I am able to stay open, I will alter my perceptions minute by minute according to what my client is telling me. I will not prejudge my client, but neither will I deny my own perceptions if they persist. I can accept my client's truth when he says that he has no awareness of being angry, but if I sense angry feelings, I will hold that in my own awareness and take it to supervision. They might, after all, be my own angry feelings– or they might be a mixture of mine and my client's.

Second-guessing my client is a sure-fire way of limiting my empathic responding. It also affects the challenge which is inherent in empathy (see Chapter 11).

FURTHER READING

Bohart, A.C. (2004) 'How do clients make empathy work?', *Person-Centred and Experiential Psychotherapies*, 3(2): 102–16.

Friere, E. (2007) 'Empathy', in M. Cooper, M. O'Hara, P.F. Schmid and G. Wyatt (eds), *The Handbook of Person Centred Psychotherapy and Counselling*. Hampshire: Palgrave Macmillan.

Haugh, S. and Merry, T. (eds) (2001) *Empathy*. Ross-on-Wye: PCCS Books.

Mearns, D. and Thorne, B. (2007) *Person-Centred Counselling in Action* (3rd edn). London: Sage. (Now completely revised and expanded.)

Merry, T. (1999) *Learning and Being in Person-Centred Counselling*. Ross-on-Wye: PCCS Books. (See Chapter 5.)

Sanders, P. (2006) *The Person-Centred Counselling Primer*. Ross on Wye: PCCS Books. (See Chapter 8.)

3

EMPATHIC
UNDERSTANDING

SIMILE AND METAPHOR

As the beginner counsellor becomes more confident, she is likely to begin to use more imaginative ways of communicating empathic understanding, and one of these ways is through simile and metaphor. A counsellor and client can develop images that sometimes give expression to the client's situation, or the relationship, in a powerful way.

EXERCISE

Think of two or three metaphors which describe something of your life at the moment, for example,

- I'm wallowing in a snowstorm of paper;
- I'm floating on a cloud in a blue sky;
- I'm an unopened letter left on the mat.

There are a number of everyday expressions – seeing the light at the end of the tunnel; fighting like a cornered animal; as light as thistledown; as heavy as lead; like a rat in a trap; like part of the furniture – which convey experiences graphically and economically. These can be used by client and counsellor as descriptive phrases. They can also be extended:

Counsellor: You were fighting like a cornered animal.
Client: [*weeping desperately*] But I didn't have any *claws*.
Counsellor: No claws, no teeth, nothing to defend yourself with.

Counsellor: You seem like a fast-flowing river, rushing along, and when I try to say something it gets swept into the current.

Client: When I first came to see you, it felt like I was in a stormy sea full of sharks. Now, it's like the sharks are still there, but the storm has cleared and I can see where they are.

Counsellor: *[to someone who said she did not know who she was, and who had been neglected and abused all her life]* I've got a picture of yourself as a timid little creature which has had to hide away to stay safe.

Later in the relationship, when the client was finding it risky to venture her self, the image was used again to empathise, this time with the fearfulness of a creature being in the open for the first time, feeling exposed and vulnerable and needing to be close to safe cover.

Similes and metaphors can be started by either person in the relationship and are often amended and expanded by the other.

EXAMPLE

The following client is hesitating on the brink of talking about a very painful memory which he has kept at bay for many years.

Counsellor: It's as though you're on the edge of a dark pit, and you don't quite know what is in it.

Client: More like a cliff, really.

Counsellor: So it feels like stepping over the edge would be very dangerous.

Client: Yes. And I wouldn't be able to get back up.

Counsellor: Mmmm. That feels quite terrifying. Once you've committed yourself, there's no going back.

Client: I don't even know whether I can *look* over the edge.

Counsellor: You might see something so appalling . . .

Client: Perhaps it wouldn't be as bad as I imagine. What do you think?

Counsellor: I think neither of us knows. That's what makes it scary.

Client: What if it's only a six-inch drop?

Counsellor: I think we need to trust your instincts. That doesn't mean we can't get down it even if it is a steep cliff. But perhaps we need to be prepared for some hairy moments, just in case.

Client: You mean it might be as bad as I think?

Counsellor: I mean that if you're apprehensive, there's probably a good reason. *[Silence]*

Client: I *do* want to know what's over the edge. But are you sure you can come with me?

Counsellor: It feels like you couldn't do it alone.

Client:	[*in a very small voice*] Yes.
Counsellor:	And it's important to know I won't abandon you.
Client:	[*nods*]
Counsellor:	All I can say is, I'm quite an experienced cliff climber, and I certainly intend to stay with you.

PUSHING, LEADING, INVITING

There are subtle but very important distinctions between pushing, leading and invit-ing clients. Leading or pushing someone down a path which the therapist has chosen is not a person-centred activity. But a counsellor might sense that her client has something on his mind. He might be hesitating for a number of reasons. Can he trust the counsellor not to judge him harshly? Does he himself feel embarrassed about something? Will the counsellor understand how important this is to him? Will his feelings overwhelm him? The person-centred therapist might wish to indicate that *she* is ready to hear him. If the client responds to such an invitation, he is ready to go down that path. The counsellor will not lead him against his will, nor will she push him in a direction of her choosing.

EXAMPLE A

Counsellor:	*I think you should talk about the death of your father.*
Client:	What's the point in raking over all that again?
Counsellor:	It was clearly a crucial point in your life. I think a lot of your present problems might stem from what happened then.

EXAMPLE B

Client:	We were so happy when we were little – before everything changed.
	[*The client is silent for some minutes, looking very sad*]
Counsellor:	Are you thinking about your father dying?
Client:	Yes.
Counsellor:	Do you want to tell me what happened?

In the first example, the therapist is pursuing a line which *she* has decided is impor-tant. In the second, she takes her cue from what is already happening in the client. Her first sentence is speculative, but based on her knowledge of the client. Her empathic response turns out to be accurate. Then she offers an invitation, saying in effect: I *am ready to listen if you are ready to talk.*

The client could refuse the invitation:

Counsellor: Do you want to tell me what happened?
Client: I don't think I could talk about it.
Counsellor: Are the feelings still very raw?
　　　　　　 [*Client nods*]
Counsellor: And you couldn't tell me about it without them spilling over.
　　　　　　 [*Silence*]
Client: It would be embarrassing.
Counsellor: You'd feel . . . exposed.
Client: I'd feel bloody stupid.
Counsellor: [*Smiles her understanding*] Big boys don't cry.

Here, the work takes a different turn and the client begins to explore how he has always had to keep up appearances. The counsellor trusts that, if it is important and when *he* is ready, the client will come back to his grief.

GENERALISATIONS

One way in which people protect themselves and others from their pain is to talk generally rather than about specific incidents. Generalities are a good 'way in' for a new client – a means of testing out whether or not a counsellor is willing and able to listen effectively. Usually, the client who feels *heard* will move gradually from the general to the specific.

Life is such a mess, it's not worth living.

Nobody really cares, do they?

People are just so cruel.

Such statements can feel a little overwhelming to the beginner therapist. How best to respond? This might depend upon the individual client and the stage of the relationship. In the beginning stages, a counsellor's empathic responses might be almost as general as the client's statements and the client will become more specific as the relationship develops. If this does not happen, though, the counsellor might become more proactive in inviting the client towards being more specific and concrete:

Nobody really cares, do they?
It sounds as though you feel pretty uncared for.

Children have to put up with getting bullied at school.
Is that what you had to do? Put up with it?

Life is such a mess, it's not worth living.
Are you feeling that your own life is a mess at the moment?

Are you wondering whether it's worth going on with the struggle of being alive?

I was scared of my dad. He was always shouting.
Is there a particular time you are thinking of?

EXERCISE

How might you respond to the following in a way that invites greater specificity?

- Work is a nightmare at the moment.
- Families! They're more trouble than they're worth.
- There's no point getting up in the morning when you feel so bad all the time.
- People are just so cruel.
- Parents are always pulling you down.
- My mum used to do some awful things to us.

Why might this be important?

Theory tells us that when we experience something as dangerous to our self-structure, we will symbolise it in awareness *inaccurately* or *not at all*. In order to re-symbolise something accurately, we have to re-experience it fully. This means thinking and feeling it once more. So the client who continues to generalise in order not to re-experience the pain is not re-symbolising the experience. The pain will remain – it is what brought him into counselling in the first place – until it has been revisited.

The power of counselling lies in the fact that another person is hearing such experiences without filtering them through the self-structure that caused the distortions in the first place.

Since the self-structure is in the process of development when we are children, it can be important to revisit childhood events so that they can be re-symbolised accurately. It is sometimes said that person-centred therapy deals only with the present and not the past. But anyone who has worked as a counsellor knows that clients themselves often bring their history into the counselling relationship. The events might be in the past, but the *experience* is very much 'here-and-now'. Person-centred theory tells us that this is something that *will happen* if the six conditions are there. There is no need for the counsellor to direct or lead the client. But the counsellor who is attuned to her client might well suspect that he is censoring his thoughts, either because he does not see the use of 'going over old ground', or because the memories are painful, or because he does not want to show emotion or 'lose control'.

In this instance, the counsellor is still following her client rather than leading if she voices her own perception of – or speculation about – what is happening in her client:

- Are you thinking of something in particular?

- You looked then as though you were remembering something.

- Is there a specific incident that is coming into your mind?
- You seem lost in your own thoughts. Do you want to tell me where you've gone to?
- It seemed to me then as though you were seeing something in your mind's eye.
- Are you remembering a time when that happened to you?
- Sounds as though you have experience of that yourself.

People censor themselves according to their own self-structure. Common introjects are along the lines of:

- What do I have to complain about? Think of the starving in Africa.
- Nobody wants to listen to my whingeing and moaning.
- It's so trivial, it's not worth mentioning.
- Something like that shouldn't be bothering me after all this time.
- It's history. I should be looking forward, not backwards.
- There's no point in raking over old ground.

And yet it is the specific incidents which carry the emotional intensity. They might be 'trivial' in the wider scheme of things, but to the individual, they are of immense importance.

CASE EXAMPLE: ANDY

Andy keeps returning in his mind to a time when, as a young child, he was in hospital. He swiftly pushes away the memory when it occurs, believing that it is not relevant to the counselling – he has come, after all, to get over his sexual problems. His counsellor notices his expressions:

Counsellor: You looked then as if you were thinking about something. But you pushed it out of your mind.

Andy: It wasn't important.

Counsellor: Do you want to say it anyway? It might be more important than you think. And if it isn't, we've lost nothing.

Andy shrugs and begins to tell her about the time he was left alone in hospital at the age of four. His parents did not visit him for more than two weeks. If he showed any fear or distress, he was told that he should be a big boy. As he recounts the story, his emotions come flooding back. He struggles to control them. The counsellor stays within his frame of reference, believing that Andy will know when to move away from his intense feelings.

Over the next few sessions, Andy becomes much more aware of how little affection or consideration he received as a child. He returns to the hospital

---

incident and takes the risk of expressing some of the emotions he experiences as he remembers. He also remembers other times when he was expected to be a 'big boy' and grieves for the parental love and care which he did not receive.

Andy begins to understand how his fears and self-protectiveness have affected his sexual relationships. He becomes aware of how he held back from intimacy with his last partner, despite wanting desperately to be close. When he forms a new relationship, Andy's focus has changed considerably. Although the path is far from smooth, Andy is much more hopeful that this relationship will be a lasting one.

The counsellor's belief is that if something comes into the client's mind, it is usually relevant. Neither she nor her client will necessarily know how or why at the time, but if she trusts in the wisdom of the process, its significance will emerge.

Sometimes, following the client's lead will take him far away from the issue which he thought he wanted to address in counselling. Again, it is for the client and not the counsellor to determine which is the most important focus for him.

DISTANCING

Sometimes, the counsellor's own language can contribute to a client distancing himself from his experience.

EXAMPLE

Client: The anger comes up more than the pain.
Counsellor: So the anger is the thing you're aware of most often.
Client: Yes. The anger towards my father is particularly strong.
Counsellor: So there's some anger and some pain, but the anger is deepest. You talked about your father hitting you. Is this where it comes from, do you think?
Client: Yes, I think it does. But nowadays it seems to come up whenever anyone in authority doesn't listen to me.
Counsellor: Like your boss.
Client: Yes, but other people as well.

In this example, the counsellor is following the client's lead in *talking about* 'the anger' as though it is something entirely separate from the client. They examine 'it' from the outside and discuss 'it' like an object that is sitting between them. From the client's point of view, of course, this is very safe and a counsellor might decide to go along with the safety for a while in the beginning stages of a relationship. As long as client and counsellor stay with this mode, however, they will be avoiding his experience in all of its depth, colour and, of course, suffering.

This example also shows a client skimming the surface of his experience by flitting from one thing to another. He ignores the particular – *your father, your boss* – and reaches for the general – *anyone in authority, other people as well.* The counsellor contributes to this by inviting him to analyse – *Is this where it comes from, do you think?* She appeals to the cognitive, rational part of him rather than the feeling part.

This is not to deny the importance of the cognitive and rational. It is, however, helpful to give equal weight to the feeling elements – particularly when a client seems to have 'lost' his own sense of their importance.

The counsellor can pay attention to the whole of the client's experience through her empathy. She does not point out to him that he is staying with the cognitive element of his experiencing. Paradoxically, phrases like *You're staying in your head* invite clients to analyse – to consider what they are doing rather than to experience. They can also convey the message *You're doing it wrong.*

EXAMPLE

Client: The anger comes up more than the pain.
Counsellor: You feel angry a lot of the time.
Client: Yes. The anger towards my father is particularly strong.
Counsellor: So you get boiling mad with him sometimes . . . raging inside?
Client: Yes . . . like a volcano that could blow its top.
Counsellor: Sounds quite dangerous.
Client: Yes . . .
Counsellor: As though you're not sure you can control it.
Client: That's exactly it.
  [The client is resting his hand on his chest. The counsellor puts hers on her own chest.]
Counsellor: Like it builds up in here.

SPEAKING THE UNSPEAKABLE

Unconditional positive regard means accepting aspects of the client that he himself finds unacceptable. It can feel risky to speak of something which a client is skirting around. Is he uncomfortable with saying outright the thing that he is hinting at? What will be his reaction if you voice it? Will he be angry with you for charging into what might be a very delicate matter for him?

It can be tempting to remain silent on the matter until you become clearer. There are two dangers with this, though. The first is that he might be worried about whether *you* can continue to accept him if he says outright what he is thinking. His experience might be of a family or society that has judged him harshly, and he is reluctant to take the risk that you, too, will reject him. Your silence on the matter might reinforce his belief that such dreadful things are not to be mentioned.

The second is that you are not checking that you have understood him correctly. You may have misunderstood partially or completely what he is saying.

Counsellor: Are you saying that you really hate your brother?
Client: No! Of course I don't! How can you even suggest such a thing?
Counsellor: You seem quite outraged at me saying that. As though it would be *unpardonable* for you to hate him.

Counsellor: Are you saying that you really hate your brother?
Client: Yes, I suppose I am. I've tried to see his good points, but it doesn't work. I can't forgive him for what he did.

Counsellor: Are you saying that you really hate your brother?
Client: No! I don't always *like* him very much, but he is my brother, after all. Perhaps I've given you a one-sided picture of him . . .
Counsellor: Are you feeling a bit disloyal now, telling me about the difficulties? As though I might judge him harshly?

Counsellor: Are you saying that you really hate your brother?
Client: Whatever gave you that idea!
Counsellor: You seem astonished. I must have totally misheard what you were saying.

If there is an area that seems painful, or even *dangerous,* a situation can arise where you collude with your client in avoiding it. This is not to say that you should push a client into a dangerous area, but that by not speaking about it you are tacitly communicating that it is difficult or dangerous *for you.* You can acknowledge that it is difficult for your client, and at the same time convey that you yourself are not afraid:

Counsellor: Every time you come close to talking about your mother, you change direction – as though there's something very painful in even thinking about her.

Counsellor: You've told me that he hurt you – and I imagine that it must have been very bad because you've rushed away from it.
Client: I get scared all over again. I know he can't hurt me now . . .
Counsellor: But at the same time *it feels like* he can.
Client: This sounds stupid, but it's like . . . I'm only safe if I keep quiet.
Counsellor: So your *experience* says it would be very dangerous to say anything. As though . . . he might come and get you if you told on him?
Client: That's exactly what it's like. Do you think I'm being silly!
Counsellor: I think that if you've been in someone's power, you can stay terrified for a long time.

Client: I wish I could tell you what happened. But I'm so ashamed.
Counsellor: Do you imagine that I'd think less of you if I knew?
[*Client nods*]

Counsellor: How might I see you?
Client: [*in a very quiet voice*] You'd know how stupid I am.
Counsellor: So I would . . . dismiss you? . . . feel disgusted with you?
Client: [*sounding childlike*] You wouldn't want to see me again.
Counsellor: [*nodding*] . . . and it would be very hard to bear if I rejected you.

There are sometimes aspects of a client's experience which are sickening for both client and counsellor. Again, it can be tempting for the counsellor to join with the client in keeping them in the shadows. The client hints at what has happened and the counsellor hints back that she has understood. This might be enough for a client, but it does not offer the fullness of acceptance.

Counsellor: Are you talking about the smell of his semen?
Client: It was awful. I wanted to be sick.
Counsellor: It made you gag in your throat.
Client: [*breaking down into sobs*] He used to make me swallow it.

MAKING YOUR WAY THROUGH THE UNDERGROWTH

We have talked about the power of the counsellor's empathy in bringing the client's dimly sensed meanings more into awareness. But there are times when the counsellor is struggling to sense the meanings of the client – times when she feels as though she is working through fog. At such times, the client is usually re-experiencing something important to him and all of his senses are engaged in that experience. The counsellor does not wish to disturb this process and is trying, very respectfully, to follow where the client leads.

CASE EXAMPLE: LUCY

Lucy has been telling her counsellor about some bad childhood experiences over the last few sessions. Today, she begins to talk about her work and then suddenly lapses into silence. All she can do is whisper 'I'm sorry, I'm sorry', in a small, scared voice over and over again. The counsellor remembers that Lucy was not allowed to speak or cry when she was a child, or she would be punished severely. The counsellor also knows that, to Lucy, talking is a betrayal of her family.

The counsellor concentrates hard, trying to pick up Lucy's meaning. She seems very young and frightened and the counsellor voices this: 'You seem very little and scared at the moment.'

Lucy repeats 'I'm sorry, I'm sorry' with intensified fear. She seems focused in on herself.

There is a silence, during which the counsellor is mentally enveloping her with compassion. Then the counsellor murmurs: 'It's OK. I'm here.'

The counsellor tries some tentative empathy: 'Are you scared that you will be punished in some way for talking to me about what happened?'

Lucy just keeps repeating 'I'm sorry, I'm sorry'.

The counsellor reaches out a hand, in case Lucy wishes to hold on to her, but immediately Lucy shrinks away, still saying 'I'm sorry, I'm sorry'.

The counsellor is puzzled. Eventually she asks: 'Are you apologising to me?'

'I'm sorry, I'm sorry, I'm sorry', Lucy repeats quickly, nodding her head.

The counsellor begins to get a glimmer of her meaning: 'Are you feeling that you've burdened me in some way?'

Lucy looks distressed but is silent. She seems very childlike. She speaks, but so quietly that the counsellor cannot hear her. She says, gently, 'I didn't hear that. Lucy. Is it ok if I move closer?'

Lucy does not recoil, so the counsellor moves her chair so that her head is close to Lucy's.

'I'm dirty', Lucy whispers.

Again, the counsellor struggles to understand Lucy's meaning. 'Are you worried that you'll make me dirty, too?' Lucy nods, miserably. 'That by telling me about it, I'll get . . . contaminated somehow?'

IMAGINATION

At first sight, it seems difficult to reconcile empathy and imagination. One is an attempt to understand the world of another person and the other, surely, is a reaching into one's own world?

Some clients are not well attuned to their own organismic experiencing. They can recount what has *happened* to them in considerable detail, but are not able to connect with their own internal experiences. For such a client, the question '... and how did you feel about that?' will be met with a blank or frightened stare. This type of question is, of itself, profoundly unempathic. The questioner has failed to understand that the client is not able to answer such a question and moreover, that either he wishes to please the counsellor and is feeling inadequate at not being able to answer or that the client is angry at being asked about such an unimportant matter.

For much of the time, the therapist will be able to offer a tentative suggestion to her client. She will pick up clues from the words used by her client, his body language and facial expression and his tone of voice. Sometimes she will experience in her own 'gut' a feeling which might be her client's. The key word here is 'tentative'. She is offering a possibility, which her client is free to take up, amend or reject as he will.

Her purpose is not to instruct, 'show' or impose a feeling on her client, but to begin the process of alerting him to the potentialities of his own internal world. If this is too much for his self-structure to accept, he will reject her suggestions. This does not mean that her tentative empathy is inaccurate. She might, in fact, be so accurate that his self-structure is denying or distorting her words in order to defend itself. A man who has rigid beliefs about what it is to be strong, for example, might reject anything which he categorises in his own mind as 'weak'.

The empathic counsellor is aware of this, and feels compassion for the client who is so scared of his own vulnerability. She is content to stay with his current experiencing.

Client: [*angrily*] You don't have to pity *me*, you know. It's all in the past.

Counsellor: Pity makes it sound as though I'm being superior. Am I, do you think?

Client: It's a long time ago. There's no point dwelling on it.
[*Pause*]

Counsellor: I just had a picture in my mind of a little boy whose dog had died. And I was feeling sad.

Client: Well, you don't need to feel sorry for me. It was only a dog.
[*Pause*]

Counsellor: A dog can mean a lot to a child.

Client: [*clearing his throat*] What I really wanted to talk about today was the job I'm applying for. I've decided not to tell Dorcas. After all, there's no point upsetting her unless I get it. She took it very badly the last time.

Counsellor: And you're worried that she'll have the same reaction this time.

Client: Oh she will. No doubt about it.

Counsellor: You sound a little . . . impatient . . . with her?

Client: Well, the last thing you want when you're preparing yourself for an interview is hysterics about moving! I mean . . . she is quite a highly strung person. Sensitive about things . . .

Counsellor: Are you feeling a bit guilty because that came out? Disloyal, perhaps . . .?

Client: It's not her fault.

Counsellor: But it can be difficult for you to handle at times, particularly when you need your energy for something important to you.

Client: Exactly.

Although the therapist does not 'push' her perceptions at her client, she does not deny them to herself. She has no investment in 'making' her client 'see' that he was distressed at the death of his dog, but holds in a corner of her own mind the probability that he was distressed. She has experienced him as touching upon his own sadness and then moving quickly away from it, and she follows where he goes. That fleeting connection with his own distress (if, indeed, she did not imagine it), was enough for him, for now.

CONCLUSION

At the heart of empathy is the counsellor's developing sensitivity to her client and her client's world. Charging around that world like a bull in a china shop is unlikely to be helpful, but neither is dabbling on the fringes. Each relationship is different, with its own nuances, and empathic communication evolves continuously as the relationship itself evolves.

FURTHER READING

Bohart, A.C. (2004) 'How do clients make empathy work?', *Person-Centred and Experiential Psychotherapies*, 3(2): 102–16.

Friere, E. (2007) 'Empathy', in M. Cooper, M. O'Hara, P.F. Schmid and G. Wyatt (eds), *The Handbook of Person Centred Psychotherapy and Counselling*. Hampshire: Palgrave Macmillan.

Haugh, S. and Merry, T. (eds) (2001) *Empathy*. Ross-on-Wye: PCCS Books.

Mearns, D. and Thorne, B. (1988) *Person-Centred Counselling in Action*. London: Sage.

Merry, T. (1999) *Learning and Being in Person-Centred Counselling*. Ross-on-Wye: PCCS Books. (See Chapter 5.)

Sanders, P. (2006) 'Empathy' in, *The Person-Centred Counselling Primer*. Ross-on-Wye: PCCS Books.

4

CONGRUENCE

Therapists can learn quite quickly to be better, more sensitive listeners, more empathic. It is in part a skill as well as attitude. To become more genuine, more caring however, the therapist must change experientially – and this is a slower and more complex process. (Rogers, 1978: 11)

WHY CONGRUENCE?

One of the outcomes which we hope for as person-centred counsellors is that our clients begin to replace other people's ideas, values and ways of understanding the world with their own. When people are in an unaccepting, judgemental environment, they tend to reach for safety – for what they 'know' to be 'true'; for those values, behaviours and ways of relating which are familiar. If the familiar does not seem to be good enough, they may put on a façade in order to win acceptance. In either case, they are taking their cue from other people. Their *locus of evaluation* is not within but outside themselves.

Sooner or later the actualising tendency will begin to do its work and they will feel dissatisfied or downright miserable. It is not uncommon in counselling to hear people saying things like: *'It's not really me'* or *'I'm not sure I know who I am any more'* or *'I want to be true to myself, but I don't know how'*.

Learning to *be me* involves developing trust in our own perceptions and working out our own values. These may have much in common with the values of our parents, say, but they become our own when they are based in our own experience rather than upon introjects. I feel satisfied, happy, good about myself when I . . . express myself creatively/help another person/stand up for my beliefs/live on my own. As the actualising tendency moves us towards greater integration between our experiencing and self-structure, we begin to trust our experience more and distort or deny it less. We begin to make our own judgements about ourselves and the world.

In the therapeutic relationship itself, my client's experience is of *me,* and my aim as a counsellor is to create a distortion-free zone. Congruence enables my client to learn to trust his experience of me. When he feels understood, he *is* understood. When he feels accepted, he *is* accepted. When he senses my irritation, I don't pretend it does not exist. He learns that he *can* trust his own perceptions – first and foremost, his perceptions of me.

In addition to this fundamental effect, congruence can be helpful to the client in other ways: sometimes an authentic response from the therapist's frame of reference will enable the client to further explore the matter which he is struggling with at the time. At other times, an expression of how the counsellor is experiencing the client may open new ground or shed light on his other relationships. But the true value to the client of counsellor congruence lies not in the detail but in the totality of the therapeutic relationship, however long or short this might be.

WHAT IS CONGRUENCE?

Your own personality, like that of your client, consists of an interplay between organismic experience and self-structure. Congruence is the part of yourself which is open, flexible, not given to distortion or denial. In other words, the *you* in which there is no conflict between your self-structure and your experiencing. This is the area of self which can be available in a very open, non-defensive way for clients.

Congruence describes that element of your personality which is *aware,* which is able to receive all of your client. When this aspect of yourself is engaged, you can hear your client's communications and adjust your perceptions of him from minute

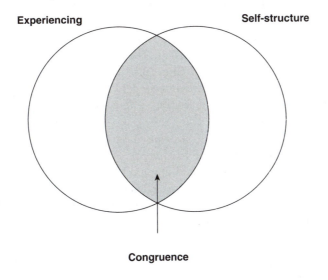

Experiencing   **Self-structure**

Congruence

FIGURE 4.1   Congruence

to minute as you receive further information from him. Your view of him is not fixed, or based on prejudice. Nor do you fit your perception of your client into a view of the world that you already hold. In fact, your view of the world is capable of being altered by what you hear from your client.

When you are able to be congruent, you are also aware of all of your own internal responses to your client. You do not distort or censor those reactions in you that are inconsistent with your idea of how a *good counsellor* should be. If you make a judgement about your client, you know that you have made a judgement. If you are impatient with your client, you can be accepting of your own impatience. This does not mean that you voice all of your responses to your client. It does mean, however, that you have the choice of whether or not to communicate them.

In person-centred counselling, helpful responses can come either from your understanding of the client's frame of reference (empathic communication) or from your own, congruent, frame of reference. The important thing here is to distinguish between that part of the personality shown in Figure 4.1 (congruence) and the choice to *communicate* to a client what is essentially something of your own awareness – your own experience within the counselling relationship. This can relate either to yourself or to your client.

As with empathy, developing the ability to communicate your own experience entails two basic processes. The first task is to learn to listen for and to become *aware* of your own thoughts and feelings in relationship with a client. The second is to learn when and how to communicate that awareness to your client.

The first task – that of developing self-awareness – is a never-ending one. As with any attempts to become more open and more self-knowing, it depends upon an environment in which the core conditions are sufficiently present. For counsellors-in-training, there are usually a number of possibilities. Their own therapy is the one in which they can focus most closely upon themselves. This has some limitations, however, in that as clients, we are working largely with our own perceptions. For this reason, most courses also have regular opportunities for course members to interact and reflect upon themselves in relationship with others. There are two main fora for this. One is the development group (also called self-awareness or personal growth group) and the other is the community meeting. The third, equally important, forum for developing congruence is in supervision, where the focus is on the counsellor in relationship with clients.

Reputable courses which lead to a counselling practitioner qualification always have as an entry requirement some baseline of self-awareness. During the course, participants will be expected to expand this and learn about authentic communication with each other, with tutors and with clients. It is a challenging and sometimes painful process. Fortunately, we do not need total self-awareness to be effective counsellors – that would be daunting indeed. We do, though, need enough openness and self-acceptance to be able to hear feedback and work with it.

Awareness of self can be more difficult to develop than the perception that is at the root of empathy. If a number of people watch a video or listen to a tape of a counselling session, there will usually be some consensus about the story and emotions that the client is expressing. The perceptions of each member of the group can be enhanced by the others' identifying and describing their 'hearing' of the client. With congruence, though, there may be no such commonality in students' internal reactions to such a tape. Each person's experience of the client will be perceived according to her own self-structure. One person's irritation or feeling discounted when a client misses an appointment without getting in touch may be another person's relief or a third's curiosity. None of these reactions is 'better' or 'worse' than another. All would be valid for that counsellor in that relationship.

You will sometimes hear the phrase '*your stuff*'. The implication is that there is material which should be sidelined or ignored as irrelevant to the therapeutic relationship. However, in person-centred therapy, all experience is of *potential* use to the client. Clearly, if you find your mind's eye focused on your own bereavement and yourself choking up, you have lost psychological contact with your client. But that same bereavement is potentially a rich source of insight and empathy – as long as your focus is the client in front of you.

A course member once likened congruence to the flame at the heart of the smoke. The smoke is the way we habitually communicate with each other. Each culture has its 'rules' of communication which cover everything from eye contact to polite phraseology. In my own culture, I learned at school that expressing the cognitive, logical, universal aspects of myself was preferred over the personal, felt and unique – reason is 'better' than emotion. We also have ways of hiding from ourselves those experiences which conflict with our self-structure, and ways of protecting our innermost feelings from being trampled upon by others. These, too, are part of the smoke beneath which we keep ourselves safe.

The flame is my authentic thoughts, feelings and past and present experiencing. Developing congruence involves believing that the smoke holds something valuable at its heart, however unlikely that may seem at first glance.

This first exercise may help you to explore the differences between 'smoke' and 'flame'.

EXERCISE

1 In a group of three or four, take it in turns for two or three minutes to tell the others about someone who (preferably in the past) got up your nose.

2 Now, again in turn, focus on your own experience. Other group members should use their empathy to help you to get in touch with your experience.

For example, from:
'He was an arrogant bastard'
to
'He didn't listen to anything I had to say. I felt utterly powerless. I lost all my ability to make an argument clearly because I got so upset and angry.'

Developing congruence can be a hard path. It means letting go of blame and recognising our own responsibility. It is the difference between '*He made me angry*' and

'*I was angry*'. It is the difference between '*It was wrong of him to do that*' and '*I didn't have a strong enough way of responding when he did that*'.

A saying which originated with Eleanor Roosevelt goes: 'Nobody can make you feel inferior without your consent' (Van Ekeren, 1988). That consent, or lack of it, lies in our self-structure. If, according to my self-structure, I am not an angry person (*Introject: It is wrong to get angry*), I may take it as a criticism or an accusation if someone perceives anger in me. I will distort or deny any angry feelings which arise in me. Common ways of doing this are to be self-righteous (*I am above such pettiness*), blaming *(He shouldn't be behaving that way)*, punitive *(I'll get him back)*, disparaging *(He's like that to cover his own inadequacies)* and so on.

Authentic communication is always centred on and held within the counsellor. It is often described as the counsellor 'owning' her feelings and experience. She knows fully that these are hers and hers alone, that congruence is always valid because it is an expression of herself in the relationship, and that the client's experience, even when it seems in contradiction to hers, is equally valid. She is self-accepting as well as accepting of her client. She *offers* her awareness to a client, to be taken or rejected by the client as happens in the moment. Her congruent experience is never imposed on the client, is never presented as 'the truth' and is usually *being* rather than doing.

AUTHENTIC COMMUNICATION

There is a 'flame' of truth to every communication which you have the impulse to make to a client, and in developing congruence you are concerned with finding that truth. Once you have found it, it will become clear whether or not it 'belongs' to you *in* the therapeutic relationship or to you *outside* that relationship.

EXAMPLE

Counsellor to client: How old is your daughter?

There are a number of possible 'truths' lying behind or underneath this question. Some of them are:

- I would like to have a picture of your daughter in my mind.
- I wonder whether she's the same age as my daughter.
- I'm worried about whether I might have to notify social services.
- How lovely, I've always wanted a little girl.
- You're waiting for me to say something and I don't quite know what to say.
- I know about medical matters and I'm working out a diagnosis in my mind.
- Oops, that question just popped out as a matter of habit.

Which of these 'belong' to the counselling relationship?
Which might you express to a client?

Although we separate the core conditions in order to consider them more closely, the overlaps become apparent very quickly. If authentic communication is centred in the counsellor's congruence, it is always unconditionally accepting of the client. If you are expressing your own responses, you are not judging your client.

We are, however, human and, without intending it, the less accepting elements of ourselves can easily 'leak'. Expressing your irritation to a client who turned up 40 minutes late for a 50-minute session is an authentic response and one which does not necessarily limit your unconditional positive regard for that client. In fact, you could argue that the pretence of a patience which you did not feel would be less respectful, and further, that unspoken irritation might make itself known in more subtle, less straightforward ways.

However, authentic and accepting responses can spill into something less appropriate to a counselling relationship.

EXERCISE

In the following examples, try to identity the elements that go beyond irritation:

- Your client is 40 minutes late for a 50-minutc session. You are irritated and you say so. But you find yourself unable to listen to your client's explanation. *You want an apology and you'll stay irritated until you get it!*

- Your client is 40 minutes late for a 50-minute session. You are irritated and you say so. He is the third client this week who has been late. You managed to be patient with the others, but this is too much. *You get rid of three lots of irritation in one go!*

- Your client is 40 minutes late for a 50-minute session. You are irritated and you say so. No one ever values what you do. You're always there for other people and they just take advantage of your good nature. *If this client does not appreciate you, there are plenty of others who will!*

- Your client is 40 minutes late for a 50-minute session. You are irritated and you say so. It's just good manners to be on time. You won't say anything more about it, but *if it happens again . . .!*

- Your client is 40 minutes late for a 50-minute session. You are irritated and you say so. He apologises. *That's easy for him to say. How does he think you are supposed to do any work in ten minutes!*

- Your client is 40 minutes late for a 50-minute session. You are irritated and you say so. *You spend the next 10 minutes telling him how much he has inconvenienced you, how he has used up a session which other clients could have taken . . .*

Some person-centred theorists and practitioners would argue that expressions from the counsellor's own phenomenal field should be rare; that they distract the client from his own process. For most clients at some times, and for some clients most of the time (those in fragile process, for example – see Chapter 9), this is undoubtedly true. However, many clients report that seeing something of their counsellor's *humanity* leads to a greater sense of equality and of trust. I remember one instance when, learning of an unexpected change of room, I became flustered and rather cross. My client's experience of this was a surprise to me. She had perceived me as always calm and in control and it was something of a relief to her that I could be caught off balance!

When the counsellor is responding from her own frame of reference she is expressing inner feelings of her own which have arisen directly from this relationship. If she is fully congruent, she will not be judging her client – although she might be expressing something that the client does not want to hear.

EXERCISE

Expressing those feelings that arise when we are with a client is one aspect of authentic communication. Such feelings may not arise from the congruent part of self, though, but from past experience or from our own value system. Becoming aware of the 'judgemental edges' of such feelings can help us to recognise when expression of congruent experience is spilling over into something else. Looking at the feelings listed below, what 'judgemental edges' might they have?

Anger

- Becoming punitive.
- Blaming.
- Being superior.

Concern

- Doing things for your client.
- Becoming protective.
- Smothering.
- 'Looking on the bright side'.

Add to the above or try one or two of the following for yourself:

| Shock | Relief | Joy |
| Anxiety | Fear | Sadness |

The beauty of a relationship is that all is rarely lost. If you become aware, through supervision say, that you have reacted in a punitive or superior or confrontational fashion, there is the potential not just for retrieving but for enhancing the relationship:

'I'm a bit ashamed of myself. I think I got rather on my high horse about your being late last week.' (*This is regretful, but it is not denying your irritation, nor is it being over-apologetic.*)

This can give a number of messages to the client, overtly and by implication:

- Your perception of me was trustworthy.
- I'm human and fallible.

- I can acknowledge my 'mistakes'.

- You too can make 'mistakes'.

- I don't expect you to be perfect.

- Making 'mistakes' is part of relationships.

- I can be accepting of myself even when I don't like what I've said.

- You can be accepting of yourself even when you don't like what you've said/done.

- You can tell me if I react in an inappropriate way in future and I won't fall apart.

- We don't always recognise immediately the impact of what we've said or done.

- We can always revisit something which is troubling us.

Person-centred counselling is, fundamentally, about relationship. What we *say* is only one aspect of our client's experience of us. We can express things clumsily or say what, in retrospect, seem totally inappropriate things and our clients will often perceive the good intentions behind the words. Conversely, our disapproval will 'leak out', even if the words are straight from a textbook.

Congruence involves being prepared to listen to other people's perceptions of you and being open to acknowledging it when there is a real basis for what they are picking up. This can feel like being 'caught out' at the time. A client said to me recently, 'You're looking really *smug*'. My first impulse was in reaction to the word 'smug'. I bristled and was tempted to deny it (my self-structure didn't like the word *smug* at all!), but I quickly realised that there was something quite accurate in what she said. I *was* feeling pretty pleased with my perceptiveness! It turned out that she was too, and she was teasing me – a fun moment in the midst of some bleak revelations.

FURTHER READING

Brodley, B.T. (1988) 'Congruence and its relation to communication in client-centred therapy', in G. Wyatt (ed.), *Congruence*. Ross-on-Wye: PCCS Books.

Cornelius-White, J. (2007) 'Congruence', in M. Cooper, M. O'Hara, P. Schmid and G. Wyatt (eds), *The Handbook of Person-Centred Psychotherapy and Counselling*. Basingstoke: Palgrave Macmillan.

Mearns, D. and Thorne, B. (1988) *Person-Centred Counselling in Action*. London: Sage.

Merry, T. (1999) *Learning and Being in Person-Centred Counselling*. Ross-on-Wye: PCCS Books.

Sanders, P. (2006) 'The Counsellor is ready to help: Congruence: Condition 3', in *The Person-Centred Counselling Primer*. Ross-on-Wye: PCCS Books.

Van Ekeren, G. (1988) *The Speaker's Sourcebook*. London: Longman.

5

CONGRUENCE IN PRACTICE

FEARS AND WORRIES

There are two main worries about authenticity in counselling relationships. The first is about our own lack of awareness. If we go back to our very simple model of personality (see Figure 4.1), the overlap between experience and self-structure, the centre section of the two circles, represents the part of ourselves which can symbolise experience in awareness. If we feel cold, we know it. If we feel tearful, we know it. If someone shouts at us, we know that it is their fury and not our 'badness'. If we disapprove of someone's actions, we know it is our own value system operating and do not imagine that 'right' and 'wrong' are absolute

In the other sections of the figure lie those aspects of ourselves which are not available to awareness or which are symbolised in a distorted way. It is these areas that we worry about in counselling, because we do not and *cannot* know when we are denying or distorting. If we could tell, then the material would not be out of our awareness.

The two-circle model, however, is too simplistic. A line between material which is in awareness and out of awareness suggests that it is either one or the other. It is perhaps more useful to imagine a band, or 'grey area' of experience which is rather dimly sensed and which can be brought into sharper focus by paying attention to it. We can feel uneasy or uncomfortable either during or after a counselling session, without knowing quite *why*. It is congruence that allows us to acknowledge the feeling, even though we cannot explain it. Another person's empathy is one of the best ways of helping us to become clearer: 'Yes, I *was* feeling resentful!', 'Of course! It *did* feel like he was pushing me', 'You're right. I *don't* want to see him twice a week'.

Supervision is vital for a counsellor because it enables us to pay attention to our more dimly sensed experience with clients. Looking back at the exercise in Chapter 4 (see p. 48), a supervisor may well perceive that the counsellor had been punitive rather than congruent and his empathy might help the counsellor to discover for herself how determined she was to make the client see it from her point of view. Alternatively, the supervisor might put himself in the client's shoes and say to the counsellor how he would have felt as the client in that situation.

Being in supervision also means that a third person, the supervisor, is responsible for alerting us to material out of our awareness which might have a bearing on our work with clients. A therapist whose impulse to punish a client was unavailable to her awareness would give a supervisor cause for concern. He might wish to ensure that she had her own counselling or a similar activity such as a personal development or therapy group to help her. More rarely, a supervisor might ask a counsellor to stop working with a client altogether until she had addressed whatever was preventing her from being open to her own or her clients' experience.

But supervision can also give us the confidence to be more spontaneous in our work with clients, knowing that we have help in monitoring our work. In practice, we will often feel ill at ease or troubled in some way if we lose our sense of acceptance for a client. A supervisor will help us to explore and become clearer about what is happening in us. This then enables us to take back to the client what is relevant to that relationship and deal ourselves with anything which is intruding in an unhelpful way.

The second worry about being congruent is of the client's reaction, for example, 'If I really say what I feel, my client might get upset/angry /hurt.'

It is very common, at work, at home, with friends, to try to avoid hurting or upsetting another person. The sense of self-blame – and others' blame – can be very strong. *It's your fault. What did you go upsetting her for!* But in any relationship, the unspoken hurts and slights can build up into a 'store' of feelings. If someone interrupts you as you are speaking, you might shrug it off as unimportant. You like this person and he's saying something interesting. The second and third times it happens, perhaps you feel yourself tensing up inside. By the time you have realised that he continually interrupts you, you have become cross *with him.* Perhaps you look for, and find, evidence that he is not such a nice person after all. By the time you say something to him, you have added self-righteousness to your store of anger. *Unconditional positive regard? For him?*

You have done all of this for the very good social reasons built into your self-structure – *Be polite; Have good logical reasons for everything; Expressing feelings is a weakness* – and because your past experience has taught you a thing or two – *The last time I got cross with someone, he hurt me badly; When I spoke up before, I got labelled . . .*

People who are hurt, upset or angry might well hit back. We know this, and it is a scary prospect. So one of our good reasons for not expressing ourselves congruently is to avoid anything which might lead to a reaction that we would be unable to cope with.

As therapists we are continuously learning to stay with and understand our clients' perceptions of the world. But it feels far more risky to stay with the perceptions of a client who is blaming *me* than to stay with him when he is angry with someone else. Can I stay in psychological contact with the client who accuses me of only listening to him because I'm getting paid for it? Can I understand how it is for the client who is feeling 'dumped' because I'm going on holiday? Can I continue to accept a client who is furious with me because I have refused to be his friend?

Can I be empathic, congruent and accepting of a client who abuses me because that is the only way he has of expressing his distress?

Another fear is not simply of hurting a client, but of harming him. Take the example of a client who wants to be your friend. This is someone who has felt himself rejected throughout his life and who is deeply hurt and vulnerable. How can you add to all this? If you say *No,* will it be the last straw for him? Will you have damaged him irreparably by rejecting him yourself?

But if you say *Yes,* this would probably be a falsehood. With friends there is a give-and-take. Could you lean on someone so needy? Would you have *chosen* this man as a friend, if you had met him in other circumstances? How eager would you be when he rang you to go out for a drink and a gossip? Would you end up hurting him far more deeply when your reserve began to show?

If you are honest with him now, he might be hurt, but he is far less likely to be harmed. If you can express your own confusions, sadnesses and worries instead of hiding behind a formula ('It's against my Code of Ethics', say), he will also learn that *No* to friendship is not a rejection of him.

We know from our theory that change is prompted by and accompanied by *feelings.* If we tread on eggshells around our clients' feelings, we might block rather than facilitate change. This is not, of course, to say that we set out to prod at our clients in order to stir up emotions. In person-centred counselling, we always work with *what arises* in the relationship, trusting that if it arises, it is ready to be dealt with.

SELF-DISCLOSURE

A common misunderstanding is to equate congruence, authentic communication and disclosure. Again, there is no consensus about how these terms are used, but for the purpose of making a distinction, I will use the term *self-disclosure* for communications which are not related to the here-and-now therapeutic relationship.

Self-disclosure includes things like:

- It happened to me.
- I have two children.
- I like skiing too.
- My father is very poorly at the moment.

There are times when self-disclosure can be very helpful to a client, but it should be treated with caution. There are several reasons for this, the primary one being to protect the *therapeutic space* for the client and his needs. This has a number of aspects. One is holding a boundary between the counselling relationship and other kinds of relationship. Mutual self-disclosure is, for example, an important characteristic of friendship.

On the other hand, never disclosing *anything* about your own life can seem like holding yourself aloof. If a client asks whether or not you have children, for example, should you answer? If he asks whether you know such-and-such a town? If he asks whether you have had a bereavement? If he asks whether you have ever been to Spain?

Such questions might arise from the client's belief that you won't be able to understand him fully unless you have had similar experiences. There are several factors which might have a bearing upon whether you give a simple answer or focus on the reason for the question, and these factors are explored in Chapter 11 (p. 138).

There are times when events in your own life might have an impact upon your counselling. You might have to rearrange an appointment, for example, or apologise for turning up late. You might realise that you have been less attentive to your client than usual. In such cases, a limited amount of self-disclosure can reassure a client that he is not the cause.

I've had a bit of distressing news and I realise I haven't been wholly here for you today.
'I'm so glad you told me. I thought I might have said something to upset you'.

On the other hand, a disclosure might switch attention from the client's material to yours, or even silence the client:

I'm sorry I cancelled without any notice. There was a death in my family.
'Oh, I'm so sorry to hear that. Was it very sudden?'
I'm sorry I cancelled without any notice. There was a death in my family.
('Oh no! I can't tell her my troubles when such a dreadful thing has happened to her'.)

The important thing is to be aware of how your disclosure has affected your client and not to:

try to dismiss his response; *or*
be drawn into giving more information than you are comfortable with.

- *I really appreciate your concern for me, but I do have lots of support.*

- *I'm touched that you're so concerned for me. It will take me a while to come to terms with it. But at the moment I'm here for you, not the other way round.*

- *You're really distressed for me, aren't you? Are you thinking about your own bereavement as well?*

ACCEPTING OURSELVES IN RELATIONSHIP

As you go through your counselling training, you are likely to focus first on acceptance and empathy. Your initial challenge will be to become *authentically* accepting and empathic with each other and with clients. But you may notice, particularly in relationship with others on the course, that there are severe limitations on your ability to be always and only accepting and empathic. Moreover, any attempt to keep this up will result in a build-up of frustration and anger. On the surface, everything might be sweetness and light, but it is a palpably false sweetness.

One of the paradoxes of writing any kind of description of congruence – or talking about it as a teacher – is that it can inhibit the very development which it describes. The quest for authenticity can easily become a condition of worth: *I am not allowed to express anything unless I do it in the 'right' way.* Once this attitude sets in on a course, participants can become very guarded – the course becomes the last place in which spontaneous communication is possible. *'That's not very person-centred'* is an accusation which is sometimes heard on courses. By its very nature, it is itself profoundly unaccepting! It usually means *'You're not listening to me'* or *'You're judging me'* and, 'underneath', *I'm hurt, I'm upset, I'm irritated* and so on.

We have seen that the self-structure under threat gets more rigid as a way of defending itself, and this is as true of counsellors-in-training as any other people. If spontaneous communication is unsafe, course members will never find the 'flame' within their 'smoke'.

EXERCISE

1 Imagine the following client, an immaculately dressed woman in her thirties who is talking nineteen-to-the-dozen. Notice your own responses as you read.

I'm under **so** much pressure at the moment. Everything at work has to be done yesterday, so either I have to stay late or I end up taking it home. Either way, Tony gets cross. It's all very well saying, I'm working too hard, but what am I supposed to do? Pack the job in? We certainly need the money, particularly with Jenny starting school in September. It wouldn't be fair to send her somewhere different from Tom. And they would really start complaining if they didn't get their holidays and their computer games and all the rest of it. Anyway, I *like* my job. There's no such thing nowadays as an easy life when it comes to work, particularly not at a salary of ninety thousand. Tony might be happy to amble along working for peanuts, but I'm not. And I can't do everything. He's just got to accept that the pressure's on at the moment. He complains that I don't spend enough time with the kids, but he's home every night by 5.30. If he wants me to do things with the kids, he shouldn't expect me to do half the shopping and cooking as well.

2 If your own responses do not appear below, add them to the list:

* Why doesn't she buy in some domestic help?
* Poor thing. She's carrying too many burdens.
* A salary of *what*?
* Oh dear. She's a pretty high-powered woman. She's bound to think I'm no good.
* Perhaps she should do a time management course.
* If she doesn't watch it, Tony's going to walk out on her.
* She'd better make a decent donation/I should be charging more.

- Sounds like she needs a holiday.
- Of course she's stressed. A mother shouldn't be trying to do a man's job.
- Lucky her. What couldn't I do with a salary like that.
- I bet she has to work harder because she's a woman.
- I'm feeling tired listening to her.

3 Preferably in a small group, identify the feeling or feelings which might be behind each response – envy, protectiveness, irritation, etc. There might, of course, be a mixture of feelings.

   If you begin to judge yourself or others, take note. The more acceptance there is, the greater is the likelihood of everyone getting in touch with their authentic responses.

4 Looking again at your own responses, see whether you can identify your good reasons for having them, irrespective of whether they seem to be useful in the counselling situation. If you are working in a group, each person should use their empathy to help the others.

It takes time and patience to help another person to find out what is *behind* or *underneath* their initial response. Time constraints on many courses make it difficult to do this, but the conditions of worth of the course (if you ask questions, you are a bad counsellor) might make it even more difficult.

EXERCISE

From time to time as your course progresses, ask yourselves: Have we built up any conditions of worth on this course? Try to differentiate between those guidelines which you are trying to follow as a matter of good practice, and any injunctions which would render someone who did not follow them a lesser or an unworthy person. As you have the discussion, check others' perceptions so that you can monitor your own self-structure. You may be predisposed to hear tutor or peer feedback as criticism, for example, in which case your own personal conditions of worth are probably operating.

Nothing that happens within the counsellor in the counselling relationship is irrelevant or inappropriate. Beginner counsellors often censor themselves heavily. Understandably, they do not want to 'make mistakes' and the early stage of training might be filled with what seem like injunctions about what to say and how to say it (and how not to say it).

- Listen, don't speak.

- Don't interrupt.

- Don't ask questions.

- Stay in the client's internal frame of reference.

- Focus on feelings.

They often learn to mistrust *themselves* in their counselling. The touchstone of the early learning, about listening to the client's internal frame of reference, not asking questions and so on, is often *Is this helpful to the client?* or *Did you say that for you or for the client?* This separation of what is yours and what is the client's is a useful early stage in developing authentic communication. But congruence is about being yourself in the relationship. The terms 'your stuff' 'and 'my stuff' are often used used in a dismissive way but I *am* 'my stuff'. All of my experience is of potential value in the relationship whether as a basis for empathic responding or sensing something happening between myself and my client.

To use the driving analogy once more, concentrating solely on your client is a little like only looking at the road ahead. To be an effective driver, you must also use your rear-view and wing mirrors. *How am I experiencing my client at the moment? What is going on in me?*

Learning to trust yourself in relationships is learning that you will not always 'get it right', either in your client's eyes or your own. But there are, of course, degrees of helpfulness and unhelpfulness. How can you recognise when congruence is spilling into your own values and self-structure – when your acceptance of your client begins to decrease? The following are some of the clues.

Be wary if:

- you find yourself doing rather than saying

- your focus shifts from your client to your own experience

- you want your client to follow a particular course of action

- you want to 'find the bright side'

- you want your client to understand *your* point of view

- your emotion takes you out of psychological contact with your client

- the action which your client might take is important to you

- you find yourself minimising the consequences to a client of your decisions

- you want to argue with your client

- you want to influence your client's decisions

- you find yourself justifying what you have said or done

Intensity of emotion is not necessarily a 'bad thing'. Nor is mentally linking your client's experience with one of your own. To some degree or another, all of our empathy is based in our own experience and we use our experiences to recognise and understand others. Again, the danger comes when we are unaware of the tie-in or when we lose the ability to focus on the client's experience. Keeping our own experiences separate in awareness enables us to recognise when our client's experience and feelings diverge from ours.

Emotion can well up in the counsellor as a client is speaking. This can be a deeply empathic phenomenon – as though the therapist 'catches' a feeling which the client is unable to express. The therapist is in close psychological contact with the client, able to experience the emotion, recognise and express it while still fully aware of the client. It is difficult to describe this experience adequately in words, but despite the feelings, which may be quite strong, there is a calm centre to the therapist. She is not lost in, or overwhelmed by the emotion. She can feel it and search for words to express it. She can be curious about whether it is her own or the client's feeling. If, when she has communicated it, the client does not recognise or acknowledge it, she can let it go and attend to the client's frame of reference.

It can be disconcerting to a client if he sees tears in the counsellor's eyes and he may well be afraid of 'causing' her distress.

Client:	I don't want to upset you.
Counsellor:	It's that poor little boy. He was trying *so* hard to be good.
Counsellor:	I'm not upset, exactly. But I am feeling for you.
Counsellor:	I don't think anyone could hear about that without it affecting them. But the difference is that I will only feel it as you are telling me. I won't still be feeling it later on today.

But the emotion that wells up in the counsellor sometimes takes her out of contact with the client and into her own world. She can either no longer focus on the client at all, or she only hears those aspects of the client's experiencing which coincide with hers. She does not find it easy to let go of the emotion, even when the client has moved on. It may be important to her that the client does not dismiss or negate the emotion and she might push the client into agreeing that it is good to have such feelings. She may feel anxious about the client's decisions or course of action. She has either become lost in her own experiencing, or so tangled up with the client that congruence is impossible.

COUNSELLOR CONGRUENCE AND CLIENT SELF-TRUST

One of the central movements for the client in person-centred therapy is that he learns to trust his own organismic valuing process. We tend to look at this in connection with the client's life outside the counselling session, forgetting that it happens – or not – within the session as well. Just as the counsellor *experiences* the client, so does the client *experience* the counsellor. But he may also have preconceptions of the counsellor which lead him to mistrust his senses.

If the client is experiencing, at a visceral level or organismically, one thing from a counsellor and hearing, in words, something different, he may well have doubts about his own judgement. The counsellor, after all, is the expert. *She* knows better than the client. In order for him to learn to trust his own experiencing, he must be able to trust the counsellor, which means that the counsellor's honesty is paramount.

For example, in the following situation the client, who is in a trusting relationship with his counsellor, feels 'pushed' in a particular direction:

Client: You're telling me what to do!

Counsellor: [*The counsellor thinks for a moment or two, taking seriously her client's perception and checking it against her own awareness*] Mmm. Perhaps you're right. I'm feeling uncomfortable now, because I don't believe in pushing you to do *anything*. Perhaps it's because I was worried for you. So, without quite realising it, I was wanting you to do what *I* would have done.

Client: Well, I want to do it *my* way.

Counsellor: You sound quite cross with me.

Client: [*Client considers*] I *was* cross. But now I've said it, it's gone away.

Counsellor: And I really appreciate the way you picked that up and told me straight away.

Client: [*Client's face brightens*] Yes, I wouldn't have dared to say that when I first started with you.

Counsellor: [*Counsellor smiles, remembering*] No, I don't think you would. You seemed very hesitant at first. Timid even.

Client: Well, I'm not now. I even told Derek where to get off yesterday.

Counsellor: You sound really chuffed with that.

Client: I do feel a lot stronger than I was.

Counsellor: Perhaps you're saying that you're getting to the point of not needing to come any more.
[*Client pauses*]

Counsellor: You look shocked. As though that's a new idea.

Client: I suppose I've got used to seeing you every week.

Counsellor: Sounds as if you're saying you would miss me. Which is a bit different from saying you need me . . .?

Client: [*Client considers*] So do you think we should stop?

Counsellor: I wouldn't like us to stop now. That would feel far too abrupt! But we could think about how and when we're going to end the work we've been doing together.

CONGRUENCE? EMPATHY? OR ...

EXERCISE[1]

Read the following extracts and discuss whether the responses given are empathic (from the speaker's frame of reference), congruent (from the listener's frame of reference), have elements of both, or are inappropriate in terms of person-centred counselling.

[1]This exercise was developed in conjunction with Maria Haines.

> *You're such a wonderful counsellor and I feel OK when I'm here with you but I just know I'm not going to be able to cope on my own over the weekend. If I could have your phone number I wouldn't feel so alone.*

a I think you've got the wrong end of the stick. I'm only a trainee counsellor, I'm afraid!

b It's very flattering of you to say so, but really you've done all the work.

c Oh, I would, but I'm afraid I've just changed my phone number and I can't remember the new one.

d I feel rather overwhelmed by that, as though I'm the only person you've got in the whole world.

e It's not allowed for me to give you my phone number.

f Sounds like you're really dreading that feeling of loneliness over the weekend.

g That's a bit scary for me because I'm worried that you're expecting more than I can give.

h So you think having my phone number would make everything feel all right.

> *He hits me – but only when he's drunk. Every time he does it I swear I'm going to leave but he's so sorry, cries, brings me flowers. But it's happening more and more.*

a I do understand. I had a boyfriend once who did that, and it's so difficult – you think of whether you could manage on your own, will the kids miss him ... oh, yes, I've been there!

b I know it must be really difficult to recognise this, but don't you think both you and the kids would be better off without him?

c Has he ever hit the kids?

d Well, in my view it's never acceptable for a man to hit a woman.

e I'm finding this a bit difficult, because something similar happened to me, and I don't want to mix up the decisions I made with helping you to work out what's best for you.

f So it's happening more and more?

g Given what you've told me before, I'm getting quite worried for your safety.

h I'm finding it quite difficult to just listen to you because I'm quite shocked by the bruises on your face.

i It sounds as though you're really torn between loving him and being frightened of what he's going to do.

BEING AND DOING

One of the characteristics of congruence mentioned above is that it is *being* rather than *doing*.

Take, for example, the counsellor who has a strong impulse to gather a client into her arms and comfort him. Acting immediately upon this impulse would not be congruence as we understand it in person-centred practice because it would not then be held within the therapist. Far from being offered to the client, it would be imposed on him. Neither would it be empathic, since it would take no account of the client's internal frame of reference.

Consider the possible effect of simply telling the client what is happening in the counsellor: 'I had a strong impulse just then to gather you up and comfort you'.

The client might:

- discover in himself a longing to be comforted

- remember a time when he was comforted and mourn the loss

- experience the pain of a life in which there is no one to comfort him

- feel embarrassed that you might want to do such a thing

- perceive you as patronising and be angry with you

The effect of such a statement is unpredictable, although with a client well known to the counsellor she might make an accurate guess. It is this unpredictability that can make congruence seem risky to the beginning counsellor. The client will 'hear' what she says according to his own self-structure and may react in a way which surprises, shocks or alarms the therapist. Foremost among the counsellor's fears tends to be that of hurting, upsetting or offending the client. Her own self-structure makes her responsible for him and instead of continuing to hear and experience him, she apologises to him.

Let us take the above interaction a little further:

Counsellor:	I had a strong impulse just then to gather you up and comfort you.
Client:	What do you mean, *comfort me* – I'm not a child.
Counsellor:	Are you feeling as though I was belittling you?
Client:	Just because my wife died, doesn't mean I can't cope.
Counsellor:	You sound quite angry with me.
	[*Silence*]
Counsellor:	Is it that, for you, someone who needs to be comforted isn't very strong – and you *are* a strong person?
Client:	[*Subdued*] I'm not being very strong at the moment.
Counsellor:	That sounded very lonely.

Counsellor:	I had a strong impulse just then to gather you up and comfort you.
	[*Client looks shocked*]
Counsellor:	You seem taken aback by that.
Client:	Well, I didn't expect you to say something like that.
Counsellor:	Do you expect me to be more . . . aloof? . . .distant?
Client:	It doesn't seem professional, I suppose.
Counsellor:	That I should have feelings, or that I should express them to you?
	[*Client looks uncomfortable. Silence*]
Counsellor:	Now I'm feeling as though I interrupted your train of thought, which wasn't my intention. You were talking about your grandmother.
	[*Silence*]
Client:	*She* used to comfort me. She was the only one who ever gave me a hug.

Counsellor: I had a strong impulse just then to gather you up and comfort you.

Client: Will you hold my hand?

Counsellor: Yes, if you want me to.

   [*The counsellor moves her chair forward and holds out her hand. The client clings to it and tears appear in his eyes. When he lets go, the counsellor speaks*]

Counsellor: Shall I move away a little now?

   [*He nods*]

Counsellor: I had a strong impulse just then to gather you up and comfort you.

Client: How dare you say that to me!

Counsellor: You sound offended.

Client: I'm going to complain about you to the BACP. You have no right to say that to me.

Counsellor: [*Counsellor looks shocked*] I'm really shocked and I'm struggling to understand what's happening. Will you tell me what you heard me say?

Client: No, I will not!

   [*Silence*]

Counsellor: I'm at a loss, really. I'd like to try and sort this out, but you seem to want to close it off.

   [*Silence*]

Counsellor: Have I been a disappointment to you in general?

Client: I've been coming here three weeks now, and nothing has changed. You said counselling would help and it hasn't.

Counsellor: I'm afraid I must have misunderstood you somewhere along the line. I hadn't realised that you expected to have finished in three weeks.

Client: All this, stuff about me. Surely you've got enough background by now. When are you going to offer me some suggestions?

   [*The counsellor remembers that not only did she mention person-centred counselling in the first session, she also gave this client an explanatory leaflet about the approach. Moreover, their initial contract was for six sessions. For some reason, the client has been unable to hear any of this.*]

Counsellor: I'm beginning to think that either I'm the wrong counsellor for you, or the person-centred approach doesn't suit you. Perhaps we should call it a day. I can help you to find someone else if you wish, and we should discuss refunding some of your fees.

Counsellor: I had a strong impulse just then to gather you up and comfort you.

   [*Silence*]

Counsellor: I've embarrassed you, I think.

Client: Yes.

Counsellor: Is there a bit of you which would quite like to be comforted?

Client: I suppose so.

Counsellor: But it's embarrassing at the same time.

Client: I remember being jeered at at school because my mum used to give me a hug in front of everybody.

CONCLUSION

Its unpredictability is one of the delights and tensions of person–centred therapy. The business of being in moment-to-moment psychological contact can have the same kind of mixture of exhilaration and scariness as a roller-coaster. *You are not in control.* Playing safe is not an option unless you abandon the person–centred approach and try to drive the roller-coaster. But, just as the roller-coaster has its own tracks, the actualising tendency works in its own way. You cannot 'steer' it. Your only alternatives are to try your best to help it do its job or to try to apply the brakes.

FURTHER READING

Cornelius-White, J. (2007) 'Congruence' in M. Cooper, M. O'Hara, P. Schmid and G. Wyatt (eds), *The Handbook of Person-Centred Psychotherapy and Counselling.* Basingstoke: Palgrave Macmillan.

Merry, T. (1999) *Learning and Being in Person-Centred Counselling.* Ross-on-Wye: PCCS Books.

Sanders, P. (2006) 'The Counsellor is ready to help: Congruence: Condition 3', in, *The Person-Centred Counselling Primer.* Ross-on-Wye: PCCS Books.

Wyatt, G. (ed.) (2001) *Congruence: Roger's Therapeutic Conditions: Evolution, Theory and Practice. Vol. 1.* Ross-on-Wye: PCCS Books.

6

UNCONDITIONAL POSITIVE REGARD

Unconditional Positive Regard. What a mouthful! This is the most difficult of the core conditions to describe and perhaps the most difficult to achieve. Words like 'accepting', 'non-judgemental', 'prizing' and 'respectful' are all used to convey something of the qualities implicit in unconditional positive regard.

If we go back to our theory, in a counselling relationship there are two people: counsellor and client. Each personality is an interplay of organismic experiencing and self-structure. As counsellors, we hope to bring our congruent selves to the encounter – the flexible, open part of our personality where there is no conflict between self and experience.

In everyday interactions, we receive communications from other people and react to them. There is no expectation that we should put our own needs or wishes to one side in order to fulfil those of the other (although we might sometimes choose to do so). So we will not necessarily monitor our own values and judgements.

Imagine a member of your household coming in late, when you are sleeping. They are noisy and wake you up. The next morning, you say, 'You woke me up last night'. This is not a simple description of what happened!

It contains a strong implication of fault, which might vary in degree according to the self-structure of the speaker, any agreements within the household about noise late at night and the relationship (for example, parent and child): *You should not have been making noise after midnight. It was insensitive of you to disturb my sleep. How dare you make such a noise when you knew I would be sleeping!* Feelings will be communicated from self-experiencing, for example: *I'm aggrieved. I'm outraged. I'm wounded. I'm upset.* If you are a parent, your belief system might say that you are *entitled* to make rules for the household – it's your house; you pay the bills.

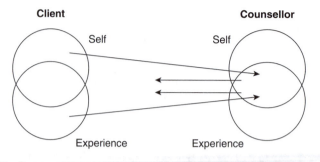

FIGURE 6.1   The Congruent Counsellor

Figure 6.1 shows the interaction of two people – counsellor and client. Each is communicating information to and receiving information from the other. Part of this information is verbal and part non-verbal. In this sense, the counsellor is *experiencing* her client, through words, tone of voice, posture and so on. Some of this experience is fully in awareness, some is at the edge of awareness and is available to be known through supervision, and some is out of awareness.

Both counsellor and client are capable of distorting or denying the information received from the other, depending upon self-structure. It would be nonsense to suggest that a therapist never makes judgements about the information she receives from her client. However, the six necessary and sufficient conditions emphasise congruence precisely because in this area of the personality, those judgements are in the counsellor's awareness and therefore less likely to impede the therapeutic work.

In theoretical terms, unconditional positive regard arises from the congruent area of the counsellor's personality. She is neither denying nor distorting her organismic experience of her client, nor filtering her experience of her client through her own out-of-awareness value system.

CASE EXAMPLE: BERNICE

Bernice, a women in her forties, has been talking about her ageing mother and the difficulties inherent in her mother living with her and her family. It was her partner's idea, she says, to invite her mother to live with them. Bernice talks about her partner and her children, 14-year-old James and 13-year-old Sophie and of how her mother has begun to criticise the children's behaviour. Bernice mentions that Helen has begun to stay out late to avoid this tension and speaks of how the entire burden of responsibility for her mother is falling on her shoulders.

- Counsellor A wonders who Helen is – Bernice's sister, perhaps?
- Counsellor B mishears the name 'Helen', hearing it as 'Alan'.
- It occurs to Counsellor C that Bernice might be in a lesbian relationship, but she is fearful of checking this out because in her self-structure, lesbian

> relationships are rather dubious. So she assumes that if she asks Bernice and is wrong, Bernice will be affronted or offended.
> • Counsellor D is perfectly at ease with lesbian relationships and simply asks 'Is Helen your partner?'

In the self-structures of Counsellors A and B, the world is constructed in such a way that the word 'family' means a heterosexual relationship, particularly where children are involved. Lesbian relationships might be something 'different', something 'other' – not of their everyday world. They experience Bernice as being 'normal' and therefore deny or distort the conflicting information which Bernice's words convey.

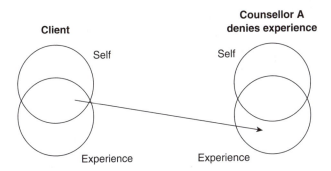

FIGURE 6.2   Counsellor A

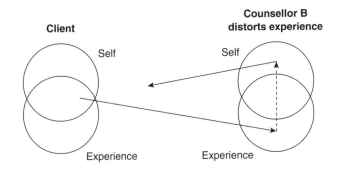

FIGURE 6.3   Counsellor B

Counsellor C has a theoretical acceptance of lesbian relationships, but is not at ease with the reality. Her self-structure might be struggling with introjected values from childhood saying that homosexuality is 'abnormal' or even 'wrong', and the values imparted through her counselling training saying 'You *must be accepting*'. So she is able to hear the possibility that Bernice is a lesbian but still treads on eggshells.

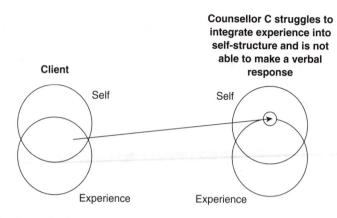

FIGURE 6.4   Counsellor C

In respect of lesbian relationships, Counsellor D has no conflict between her self-structure and her experience of Bernice as possibly in a lesbian relationship. She has no fear of offending Bernice because she does not see lesbianism as offensive. She is also aware that homophobia is a matter of introjects and if it proved that she had misperceived and Bernice herself reacted with horror, she would not judge Bernice's unaccepting stance.

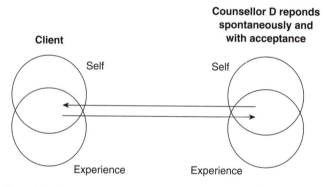

FIGURE 6.5   Counsellor D

JUDGING OTHERS

When we begin to learn about counselling, we discover that many of our spontaneous reactions have an element of judgement which we communicate in our responses: *'But don't you think ...'*, *'Wouldn't it be a better idea to ...'*, *'Surely, you're not going to ...'*.

As a starting point in learning about unconditional positive regard, we become aware of such reactions and learn to censor them. In fact, we often cut out entirely any expression of ourselves in the relationship at this stage, focusing solely upon empathic listening. This is a useful stage of learning, since in striving truly to understand another person, we have to put our own judgements to one side. As we learn more about others, we begin to let go of our certainties about the world, particularly of the nature: *Anyone who does X is a bad person*.

What is harder is not to collude in clients' judgements about themselves '*I shouldn't have done it*', says your client. '*Good*', you think, '*at least he knows it was a bad thing to do*'. This, though, takes no account of what led your client to do whatever he did. And it does not differentiate the action from the person, '*I shouldn't have done it …*' can mean the same to the speaker as '*I am a dreadful person*'.

Unconditional positive regard means believing that everyone has their own reasons for everything they do. All human effort is an attempt to reconcile organismic needs and self-structure in the best way possible for that person at that time.

JUDGING OURSELVES

Before accepting another, we must have achieved some degree of self-acceptance.

EXERCISE

1 On a sheet of paper, write down three qualities which you like in yourself, and three with which you are not so happy. Do not read further until you have done this.

None of these qualities is intrinsically 'good' or 'bad'. Each one has the potential to be creative or destructive, positive or negative. Each has an up side and a down side or a shadow and a bright side.

Take, for example, *competitiveness*. The *up* side of competitiveness is a striving for excellence, high standards, to be among the best. The *down* side is a desire to defeat others or put them down.

2 Looking at your own list, consider the *up* side and the *down* side of each of your own qualities. If you can, do this in a small group, since others can help you to see the pitfalls in those qualities you like in yourself and the potential in those you dislike.

When you wrote down your qualities, you were invited to make judgements about yourself.

- I like to control people

Hearing this, you might find yourself making a judgement – that controlling people is *bad*. But your client might be saying it with pride. Getting into *his* frame of reference could be a struggle. What is he telling you? Can you hear it?

Which of the responses below seem judgemental to you?

- It gives you a buzz when you have some power over others.
- You rather like bossing people around.
- You enjoy using your authority.

In fact, all or none of them are judgemental. If they are said with critical intent, they are judgemental. If you accept that *this is how it is* for your client and you are checking out his meaning, then you are not judging him. Acceptance lies in you, not in any form of words.

Unconditional positive regard comes from a basic belief that everyone has reason for everything they feel, think and do. The 'good reason' may not be immediately apparent to you or to your client, let alone the other people around him. The 'good reason' might be in the past and it might be totally out of date, but it is there and it will come to light when and if it needs to – if you are open to hearing it.

PARTIAL HEARING

Hearing and accepting *all* of your client's world is a complicated business. It is easy to fall into the trap of limiting your positive regard by paying more attention to one aspect of your client's communication than another.

For example, paying attention to your client's expressed goals can, paradoxically, prevent you from fully accepting her. Take, for example, a client who has been talking about a relationship in which her partner abuses her in some way. During one session, she says with great decision, '*I want to leave him. I know it's going to be difficult, though, so please help me*'.

Perhaps you have been worrying about her safety. You may even have felt some relief at her decision. From then on, without you quite realising the effect of it, it becomes your goal to help her to leave her partner.

She says, sadly: '*I loved him so much*';
'*But he's changed*', you reply, also with sadness.

You have chosen to respond to a previous communication. *He has changed*, in preference to paying attention to the loving feelings which your client had, and may still have, towards her abusive partner.

She says, in worried tones: '*I'll have to move away from all my friends*'.
You reply: '*Why does it have to be you who moves away?*' or: '*Do you find it difficult to make new friends?*'
It might not be so bad, you are suggesting, or even, *It has to be done, though*.
Eventually, she begins to blame herself for not making the move: '*I know I'm being stupid ...*', '*I know I should just go ...*'
'*You're not being stupid*', you reassure her. '*It's very difficult to make a move like this*'.

What has happened? You were being person-centred, weren't you? *She* was the one who said she wanted to leave. You may even be feeling impatient with her for procrastinating instead of getting on with it.

Without realising it, though, you have blocked exploration of two important areas: first, the possibility that she might stay with her partner and, second, her loss and grief if she goes. It is as though by paying attention to the love she has (or has had) for her partner, you believe yourself to be undermining her decision to leave. But she has reason for being in that relationship and, whatever her eventual decision, she will be mourning the loss of those things the relationship held for her.

Were you being person-centred? Or were you being goal-centred?

Had you stopped listening to and accepting *all* of her, in favour of listening only to those parts of her communication which moved forward the goal of her leaving the relationship? Was your own self-structure so outraged by her partner's behaviour that you were unable to hear that she loves him still? Did you worry that if you paid attention to her loss and grief, she might decide to stay? Did you, without intending to, block off her exploration of how she might protect herself *and* remain in the relationship?

When you hear and accept her reasons – love perhaps, companionship, solvency, fear of being alone, disapproval from friends or family, religious beliefs – so will she. Instead of worrying about *your* opinion of her, she will listen to herself.

LISTENING TO THE WHOLE PERSON

One danger is to listen more to the organismic experiencing than to the self-structure. In the example above, the woman might be risking her own acceptance in her family or social circle if she leaves. In some cultures, the honour of her entire family might depend upon her staying.

'I *can't* cry', says one client. The counsellor hears this as a plea for help. According to her theoretical understanding, her client's inability to express his distress is caused by his conditions of worth. It is entirely logical, therefore, for her to accept the task of helping her client to overcome this barrier to true expression of his feelings.

She comes to supervision and reports being 'stuck' with this client. He seems to be going round in circles and she cannot seem to help him to release his tears. Without realising it, she has fallen into the judgemental trap of valuing his distress more highly than his apprehension. The client knows better. He is of a family, of a workplace and of a society which see men who cry as weak. Realistically, if he were to cry in front of his family members, he, and they, would suffer considerable embarrassment. If he were to cry in front of his colleagues, he would jeopardise his prospects of promotion. Instead of receiving acceptance and understanding from his therapist, he has received the subtle message that he should learn how to cry. His self-structure is under threat and it has marshalled its defences.

The self-structure is fulfilling its function admirably in ensuring that this client does not receive censure or disapprobation from others. However, the actualising tendency is at work. His uncomfortable feelings are its signal that there is an important matter that needs to be symbolised in awareness and incorporated into his self-structure. By failing to empathise with the self-structure and to accept its validity, the counsellor is failing to provide the climate in which the self-structure can loosen and integrate the distorted or denied material. If this climate were to be provided, '*I can't cry*' could become '*I can sometimes cry, but not in front of …*'.

In practice, it can be very difficult to accord equal unconditional positive regard to every aspect of a client's self-structure: an anorexic who perceives herself as fat; an abused young woman who is convinced that she is worthless; a convicted criminal who 'knows' that no one gives a shit, so why should he? How tempting it is to 'show' such clients that they are wrong! But any attempt to do so, however subtle, is an attack upon the self-structure and it will respond by defending itself and becoming more rigid.

EXERCISE

If a client made the following statements, what might you *not* hear as clearly as you hear the goal?

'I really want to pass these exams, but I'm useless at studying. Everyone's telling me I should get good grades but when I get the books out, I don't seem to take anything in. Will you help me?'

'I know I shouldn't hit my kids when I get wound up. It's not their fault, and I feel so *guilty* afterwards. But they're really naughty sometimes and I don't know what to do with them. I want so much to be a good mother, I really need your help because I'm frightened that they'll take the kids away from me.'

'I just *can't* lose my job. The hearing is in three weeks and I've already got two verbal warnings against me. I know I should have got in touch with the Union before now, but they weren't very helpful last time. What do you think I should do?'

'It's the kind of opportunity I've always dreamed of. Pat's *very* excited about it, living in the United States for a couple of years. And the Company is being very generous with expenses as well as the salary. It's a once-in-a-life-time thing, really – all my colleagues are green with envy. To tell you the truth, it's making things a bit difficult, me being chosen like that. But I couldn't turn it down, now could I?'

CONFIGURATIONS OF SELF

Mearns and Thorne (2000a) have taken further the concept of the self-structure to acknowledge that we all draw upon different aspects or 'parts' of our selves at different times. These they call 'configurations'. They might be named by a client as 'the strong, coping me' or 'my scared little girl part', or even given a name as in 'Bully Brian' or 'Whining Mary'.

Again, we might be tempted to 'hear' one configuration more strongly than another, particularly if we see some configurations as less attractive, or even less truthful, than others. But the therapist's task is to accept all aspects of our clients and accord them equal respect.

BEING 'POSITIVE'

One of the common misunderstandings about unconditional positive regard arises from the use of the phrase *valuing the client*. This becomes confused with *praising* the client, which is just as much a judgement as condemning the client.

One of the outcomes that we hope for in person-centred therapy is that the locus of evaluation moves from external to internal. In other words, instead of looking to others for judgements about how to live his life, a client begins to clarify his own values and make his own judgements accordingly. He comes to recognise that some of the tenets he has held as 'truth' do not mesh with his experience and he is able to revise his belief system to take account of this. He comes to trust much more in his own perceptions rather than taking on other people's points of view.

When a counsellor praises a client, this can be as much a threat to the self-concept as any other experience which conflicts with the self-structure. In fact, anyone will be able to hear and believe condemnation which accords with his self-structure more readily than praise which conflicts.

EXERCISE

In a small group of people who are known to each other and trusted by each other, each person in turn takes two minutes in the 'hot seat'. During this time, the others say the things which they like, value or appreciate in the person. The rules are:

1 Everything that is said must be truly meant. It is important that the hearer can trust the others so that s/he knows any twisting of the meaning to be entirely in her/his own head. If one of the group does not like, appreciate or value anything, they must remain silent.
2 If another member of the group says something with which you agree, you should voice that agreement, so that the person knows that you, too, have that perception.
3 The person in the 'hot seat' should try not to respond to the others, but should notice his or her internal reactions to what is being said.
4 No one should be pressurised to be in the 'hot seat'. This can be a challenging exercise.
5 After everyone has had the opportunity to be in the 'hot seat' (even if some of the group do not take up the opportunity), the group discusses the exercise.

Some group members will dread, or even expect, silence, wondering whether the others in the group like anything about them. Commonly, each group member will find her/himself distorting some of the feedback to fit in with his/her self.

- 'You're really good at organisation' might be distorted to *She thinks I'm bossy.*

- 'I love your clothes – they're so colourful' might be distorted to *He thinks I'm too old to dress like this.*

In one of those many overlaps between the core conditions, it begins to become clear that when we talk about self-acceptance, or unconditional positive self-regard, we are also referring to our own congruence. In order to accept ourselves, we must first know ourselves and not distort or deny significant aspects of who we are or how other people perceive us. However, there may be aspects of ourselves, either past experiences or character traits, which are known to us but about which we feel discomfort or shame. Can we, in truth, perceive similar aspects in clients without judging them as we judge ourselves?

HEARING AND RESCUING

There are some things that may be particularly difficult for a therapist to hear fully and offer an empathic response to. Usually they involve the client's non-acceptance of himself:

- My life is not worth living.
- I am a disgusting person.
- It was my fault that I was raped.
- I am obscenely fat. (An anorexic speaking)
- He didn't mean to do it. (An adult survivor of repeated childhood abuse speaking of her abuser)

For the beginning counsellor, voicing empathy might seem too close to agreeing with the client. It is as though by saying something which is understanding of the client's frame of reference, she might make the awful thing bigger.

And what of congruence? If she is appalled by the client's terrible and unrealistic view of himself, may she not say so?

As always, the three core conditions need to be in balance. If a client were in the throes of distress because his child had died, would the counsellor rush into saying that she saw him as a strong, coping person? Probably not. This would be inappropriate because she would not yet have fully *heard* his grief. Neither would it be accepting of his distress. She would almost be dismissing his pain in her wish to 'make him feel better'. When we distract someone from their feelings in this way, it is called 'rescuing'. It is unlikely to be really congruent because it arises from the counsellor's unwillingness to accept her client's believing such awful things. She wants to reassure him that he *is* a nice/good-looking/worthwhile/intelligent person and that life *is* worth living or *will* get better … .

In doing this, she fails completely to offer unconditional positive regard. The client learns that his certainty about his own slimy core is unacceptable. His counsellor is not willing to *understand* what this feels like. She would rather he pretend that it is not there. He learns that his counsellor cannot accept that he feels responsible for his own abuse. She would rather persuade him otherwise. In doing so, she prevents him from expressing freely what he wants to express.

EXERCISE

In the examples below, what might the client be wanting to express or explore?

Client: I hate myself.
Counsellor: Oh, but you're a lovely person!

Client: I'm a dreadful mother.
Counsellor: But look at the way you care about Sonya! You can't be such a dreadful mother when you love her so much.

Client: I'm so fat and ugly.
Counsellor: That's just not true. You're nothing but skin and bone.

Client: I'll never be able to pass the exams.
Counsellor: Of course you will. I've seen how intelligent you are.

LABELS

There are many ways of describing people who use services such as housing, education and health. Some of these are also used of counselling clients: this client is 'manipulative', that client is 'dependent', another client is 'attention-seeking'. What is happening when we use such labels?

The first thing is that we can lose sight of one of the basic premises of person-centred theory: that people have reasons for everything they do. Take someone who is described as 'manipulative'. He might have learned early and painfully that asking directly did not result in his getting his needs met. He might, for example, have had a parent or carer who was impatient and needy herself and who could not cope with the demands of a young child. He might have absorbed a condition of worth along the lines: *It is bad to ask for things. Wait until they are given*. In his experience, the only way to get his needs met without being punished is to wheedle or 'trick' others.

Another person is described as 'attention-seeking'. Who among us does not want attention? Once this label is applied, though, the covert message is that to *give* attention to such a person would be in some way encouraging them to continue with a bad habit. One can argue that people need attention as much as they need food. And the parallel – that we should not encourage someone to eat today, because they will only want more food tomorrow – is clearly nonsense.

The third example is of a 'dependent' client. Many among us will have depended upon others, particularly when we have being going through a painful or traumatic time in our lives. How many times have you heard someone say, 'I wouldn't have got through it without X'? They may not mean literally that they would have died, but the phrase does express something of the neediness and desperation they felt and the gratitude they experience for the person who was able to respond.

There is a subtle shift in wording from 'depending upon' to 'being dependent' which changes the natural activity of turning to others for help when in need to some kind of fixed way of being. This is the real danger of labels. Implicit in the sentence 'X is dependent' are the notions that X's dependency is unnatural or even dangerous and that it would be counterproductive to meet her needs. The counsellor becomes a superior being who has made a judgement about X which makes it ok for her to become detached from X's feelings.

What is happening here for the helper? *Being depended upon* can feel quite overwhelming. As a counsellor, I can become aware that I am the *only person* in someone's life, that their hour with me is so important that their survival seems to them to depend upon my being there. I can feel trapped by this intense neediness – perhaps I feel inadequate in the face of their pain and the barrenness of their life.

Here, yet again, theory is my lifeline. I must – and do – trust that this person's self-structure is gradually loosening, that they are integrating more and more of their experience, that when the time is right they will begin to form new and more honest relationships based upon a growing sense of their own worth and the trustworthiness of their own instincts. Their need for me will lessen but their *experience* of me and our relationship will be carried forward.

When we classify or label someone, we are often disguising our own worries and insecurities. We try to make it *their* problem and nor ours.

EXERCISE

1 Add any more you can think of to the following list of labels commonly used for clients of a range of services:

- Dependent
- Manipulative
- Compliant

- Disruptive
- Moody

2 Taking each label in turn:

   a what kinds of behaviour are likely to have given rise to the label?
   b what might be your own worries and anxieties in working with such a person?

Nowadays, clients themselves often have preconceptions about therapy and what makes a 'good' client. They might say something like 'I know I mustn't turn you into a substitute for my mother' or 'I know I mustn't get dependent on you'. Such statements might be expressions of a deep longing for something they have never had.

Our knowledge of, understanding of and belief in our theory and our hypotheses, are being challenged all the time. What if it doesn't work? What if it doesn't work *for this person*? What if it takes years and years? These are questions which do not seem to go away, no matter how much experience we have.

I think I must once have imagined that after a number of years of practice, I would never have any doubts, either about the validity of person-centred theory or about my own inadequacies. But although in my head I *know* that person-centred counselling is effective and that all of my experience bears out the fact that the six conditions bring about change, each time I am in contact with a client in the depths of pain and hopelessness such knowledge is challenged. I have come to believe that if I am truly empathic – if I enter into someone's world in such a way that I can *feel* their despair – my certainties must become shaky. It is *this* person who is suffering, *this* person who has no expectations of happiness, *this* person whose life and experiences are unique. If I am in touch with this person, I must somehow be less in touch with global certainties. I find myself believing and doubting at one and the same time.

DECEIT

Alan Brice's account of his work with a deceitful client, which follows this chapter, illustrates several aspects of person-centred theory, particularly that 'objective truth' is not a useful concept in therapeutic work and that the actualising tendency is still at work, even in the most unpromising of circumstances.

If a client is deceiving you, it is the meaning which is important. Why does he need to lie to you?

- Because he doesn't believe that he is interesting enough for you to give him time?
- Because he wants you to see him as important or successful?
- Because his experience says that if he tells the truth people betray his trust?
- Because if he told the truth, you would have a hold over him?
- Because if he trusts you, he is risking too much disappointment?

In many cases, a counsellor will not know at the time that the client is not telling the truth. But sometimes counsellors have suspicions, or even evidence, that a client is lying. If the counsellor becomes troubled by what the client is telling her, how might she raise it with the client?

This is always a matter of congruence. We will each have different feelings if this happens, depending on our own personality and on the client we are working with. Sometimes we might have an understanding of why a client is concealing or misrepresenting something – and it might seem unimportant to raise this if the work is focused elsewhere. But sometimes something will 'niggle' at us so that *not* saying it is getting in the way of the work.

Counsellor:	I'm a bit confused about what you're saying. I thought at one point you said your father was a barrister. It doesn't matter very much, but did I get that wrong?
Client:	Well – er – he's had several different – er …
Counsellor:	I was wondering whether you thought that I might – I don't know – treat you with more *respect*, if your father was a barrister.

Counsellor:	I found out by chance that you're back living with your family and you've been talking to me as though you're still in your flat. I'm feeling rather hurt – because I don't understand why you feel you have to conceal it from me.

Counsellor:	I'm finding it difficult to say this because I think you might take it as an accusation. But you're so *detached* at the moment, I'm not sure I can believe you when you say you haven't been drinking.

Counsellor:	Some of what you're saying doesn't seem to hang together. I was wondering whether you've gone back to Paul and you didn't want to tell me because you thought I might – *disapprove?*

CONCLUSION

Unconditional positive regard is difficult to assess because it is an attitude on the part of the counsellor – a willingness to believe that any client is doing the best he can in the circumstances in which he finds himself. It involves patience – moving with the client and allowing the process to unfold in its own time. Paradoxically, this is usually the quickest time, since a client who is censoring himself to avoid a counsellor's judgements or to please his counsellor does not have the best conditions for development.

FURTHER READING

Bozarth, J. and Wilkins, P. (eds) (2001) *Unconditional Positive Regard.* Ross-on-Wye: PCCS Books.

Bozarth, J. (2007) 'Unconditional positive regard', in M. Cooper, M. O'Hara, P. Schmid and G. Wyatt (eds), *The Handbook of Person-Centred Psychotherapy and Counselling.* Basingstoke: Palgrave Macmillan.

Kearney, A. (1996) *Counselling, Class and Polities.* Ross-on-Wye: PCCS Books.

Mearns, D. and Thorne, B. (2000) 'The nature of configurations within self', in D. Mearns and B. Thorne (eds), *Person-Centred Therapy Today.* London: Sage.

Purton, C. (1998) 'Unconditional positive regard and its spiritual implications', in B. Thorne and E. Lambers (eds), *Person-Centred Therapy Today, a European Perspective.* London: Sage.

Sanders, P. (2006) 'Unconditional positive regard', in, *The Person-Centred Counselling Primer.* Ross-on-Wye: PCCS Books.

CASE STUDY: ACCEPTING A CLIENT WHO TELLS LIES

ALAN BRICE

Many people relish the chance to try to be free of visiting their dangerous and shameful places. After years of suffering the agonies of their lives, they have had enough of that. In the context of a counselling relationship they can have the chance to step outside of the critical and negative judgement they are familiar with. They can begin to value and appreciate themselves. On occasion, in being keen to move on from their past, clients can get into difficulties when trying to create a new life within the context of the rest of their world. I have sometimes seen clients who have wanted to block out part of their world that they have not wanted and then hoped that they will be all right. I was intrigued to find that Marcel Proust wrote: 'But the absence of one part from a whole is not only that, it is not simply a partial lack, it is a derangement of all the other parts, a new state which it was impossible to foresee in the old' (Proust, 1996: 368). It is that derangement, this new state, that can be troublesome.

MY CLIENT

One of my clients, a young man in his twenties, told me his mother suffered from schizophrenia, and she was regularly in and out of hospital. He feared being as disturbed as she was. He felt terribly guilty about this, because he couldn't cope with it and he kept away from her. His parents had separated when he was quite young, and he felt he had been left with his mother to help look after her. In addition he told me that his male baby-sitter, selected and trusted by his mother, sexually abused him.

We met many times over a period of a year as he tried to find himself amongst all that had gone on.

When he told me he had heard the news that his mother had died, he was, especially confused, disturbed and unsure. It seemed unclear whether she had killed herself or taken an accidental overdose. She had taken a number of tablets. It seemed that there was no suicide note, so perhaps she had been confused, drunk possibly, rather than intending to die.

We worked through his bereavement for some time. He was drained by sleeplessness, as when he did sleep he had the most awful dreams of seeing his mother in her coffin getting up, moving around, speaking to him. It really seemed hard for him to cope with the complexity of his relationship with her and with the tragic ending to her sad life. The amount of unresolved material was very hard for him to cope with.

At this point I felt confident of our working relationship. My mother had mental health difficulties and my parents had separated too. Supervision was helpful to me in making sure my material was separate from his. Yet I know I felt connected to him. I had a real warmth, Rogers's 'non-possessive love' perhaps, for him. I felt we both believed that the process of counselling would work and that, although damaging to him, this bereavement could be worked through. My belief in this work was sufficient that I thought that I might use this bereavement work for a case study for my BACP accreditation, which I was completing at that time.

Indeed, over a period of time, he did seem to become more resolved and able to move on. He was noticeably less affected by his mother's death and more concerned about current events in his life, such as trying to re-establish contact with his father.

After a while he became troubled by suicidal thoughts and began cutting himself and drinking excessively. He talked more and more about his own suicide and the ideas he had had for that. I was very worried about this and told him that it seemed he was becoming more fixed on his feelings of worthlessness and pointlessness, and that the idea of dying seemed increasingly attractive to him. He acknowledged that and we spent several sessions facing the bleakness of this.

He arrived at my office on a Sunday when I was sorting some paperwork. I saw him because I was concerned for him and his 'out of hours' visit was sufficiently unusual for me to suspect an emergency.

He told me he had just taken a big overdose of a cocktail of medicines. We sat together reviewing what had brought him to this state. I really did not want him to die, and told him so. He didn't want me to call the ambulance and I feared that if I did he would leave the office, disappear into the city, and be found dead in an alley or park. I determined to call an ambulance when he started to lose consciousness to the extent that I could prevent him from leaving, and I really hoped it would not be too late.

I was hugely relieved when he decided to go with me to the casualty department of the local hospital, which conveniently was a few hundred yards away.

He telephoned his flatmates to let them know where he was, because he had left a note for them, and now did not wish to frighten them. They arrived at the hospital while he was being assessed by the medical staff, and they told me that his mother had telephoned and wondered where he was, that they knew he was lying continuously, and that they liked him but couldn't put up with all his lies.

I was almost thrown into a state of shock, really not sure what to believe. This was a moment when the world seemed to swim around my head. Perhaps his mates were lying? He couldn't be lying. Could he? I was doing my absolute best to keep a professional aspect of calm as I listened to them. Congruence was not in my mind. How could I stop from slumping down and crying about how awful it all was? Had my pathetic, foolish, complacent counselling almost led to this young man killing himself? How could I ever counsel again?

When I went into his room, he realised they had told me about his lies and I saw from his reaction that they were right and he had been lying. I remember smiling at him, with a rueful laugh.

When they had gone, he told me he had lied to me about many, many things, but he felt worst lying about his mother's 'death'. He feared that I would not be able to trust him at all, and that I would no longer believe he had been abused.

I was quite shaken, and confused – how had I been so foolish as to not realise? How had he sustained it all for so long? What did I believe about him? I felt angry at being deceived. I felt stupid, a fraud and really challenged about my worth as a counsellor.

I also realised that this did not stop my love and care for him. Even at that moment I was thinking about how helpful it must have seemed to him to live as if his mother were dead. What he hadn't expected was the derangement that Proust wrote of, the new state, where rather than it being easier, it actually was worse.

He recovered from the overdose and came and saw me a couple of days later. He explained how he had lived in a fantasy world, which was part real and part false. He couldn't sustain it when he saw how much I believed him, trusted him, cared for him and had tried so hard to understand his experience. That had challenged his sense of himself. He could not face himself as someone lying that much. It seemed that his only option was to die, and yet he came to see me because, at the same time as needing to die, he did not want to die. When I started to write this and brought it back to my attention I cried because the world was so close to losing a very lovely young man who had suffered terribly.

By mere chance his friends had broken the deceit, and yet I wondered whether this was chance or by his design. I realised that he wanted to live, and to live well, and that he had a small flame of hope flickering within him. In the end I don't think that at any conscious level he tried to stage-manage his friends telling me the truth. I do think that this was me questioning truths and becoming hyper-suspicious of people's motives! Immediately after the overdose and for some time I was quite unsure whether what he or anyone told me was true. My vanity was certainly damaged and I was so glad I didn't write this case study for my BACP accreditation!

I did feel terribly unsettled by this, and yet perhaps oddly reassured about the importance of trusting the client's process.

If I had questioned his mother's death, what sort of relationship would we have had? Would we have had a factually true series of social worker interviews or would we have had a relationship based on value and respect? I see it as something close to the difference between taking a patient's history, which would include getting the facts, and trying to generate a process of therapeutic movement.

I explored not needing any 'truth'. Indeed having studied philosophy at University I started to reconsider issues such as truth, certainty and knowledge. I became fearful of naivety, of foolishness. I read about the psychology of lying, thinking that I needed to resource myself so I could tell when someone was deceiving me.

I learned a lot at this time. What I learned was to trust in the quality of our relationship. No matter that he had lied to me, he came to me when he could have died. He trusted me. He believed I would be there for him. It might seem unlikely but from then on we had an amazingly close, deep, powerful connection. We both see that time as a crucial turning point in our lives.

I recall laughing with him as he told me about a new relationship he had started, as we joked about him making it all up. All the books and the philosophy had given me nothing compared to what we had between us.

For me it did confirm my belief in working in a person-centred way, and it gave me what I can only call a faith in my way of being with my clients. That I could stay with him after finding that out, and that I stayed with the 'real' him with all the damage and disturbance we had been through was deeply healing for him, and certainly surprising to me.

For him, well, he has now been in a stable and very loving relationship with his partner for nearly three years, and has a settled job. He keeps in contact with a postcard, e-mail or a note every few months.

MY LEARNING

All the work on sub-personalities including Mearns's work on configurations of self (Mearns and Thorne, 2000b) and Warner's work on fragile and dissociated processes (Warner, 2000), as well as my reading of literature really helped me to get a sense of what this was all about.

It isn't so odd to present ourselves as more than we are, or to emphasise certain aspects of ourselves. I certainly couldn't be judgemental about that. I see that he was further out on the '*completely solidly real* ↔ *invented and exaggerated*' continuum than many people.

He talked about a part of him wanting to be free of all the shame and guilt about his mother. He wanted to be a different person in so many other ways, and so he lived those other ways. He put aside his abused past. He 'killed' his mother off. He read literature and studied art. He talked about travelling around Europe.

I recognised that some of this was similar to how I can present myself, and saw that in some way he was modelling from someone important to him whom he respected – me. Yet it was too hard to tell me that, and I didn't know about it.

Other parts of him knew he was lying, and he couldn't quieten them even by cutting or drinking. The dreams of his mother in the coffin were real, and make a different sense now. The internal turmoil nearly killed him.

I have wanted to come to an understanding of what encouraged him to lie, or prevented him from telling me the truth.

Did I, in that relationship, contribute to his going beyond who he was into something quite fantastical? Did he feel some sense of falseness in me that encouraged him? My room has art prints by Hockney, Rothko, Moore, an Italian espresso machine, photos of countryside from Scotland, Ireland, and from recent holidays to Italy. Do I present myself as the fullness of me or suitable aspects of me for the role I live out in the context in which I work? My family background is neither artistic nor of the subculture that I choose to live in. Did he see me stepping beyond my own troubled past to a brighter, newer world that I have created?

How true it is that I learn from my clients. It made me even more determined not to give a toss if someone turned out to be lying. Actually, that isn't true. I am happy, so life-affirmingly happy, to accept them and their lying, without rancour, without regret for me and with as much positive regard for them as I can find.

7

PSYCHOLOGICAL CONTACT — BASIC AND COGNITIVE CONTACT

ROSE CAMERON

The first of the six conditions that Rogers considered necessary and sufficient for therapeutic change is that two people are in psychological contact with one another. All that he means by this is that some minimal relationship exists between them, even if this is merely that they are, at some level, aware of each other's presence. The importance of this in counselling is, Rogers says, so obvious that it hardly seems worth mentioning. What is very much worth mentioning, but he makes psychological contact the first of the necessary and sufficient conditions for therapeutic change because the other conditions are meaningless without it. He says it is more of an 'assumption' or 'precondition' (Rogers, 1957) than a condition in itself, and in a very late and little known re-working of the conditions necessary and sufficient for constructive personality change (Rogers and Sanford, 1984), he dispenses with mentioning it altogether.

Rogers conceives of psychological contact as either being present or not, and, if present, as something that we can take for granted. Later writers (Ellingham, 2002; Van Werde, 2002a, 2002b, 2005; Warner, 2002; Whelton and Greenberg, 2002), including myself, have conceived of psychological contact as being on a continuum, or of there being different qualities or degrees of contact. Margaret Warner highlights the importance of meaning in writing that '(p)eople feel out of contact with each other when they can't sense the other person as meaningfully present'. She goes on to discuss Garry Prouty's 'pre-therapy' work with clients who are experiencing 'schizophrenic or retarded psychoses' (Warner, 2002). This chapter will begin by looking briefly at pre-therapy (there is more about this in Chapter 14) before discussing other aspects of contact that are related to what is said. The following chapter will explore some non-verbal aspects of psychological contact. Both chapters will invite you to explore how available you make yourself, and will look at how we may respond to a client who is, in some way, making him or herself unavailable.

MEETING: BASIC PSYCHOLOGICAL CONTACT

Psychological contact is a mutual thing. Each person must receive the other: I must know that you are here, and you must know that I am here. I may, for example, on the first day of a counselling training course, notice you as somebody I know by sight. If you also notice me we are beginning to make psychological contact. We are affected by each other's presence.

However, we will not experience ourselves as being in contact unless we acknowledge each other in some way; I must know that you know that I am here, you must know that I know you are here. You may warmly return my smile, glad to see someone you recognise, or you may think, 'Oh God, there's that awful woman', and stare at me blankly. We choose whether we want to be in psychological contact with someone or not, and we communicate our receptivity towards the other.

THE COUNSELLOR'S AVAILABILITY FOR MAKING BASIC CONTACT

We are not indiscriminately available for psychological contact. We put limits and conditions on our availability, on our willingness to receive another person. Some limits are a response to our own needs: I may, for example, choose not to answer the phone if I am very tired. Conditions arise out of judgements we make: I may avoid someone in the street because I deem them to be mad, bad or boring.

The limits we put on our availability for psychological contact depend partly on our cultural norms. I, for instance, grew up in a city in which it was relatively usual to acknowledge strangers whilst passing in the street. I quickly learned to stop doing this on moving to another city in which it was not at all usual, and regarded with bemused suspicion. So it may be necessary to put limits on our availability for psychological contact in order to remain socially appropriate. We may also feel it necessary in order to maintain a sense of having personal space.

However, we may also put conditions on our availability for contact in much the same way as we put conditions on our acceptance of others. Rogers called the conditions we put on our acceptance of each other 'conditions of worth'. He saw conditions of worth (the messages we receive that we are only worthy of acceptance if we are polite/successful/don't get angry/frightened, etc.) as fundamental to the process by which we lose self-acceptance and eventually lose trust in our organismic experiencing. They can be profoundly damaging.

Conditional availability for contact can be understood as an extreme condition of worth. It gives the message, 'If you are not as I want you to be, you are not only unworthy of my acceptance, but unworthy of my paying any attention to you whatsoever. I will treat you not just as a bad person, but as an invisible person. You're not fit to exist.'

We may make our willingness to receive another person conditional on who they are. We may have a prejudice against certain groups of people, and perhaps look through individuals of a particular race, class, gender in a manner that is particularly annihilating. We may express our discomfort with people who are in some way different to us, perhaps disabled or homeless, by acting as if they are not there. We may also make our willingness to receive another person conditional on how they behave.

EXERCISE

Circle the situations below in which you might choose to block someone out.

- when you see someone begging in the street
- when you notice a stranger behaving oddly
- when you are angry with someone
- when someone is angry with you
- when you are frightened of someone
- when you find someone's behaviour towards you hurtful
- when someone is ignoring you
- when you feel anxious in a new group
- when someone is boring you
- when you pass someone collecting for a charity you do not feel strongly about

What judgements might you be making?
What might you be feeling?
How might you communicate your unwillingness to make contact?

We may block psychological contact when we feel uncomfortable, hurt, angry or threatened, instead of making, or staying in contact and communicating a response. Imagine deciding that you will not block contact in the situations you circled.

- What might you do or say?

- What do you feel as you imagine this?

THE CLIENT'S AVAILABILITY FOR MAKING BASIC CONTACT

Hopefully you will not actually ignore your client during the course of your counselling work. It is possible, however, that your client may ignore you.

Responding to a client who appears to be ignoring you depends very much on the context and meaning of the client's unavailability. Before reading on, make some speculations as to what might be going on in the following situations.

> ## EXAMPLES
>
> A client with whom you have had quite a difficult session arrives for the subsequent session, gives you a terse hello, and then sits silently without looking at you.
>
> You are seeing a 14-year-old client, referred by a teacher, for the first time. She sits with her arms folded, raises her eyes to heaven and sighs dismissively when you make an opening comment.
>
> You are with a client who has recently been in a terrible accident in which she lost two children. She has been sitting silently, looking past you for what seems like a very long time.
>
> You are seeing clients on a psychiatric ward. A client, whom you are meeting for the first time, does not communicate or respond to you at all, she just rocks back and forth.
>
> Another client from the same ward seems highly agitated, and talks a lot, but to himself rather than to you. You cannot make sense of what he is saying.

Clients may be unavailable for psychological contact because they are angry, frightened, or overwhelmed by what is going on inside them. Clients behaving in a similar way to the clients in the final two scenarios are often seen as needing 'more' than person-centred or, indeed, any other kind of counselling. In the Wisconsin Project, Rogers and his colleagues did work with people diagnosed as schizophrenic, who tended to either remain silent or fill their time with talk that was incomprehensible to the counsellor. They found that when therapeutic movement did occur, it was as a result of the counsellor's empathic, respectful and genuine attitudes, but that mostly the clients had difficulty perceiving these attitudes, and there was no significant therapeutic movement. 'Our schizophrenic individuals *tend* to fend off relationships either by an almost complete silence – often over many interviews – or by a flood of over-talk which is equally effective in preventing a real encounter' (Rogers, 1961: 188).

Gary Prouty (1990), an American psychiatrist working from a person-centred perspective, has recently developed a way of working with clients who do not acknowledge our presence – clients who do not indicate that they know we are here, or, indeed, that they know they are here. Prouty suggests that institutionalisation, over-sedation, social isolation and psychological withdrawal may impair a client's ability to make contact. His 'pre-therapy' aims to help such a person make psychological contact with themself, their environment and with other people.

Prouty categorises various reflections counsellors, or others, may make in order to establish psychological contact with a client who does not communicate:

- *Situational reflections* (SR) acknowledge the environment shared by client and counsellor and help the client make contact with a shared reality.

- *Bodily reflections* (BR) help the client become aware of what they experience within their own being, the sensations and feelings they experience.

- *Facial reflections* (FR) verbalise the feelings implicit in the client's facial expression.

- *Word for word reflections* (WWR) acknowledge what the client says and confirm them as somebody who can communicate.

- *Reiterative reflections* (RR) help to re-establish contact by inviting the client back to a point at which the counsellor experienced being in contact with them.

I think it is useful to think of Prouty's reflections as expressions of an attitude of receptivity. Each time the counsellor makes a reflection she says, 'I know you are here. I can see you do this, hear you say that'. She lets her client know that she is receiving him. She acknowledges him, communicates with him, invites him to enter into a relationship with her. She does not withdraw in frustration, irritation or boredom, but continues to be interested in, and receptive towards the client, and lets him know this by acknowledging what he does and says. The counsellor invites the client to open up by remaining open herself.

So far we have been looking at instances in which a client is obviously and clearly unavailable for contact. In most working situations, it is likely that a client's unavailability for psychological contact will be subtler and less absolute.

Psychological contact is established when both people experience themselves as being in psychological or personal contact with each other. It is subjective – we have to rely on our own experience.

We may experience our client as rather remote, 'not quite with it', 'a bit out of it'. The most appropriate response to this again depends very much on why the client is absent. Their ability to make contact may be impaired by alcohol or mood-altering drugs, including prescribed medication. Clients may be withdrawn because they are depressed, anxious, frightened or in shock. Keeping a psychological distance from other people may be habitual and an important issue to work on in counselling, or they may just be very tired, or coming down with the flu.

Whatever the reason, it is important to acknowledge that you do not feel in contact. Such an acknowledgement might be enough to bring the client back into contact. It may lead to a mutual decision that therapy would be more useful once your client has stopped or reduced whatever substance they are using, or that the degree of contact that is possible is sufficient to make the relationship workable. Using your experience of the client's remoteness may help them make contact with their feelings of isolation – or decide that they'd be better off going home to bed.

MAINTAINING BASIC CONTACT

Your client is not the only one whose availability for contact may vary.

EXERCISE

Can you remember instances in which you have been distracted by any of the following, and temporarily withdrawn from contact with a client?

- worrying about whether you are making the 'right' responses
- feeling shocked
- being reminded of something similar in your own life
- feeling criticised
- wondering if the tape you are making will pass an assessment
- boredom
- preoccupation with your own thoughts
- tiredness
- feeling attracted to your client
- annoyance
- making a judgement about the client, perhaps that they are 'in their head'
- analysing the client

1 What did you do, or what might you have done in the above situations to bring your attention back to your client?

2 Imagine that you've been considering the possible causes of your client's problem. Suddenly you realise that while you've been doing so, you haven't heard a word your client has been saying. Do you say anything about this to your client? What might you say? You may find it useful to explore potential responses with a partner or in a small group.

Although it is not strictly true, it may be useful, in the interest of maintaining focus, to adopt the belief that you can't listen and think at the same time. In suggesting this, I am not suggesting that you neglect to use your brain at all. Understanding our client accurately, being in what we might call cognitive contact, may require considerable mental flexibility.

UNDERSTANDING EACH OTHER: COGNITIVE CONTACT

Cognitive contact involves our mental processes – thinking, understanding and so on. Cognitive contact is about shared meaning, and like basic contact, it is a mutual thing. Each person must make their meaning available to the other, and be able to receive the other person's meaning. It seems reasonable to expect the counsellor to work harder at this than the client: the contract we make, explicitly or implicitly, with our client is that we will try to understand them as best we can. In order to understand our client's meaning as best we can, it is important that we have some understanding of the ways in which the client constructs meaning, that we are able to understand their perceptions, their point of view, to enter their frame of reference.

The counsellor's availability for cognitive contact

In some forms of therapy the client must be willing to understand and work within the therapist's theoretical frame of reference. The person-centred approach, on the other hand, makes the individual client's frame of reference the meeting place. A client in a person-centred counselling relationship does not need to understand concepts such as conditions of worth in the way that a psychoanalyst's client would need to understand the concept of the unconscious. This does not mean that the person-centred therapist should not be explicit about her theoretical framework if asked. It does mean that the onus is on the counsellor to understand the client's way of looking at the world in the client's terms, rather than the other way round.

In order to receive our clients as they really are, rather than as we expect them to be, we have to recognise the influences that shape our clients' frame of reference, and the influences that shape our own frame of reference. We must recognise our own perceptions, values and beliefs as our own rather than assuming that they are 'right' or are shared by everyone.

We live in a multicultural society, and we are multicultural beings: we live within our national culture or cultures, the culture of our class, family, generation, group of friends, office, company, profession and training institution. We speak the languages of our different cultures and, to varying degrees, adopt their value systems. If I am going to really hear another person, I will probably have to make some effort in order to understand the real meaning of their words; I will probably have to widen my knowledge and understanding of different communities and cultures.

Learning about other cultures is important if we are to recognise, understand and value our clients' difference (I recommend reading fiction by writers from different places). However, knowledge is only useful if used wisely. However much knowledge we may acquire about another culture, we will never really grasp its subtleties and complexities. To imagine otherwise is to risk misunderstanding, missing our client's meaning.

We also risk missing our client if we use our knowledge to stereotype. To be in a client's internal frame of reference is to enter their inner world. When we stereotype, we trap people in a world that is not theirs, a patchwork world we have created out of bits of information and partial understandings.

The client's availability for cognitive contact

Words will probably be the door through which we will most often be invited to enter our client's world. The importance of basic comprehension – understanding what the words mean – is obvious. Achieving it, however, may not be without its difficulties.

EXERCISE

A client uses a word you don't understand. What might you think, feel and how might you respond in the following situations?

- Your client's first language is not English, and you are struggling with their accent.
- Your client's first language is English, and you're struggling with their accent.
- Your first language is not English, and although you are really fluent, you find this client seems to be using a lot of words you don't know.
- Your client is using a lot of slang that you don't understand.
- The word your client has used is quite a long one and you don't know what it means. You think your client must be using the word without really knowing what it means. In social conversation you would let it pass for fear of embarrassing the other person, but it really is affecting your understanding.
- Your client is a drug user. It is the first session. You have no idea what brown/rocky/skag/blow/snow/draw/whizz/jellies are. You didn't ask when she first used the word, and now it seems rather late to do so.
- Your client, who is perhaps from a different cultural background, or much younger than you, uses an ordinary word (wicked, sad, sick, bad, etc.) in a way that suggests a meaning different from the meaning it has for you.

SPEAKING IN CODE

Our accent, choice of words, and the meaning we ascribe to them vary according to our culture, class and generation. Culture, class, generation, and even our gender and our sexuality, also affect our use and understanding of language in less obvious ways, as we will see towards the end of this section.

Unless we belong to the same community as our client, it may seem to us as if they are speaking in code. They are. We all speak in some sort of code all of the time. Fully receiving our client at a cognitive level means accurately receiving their encoded messages as well as the more apparent content of what they say (or don't say).

Some of the codes we use – street speak, technical jargon, family phrases and words – are easily recognised as such. They indicate our membership of particular groups. We encode information about ourselves by using language in a way that indicates our ethnicity, class, religion, politics, etc. We may, like the client in the excerpt below, intentionally use such codes to indicate our membership of a particular group.

EXAMPLE

My line manager sent me to see the counsellor at work. I work in quite a homophobic environment, and nobody knows I'm gay, so I wanted to check out the counsellor's attitude quite carefully. I mentioned my partner a few times without mentioning his gender. I could tell she noticed because she, too arranged her words so that she could avoid saying he or she without it sounding awkward. It felt as if she got the message straight off, and was letting me know that, and telling me she wasn't going to push it. I ran a couple more coded words by her. She matched me perfectly, catching everything, returning code word for code word. I was really warming to her. It felt like we were doing a formal dance, increasingly tongue in cheek. Later I dropped in a reference to a gay icon and we smiled together in recognition of the fact that she'd got the message loud and clear.

Had the counsellor not picked up on the client's encoded messages, she would have missed the client's invitation to understand him better, his invitation to greater psychological contact. We use code of some kind to indicate the degree of psychological or personal contact we want, expect, or think is appropriate, in all our exchanges with each other. We may maintain a distance by using a formal code, predictable, polite, the socially sanctioned script for that situation, or we may use a much more informal code which invites familiarity.

The beginning of a counselling relationship is often characterised by a formal code of careful wording and stock phrases till one person initiates the change to a more informal code.

Counsellor: It's good to see you again. Please, feel free to begin whenever you're ready.

Client: Well, I felt much better after last week.

Counsellor: You felt better after talking last week.

Client: Yes, I did some of the things I said, including ringing my father. Is it ok to talk about anything?

Counsellor: Yes, this is your time.

Client: My father said that the cousin I told you about has been sent to prison for armed robbery.

Counsellor: Bloody hell!

Client: [*looks surprised, then relieved, relaxes, then starts to shake*] I've been going mad –...John's a ****, but now he's gone down I feel dead sorry for him.

At the beginning of the above extract, the counsellor is using a formal code of learned stock phrases – 'counsellorese'. The counsellor is probably unaware of the fact that she is using a code, and almost certainly unaware of some of the implications of doing so. By using a formal code, she indicates her membership of a group – the Counselling Profession – and does so in an exclusive way. The gay client earlier used code in an inclusive way: 'Do you recognise these reference points?' he asked his counsellor. The counsellor in this extract is not asking this question. She is probably just not thinking about what she is saying. Or rather, she is probably thinking too much about what she is saying, perhaps wondering if what she says would be approved of on her course, rather than responding spontaneously.

Because the power imbalance between counsellor and client is likely to be particularly pronounced at the beginning of the relationship, the client may well use a formal code out of respect for the counsellor's status as a professional. This client does not use a specialised code like counsellorese, but is careful to 'speak properly'. The counsellor above successfully invites a person-to-person encounter, gives the client permission to be human, by being human herself, expressing her shock in a spontaneous, unmeasured, everyday way.

Formality marks social as well as professional boundaries. We are expected to show particular respect to those who have more status than ourselves by virtue of age, class, social standing, etc. Formal language codes reinforce these inequalities in power, and may do so within a counselling relationship. The client in the above extract was careful to 'speak properly' not just to match the psychological distance indicated by the counsellor's relative formality, but also in an attempt not to appear uneducated to a middle-class professional. The therapist's shift into an informal code was a huge relief to her, and turned the session into something to be used rather than endured.

Moving from a formal to an informal code is a delicate negotiation. Informality has become the new way of being warm and welcoming in America, and to a lesser extent in Europe. This does not mean that informality has acquired this new meaning for everyone. Too familiar a code may be received as rude, intrusive or disrespectful. Informality may help some clients feel at ease whilst the absence of appropriate social rituals may leave others feeling insulted.

Other forms of linguistic code are more subtle, and very likely to be used out of awareness. Codes assume common ground, shared meanings: we do not necessarily restrict our use of shorthand to those who are likely to understand it, especially when we are not aware that we are using a code in the first place. When the use of code is out of awareness we are most likely to misunderstand, and be misunderstood.

THE PROCESS OF FRAMING

It's not what we say, or even the way that we say it that matters. What matters is whether the meaning we intend matches the meaning that is taken. Codes assume shared meaning, and shared meaning requires common reference points. If our frames of reference are very different, what we hear may not be what our client intended to say, and vice versa.

Our frame of reference is constructed from our life experience, and the contexts and cultures in which that experience takes place. Attributing meaning, framing experience, is not a static thing but a process. If we are to enter our client's frame of reference, to understand their personal meanings, it is useful to understand some of the ways in which they are likely to frame their experience. It is also useful to have an awareness of how we frame our own experience. 'Whites who are effective seem to learn two attitudes', writes Rogers. 'The first is the realisation and ownership of the fact that "I think white". For men trying to deal with women's rage, it might be helpful for the man to recognise "I think male"' (1978: 133).

Men, claims linguist Deborah Tannen (1992), tend to understand relationships in terms of hierarchy and status, whilst women understand relationships in terms of interconnectedness and intimacy. Many women, she says, are surprised that their partner doesn't know how many children his boss has, and are likely to interpret this as a lack of interest and warmth because the woman is more aware of what she has in common with the boss – kids – and uses this common interest to make a personal connection. Her partner, however, makes contact through the more formal relationships dictated by status. He acknowledges his boss's status by keeping a respectful distance, not being 'too personal'.

In talking to anybody about anything we inevitably express something about how we understand our relationship with that person. The person with whom we are talking will invariably hear something about how we see our relationship with them. What they hear may, or may not, be what we intended to communicate, depending on whether we are framing something in the same way.

EXAMPLE

Counsellor says: 'I really want to help you all I can with that'.

Female client smiles and nods in receipt of the implicit message: *I've nothing particular in mind, I just want you to know that I care about you and want to support you.*

Male client quickly replies, 'Oh I will work it out in my own way', having heard, *I'm a professional with more status. I've got much better ideas than you. I want to take over and tell you what to do.*

Letting the client know that you understand what they are saying is something you probably will, or will have, practised with some persistence during your early training. You will, hopefully, also have practised checking out what your client has understood you to have said. Making verbal contact is important, but the non-verbal aspects of psychological contact are more important. They are also more difficult to discuss, but I will attempt to do just that in the following chapter.

FURTHER READING

Clarkson, P. (1995) *The Therapeutic Relationship*. London: Whurr.

Joseph, S. and Worsley, R. (eds) (2005) *Person-Centred Psychopathology: A Positive Psychology of Mental Health*. Ross-on-Wye: PCCS.

Joseph, S. and Worsley, R. (eds) (2007) *Person-Centred Practice: Case Studies in Positive Psychology*. Ross-on-Wye: PCCS.

Prouty, G., Van Werde, D. and Partner, M. (2002) *Pre-Therapy*. Ross-on-Wye: PCCS.

Rogers, C.R. and Sanford, R.C. (1984) 'Client-centered psychotherapy', in H.I. Kaplan and B.J. Sadock (eds), *Comprehensive Textbook of Psychiatry, IV*. Baltimore: Williams and Wilkins Co. pp. 137–88.

Sanders, P. (2006) 'Psychological contact', in *The Person-Centred Counselling Primer*. Ross-on-Wye: PCCS.

Sanders, P. (2007) *The Contact Work Primer: An Introduction to Pre-Therapy and the Work of Garry Prouty*. Ross-on-Wye: PCCS.

Tannen, D. (1986 reprinted 1992) *That's Not What I Meant: How Conversational Style Makes or Breaks Your Relations with Others*. London: Virago.

Tannen, D. (1991) *You Just Don't Understand: Women and Men in Conversation*. London: Virago.

Wyatt, G. and Sanders, P. (eds) *Rogers' Therapeutic Conditions: Evoluation, Theraphy and Practice. Vol. 4: Contact and Perception*. Ross-on-Wye: PCCS.

Wyatt, G. (2007) 'Psychological contact', in M. Cooper, M. O'Hara, P. Schmid and G. Wyatt (eds), *The Handbook of Person-Centred Psychotherapy and Counselling*. Basingstoke: Palgrave Macmillan.

8

PSYCHOLOGICAL CONTACT — SUBTLE CONTACT[1]

BY ROSE CAMERON

SUBTLE NON-VERBAL CONTACT

Paying attention to the more subtle, non-verbal aspects of how we make ourselves available for contact makes the difference between a rather mechanical and lifeless therapeutic relationship and one that shimmers with energy and involvement. It is difficult to say what exactly the non-verbal aspects of psychological contact are, but most readers will have experienced the difference between talking with someone who is really 'there' and someone who is 'not really there'. Both interactions might look and sound exactly the same, but there is a very real difference in quality: they *feel* different.

The non-verbal aspects of how we indicate our availability for psychological contact certainly involve our expression, posture and gestures, but they also involve something more elusive. When I run training workshops on this subject I demonstrate this by sitting in silence with a volunteer while the other workshop participants observe. Without moving or changing my expression, I shift my attention away from the whole group, relax, and allow myself to silently 'reach out' to the volunteer. I might equally say that I make myself 'available' to them, or even that I 'open' towards them. Then I 'pull myself back in'. The volunteer notices a change immediately, as do some of the observers.

---

[1] This is a thorough re-working of the chapter in the original edition of this book, and draws upon Rose's work towards a PhD at the University of Edinburgh.

EXERCISE

Ask a counselling colleague, or even a friend, to sit with you for a few minutes and just experience what it is like to be in your presence. Gather yourself together, then turn your attention to your partner and allow yourself to gently 'reach out' to them. Don't do or say anything, just have the intention of making contact with them. When you feel you have done that for long enough tell them that you are going to do something different, then 'draw yourself back in' or 'shut down'. You will probably find it harder to 'draw yourself back in' than you found it to 'reach out'. You can 'pull yourself in' first and then 'reach out' if you find that easier. When you have finished give yourself a shake and return to you usual state.

Ask your partner to describe what it was like being with you while you did the above.

The volunteer I do this experiment with usually feels that we are in contact, or in better contact, when I 'reach out'. Sometimes the volunteer notices a change in my eyes, and sometimes the observers notice a change in the rhythm of my breath, but the most obvious difference is in the emotional atmosphere. I invite the participants get into pairs and try the experiment for themselves. I suggest that once they have done so, they then try doing it with their eyes closed. They find that they can still sense a very distinct difference even when they can't see anything. Sensing variations in someone's availability for contact in this way is a very ordinary, every-day experience, although it can seem strange when it is isolated from other aspects of communication. We all notice changes in someone's tone, expression, posture and gestures when they become bored or distracted. We also *feel* a change – the 'vibe' is different.

THE DIFFERENCE BETWEEN PERCEPTION AND INTERPRETATION

Words such as 'vibes' or emotional 'atmosphere' are often used in discussing this level of contact. We rarely talk about 'vibes' or 'atmospheres' without making a value judgement – we talk about 'good vibes', 'bad vibes', a 'good atmosphere' or a 'bad atmosphere'. We usually imagine that we know what the other person is feeling. We are not necessarily right.

In the original version of this chapter I made rather too clear a distinction between this quality of contact, which I called 'subtle contact' and emotional availability, or 'emotional contact'. The two *are* distinct. The volunteer who helps me with my demonstration usually experiences me as warm and interested when I 'reach out' and as uninterested and cold when I 'pull myself back in'. In fact, my feelings, emotional availability and degree of interest have not changed. I 'reach out' and 'draw myself back in' not because I am experiencing a strong emotion, but simply because I choose to.

However, it is unusual to 'reach out' or 'draw oneself back in' simply to demonstrate that one can. Although distinct, 'subtle contact' and 'emotional contact' are two inter-twined strands. In real life we usually do 'reach out', 'open up', 'draw ourselves in' or 'close down' because we are experiencing emotion. 'Reaching out' or 'drawing back in' are like smiling or frowning. They arise with emotion, but only the person experiencing that emotion knows exactly what it is. Smiling often indicates that someone is experiencing pleasure, but not always. We may also smile because we are uncomfortable, and frown when we are concerned. Similarly we may 'reach out' because we are very needy or 'close down' because we feel ill.

Those workshop participants who experience me as warm and interested when I 'reach out' and as cold and judgmental when I 'draw myself in' accurately perceive a change, but their interpretation of that change is a misinterpretation. This is not at all unusual. We all interpret the subtle fluctuations in the quality of each other's presence, and we usually do so in terms of what we imagine the other person feels towards us. We sense the other person 'shut down' and conclude that they are bored, shocked, angry or dislike us. It is almost impossible not to take it personally.

For some people, particularly those of us who trust our intuition, it can also be almost impossible to accept that we might be wrong. We *know* we have sensed a change in the other, and we are right. But we do not know what has led to that change. The other person may well be angry, or they may be distracted, tired, unwell or be a therapist whose internal 'time's running out' alarm has just gone off. It is really helpful to develop an awareness that therapists and clients are particularly well attuned to such changes in the each other, and in a constant process of interpreting (and misinterpreting) them. You may well be able to sense an emotional change in a client, but you do not necessarily know what that change is. Acknowledging and enquiring about such changes is usually helpful (if sometimes challenging); interpreting them – effectively *telling* your client what they feel – is as likely to result in your client feeling missed as received. Your clients will be at least as well attuned to these changes in you, but perhaps less likely to enquire about them.

Nobody likes to be misunderstood, and most of us are quick to correct such misunderstandings. It is important that therapists do not, in the process of correcting a misinterpretation, dismiss the client's accurate perception that something has changed. Compare the following responses:

Client:	You're shocked. I didn't think you would be.
Therapist:	I'm not shocked.
Client:	You are. I can feel it.
Therapist:	Really, I'm not.

The client does not return, but does move on to a new therapist. Predictably the same thing happens to the client again, but this time the therapist manages to affirm the client's reality whilst standing up for their own:

Client:	You're shocked. I didn't think you would be.
Therapist:	I'm not shocked. [*Checks her own reaction*] But I did withdraw. I feel frightened for you.

A client's perception of the therapist's relative distance or closeness – and more importantly, their interpretation of that closeness – will affect their perception of the therapist's congruence. If the therapist is trying to convey acceptance, but the client is interpreting their relative distance as disapproval then whatever affirming things the therapist may say just won't 'feel right' to the client- they will seem insincere.

BOUNDARIES

The interpretations we make at this level of contact depend very much on where our invisible boundaries are. In workshops, I am usually experienced as open and warm when I 'reach out' towards the volunteer, and as cold, uninterested and distant when I 'pull myself back in', but not always. Sometimes the volunteer (or an observer) experiences me as hostile and aggressive when I 'reach out'. We all have our own (variable) boundaries at this level – a sense of what is too close or not close enough. I do not intend any hostility when I reach out but sometimes I inadvertently invade someone's personal space. Respecting a client's personal space – and indicating your availability for contact – are both more complex negotiations than the simple matter of how closely you position the chairs.

EXERCISE

Imagine you are with a new client who seems uncomfortable. What might you say in order to check out whether there is the right amount of psychological 'space' between you?

Hard, isn't it? We do not have a commonly understood way of thinking about this level of contact, and it is rarely written about. Yet we do have a number of terms in ordinary, everyday speech that refer to it:

Therapist:	I know that I can be a bit 'full on' for some people, a bit too 'in your face'. I'm wondering how comfortable you're feeling with me?

Or:

Therapist:	Some people find me a bit distant. I'm wondering if you do?

The client may still find it difficult to answer even when a therapist finds the right way to ask. Then there is the question of how to respond if a client indicates that they are uncomfortable. It is possible to change what you are doing so that they feel more at ease with you. You can choose to 'open out' a little more. You can also choose to 'draw yourself back in' a bit. However, I would caution you to be careful in how you do this. I find that holding a 'drawn-in' position quickly makes me feel as if I'm wearing a shoe that is too tight. I find that I can get out of my client's space without adversely affecting my own comfort by mentally deciding to 'sit back'. I do not disengage, but I do 'back off'. The important thing is that I can feel myself return from 'over there' with the client to 'back here' in a way that is comfortable and sustainable.

You may not want to change what you are doing to suit your client, or it may be that the most therapeutically useful thing to do is to stay as you are and work with the client's discomfort.

Therapist:	I'm sorry you're finding me distant – it's not because I'm uninterested. I'm curious about what you're maybe doing in response. I have a sense of you trying to 'search me out', as if your antennae...
Client:	[*laughs and indicates that indeed she is trying to 'search out' the therapist*]
Therapist:	Actually – and I mean this as feedback, not a criticism– I think that's making me a bit uncomfortable. I feel kind of peered at.
Client:	My husband says that!
Therapist:	Really? Do you find him distant too?
Client:	He retreats into himself.
Therapist:	And you feel shut out?
Client:	I feel alone when he's like that. I can't get through to him no matter what I do.
Therapist:	You sound really sad. And frustrated. I have an image of you wanting to poke a hedgehog out of its curled-upness.
Client:	Yeah. That doesn't really work, does it?
Therapist:	It sounds prickly…
Client:	It is.

The relative closeness or distance between a client and therapist, and the degree to which the client welcomes it, affects what the client hears. A therapist can be exactly the same way with two different clients, say exactly the same thing, and be experienced in radically different ways. A client who is feeling invaded is likely to hear an empathic response very differently to a client who feels comfortably in contact, and a client who feel out of contact is likely to feel 'missed' even if the therapist's empathic response is entirely accurate. In other words, condition six, that the client perceives the acceptance and empathy that the therapist experiences, very much depends upon the quality of the first condition, psychological contact. By Rogers' definition we are still in contact if each person is still making some sort of a difference to the other's experience, but the quality of the contact will be radically different – and that matters.

The degree to which the client feels in contact with the therapist affects not only what the client hears, but also the way in which they talk. Once workshop participants have experimented with 'reaching out' and 'drawing back' in silence, I suggest that they put this into a more realistic context by 'reaching out' and 'drawing themselves back in' while their partner talks about something non-emotive. The person who is talking feels met, received, accepted and understood when the degree of subtle contact is right for them, and talks easily. Many dry up or lose the thread of what they were talking about when the listener 'draws themselves back in'. Occasionally someone feels that a pressure has been removed when the listener 'draws themselves back in', and talks more easily.

RETURNING TO INTUITION

Negotiating a comfortable distance between ourselves and the people we relate to is an everyday thing that normally happens out of awareness. We get it right much of the time and it isn't an issue. However, mismatches and misunderstanding happen so it is really helpful to try to develop an awareness of your process at this level in order to reflect about its possible impact upon the therapeutic relationship. I have found that it is helpful to call on whatever ability it is that I (and most other people) have that enables us to get it right most of the time. I do this by asking myself to 'do the most appropriate thing' and then noticing what changes. This passive–receptive mode of asking myself, as opposed to actively trying to work it out or making a guess based on my knowledge of the person, seems to be the most helpful thing to do.

EXERCISE

Think about a client who, for no apparent reason, suddenly stopped coming. As you think about them notice whether you sense yourself 'closing down' or 'opening out'. Imagine being in the last session you had with them, and again notice whether you 'open out' or 'close down'. Now ask yourself to be in the way that would have been most appropriate. Do you 'open out' or 'close down'? What do you think your client might have made of how you were, and how might this have impacted the relationship?

Developing an awareness of your own process at this level, and reflecting on its possible impact is a more realistic (and possibly a more helpful) aim than getting the distance between yourself and client 'right' at all times.

AVOIDING CONTACT

As well as 'reaching out' or 'drawing yourself back in', you might 'jump out of your skin', be 'beside yourself', 'sink' into the doldrums or be 'all over the place' etc. These are all ways of not being fully present. It may not be your intention to avoid contact, but you will be experienced as 'not really there'. Your client *will* notice your relative absence, even if they don't comment on it.

EXERCISE

Close your eyes and take a moment to notice where you are in relation to your body. Are you wholly inside your own skin, or is your attention reaching out beyond it? Are you floating around your head? In your belly? Have you collapsed?

Inhabit your body as wholly and completely as you are able.

Now think of an instance in a counselling relationship that was difficult for you. Notice what you do. Do you 'close down'? 'Jump out of your skin'? 'Step to one side'? …

Return to inhabiting your body as fully as you can. Notice the changes that you sense – they will tell you something about where you have been. Tingles or shivers moving downwards, for instance, suggest that you came back **down** into your body, whereas a sense of opening out suggests that you have been closed up inside.

Open your eyes and give yourself a shake.

Were you really fully present in the session or moment that you were thinking of? What effect do you think the quality of your presence had on the therapeutic relationship?

Self-care

Many therapists take a moment to make sure that they are grounded and available for contact at the beginning of a session. It is also very useful to take a moment once the session has ended. This chapter has been mainly concerned with how a client may be impacted by what the therapist does, but it is important to attend to the ways in which you are affected by the interaction. There are three ways in which the therapist may be impacted at this subtle level of relationship:

- the therapist may get stuck in a response that they have had to a client and spend the rest of their day overly 'drawn in' or 'all over the place' and so on;
- the therapist may empathically resonate with the client's state of collapse, or being beside themselves etc, and become stuck like that;
- the therapist may continue to 'reach out' to the client after the session has ended.

Some therapists develop habitual ways of bouncing back into their own shape after their last session, perhaps listening to a particular kind of music or doing some kind of exercise. Whether you like to jog or lie in a warm bath, it is important to find some way of letting go at the end of the day. It may also be helpful to so something between sessions in order to return to a neutral state before seeing the next client. Paying attention to your breathing is one of the quickest and most effective ways to do this.

CONCLUSION — THE DANCE

We 'reach out' or 'take a step back'. Our client responds by 'reaching out' to meet us, or maintaining a safe distance. We respond to their response, they to ours, and so on. An invisible and inaudable level of relationship arises as we dance closely, then further away, then closer again. Rogers does not conceptualise psychological contact in this way, but would, I think, recognise this dance. He does write, latterly, about 'reaching out',

> When I am at my best, as a group facilitator or as a therapist, I discover another characteristic ... it seems that my spirit has reached out and touched the inner spirit of the other. Our relationship transcends itself and becomes a part of something larger. Profound growth and healing and energy are present.

(1980: 129)

Rogers observes that there is nothing he can do to force such an experience. I agree absolutely. The profound growth, healing and energy that he describes come into being only if the client welcomes our 'touch'. These moments are co-created and therefore not wholly within the therapist's control. However I do think that there is much we can do to make ourselves available for this quality or contact — and much we can do to respect the rights of clients who would not welcome it.

Developing a more continuous awareness of how fully present we are, of when we 'reach out' and 'draw ourselves back in', and increasing our sensitivity to how this impacts upon each relationship is as difficult as developing any other kind of self-awareness. It requires a quiet reflective space inside, and that can be difficult to find if you are at the stage of having to really concentrate to remain aware of your own process whilst also listening to your client and trying to sense their inner world. It might be useful to take a moment at the beginning of a session just to hold the intention of making contact in the most appropriate way with this particular client, and then to relax and trust that you will sense when your client welcomes your 'touch' or needs you to take a step back. Hopefully, using the exercises above will help you to reflect in retrospect and become increasingly able to catch a mis-step in real time.

FURTHER READING

Cameron, R. (2002) 'In the space between', in G. Wyatt (ed.), *Therapeutic Conditons: Evolution, Theory and Practice. Volume Four: Contact and Perception.* Ross on Wye: PCCS.

Cameron, R. (2002) 'Subtle body work', in T. Staunton (ed.), *Advances in Body Psychotherapy.* Hove: Brunner-Routledge.

Cameron, R. (2002) 'Subtle energy awareness: Bridging the psyche and soma', *Person-Centred Practice*, 10(2): 66–74.

Cameron, R. (2004) 'Shaking the spirit', in K. Tudor and M. Worral (eds), *Freedom to Practise.* Ross-on-Wye: PCCS.

9

THE THERAPEUTIC
PROCESS

In a world where we have been taught to follow rules, to use reason and logic, to solve problems, to strive for success – in short, to be *active* – it is not surprising that it comes hard to lay all of that aside. And yet the fundamental hypothesis of person-centred therapy, the absolute bedrock upon which it is based, is that we all have within us the momentum of the *actualising tendency*, that force which moves us always in the direction of wellbeing and the fulfilment of our potential.

The implications of this are profound. It means that advising, guiding, problem-solving, directing people's behaviour, telling them what is best, are ultimately redundant activities. We may strike lucky and find that our advice coincides with what someone feels is right. But we probably all have experiences of urging someone to do something which *we* believe they should and finding that they have all sorts of 'excuses' for not taking our advice. Or they may *seem* compliant – so as not to hurt us or not to get into an argument – but totally ignore us. Aren't such people exasperating? We try to help and look what happens!

'I need help', they say. So we suggest what they might *do*. 'Why don't you talk to her', 'See a solicitor', 'Look for a different job', 'Move so you can be closer to him'. The trouble is that such suggestions are based on *our* experience, *our* skills, *our* confidence levels.

But putting all of these activities to one side is scary, to say the least. It is impossible if we do not believe that we can trust each and every person to find their own way forward.

Person-centred work is predicated on the notion that the client's process is always trustworthy. This can be a hard concept to grasp at first, but without it there is no basis for person-centred counselling. It is as important as that. Everything we do as person-centred therapists is dedicated to freeing up our clients so that their innate drive, the *actualising tendency*, can work more effectively.

Our theory tells us that any threat to the self-structure, for example a contradiction or criticism, makes it 'tighten up' or become more rigid in order to defend itself. Maintaining the six conditions has the opposite effect. If there is no threat, the person can relax enough to allow himself to become aware of his self-experiences and to integrate the evidence of his senses within his self-structure.

This is not to say that the self-structure is 'bad', or that the person will necessarily act upon his organismic experiencing once it is available to awareness. It does, though, mean that the individual has more choice in the way he acts and reacts. If he has been taught that dancing is silly, for example, this introjected condition of worth will make it difficult or impossible for him to be aware of how much he wishes to express himself through dance. Through a loosening of his self-structure, he might become aware of this. But he still might choose other priorities in his life.

If he has an introjected condition of worth which adjures him to provide for his wife and children, he might be resentful that he 'has to' stay in a job which he hates in order to maintain their standard of living. Over time, he realises that his self-worth is tied in with material possessions and job status. He begins to become aware that he can make different choices, if he so wishes. Here, the counsellor might have become so caught up with his resentment and anger that she is almost willing him, or even urging him, to change to a less demanding job. This 'siding with' the self-experience would be to lose sight of the process. Her empathic *receiving* of his bitterness and his sense of being trapped paradoxically enables him to accept other feelings which have been pushed into the background. He discovers that there are some aspects of having status and material wealth that are important to him and give him pleasure. Now, he is able to be aware of the full range of his experience and he can make choices accordingly.

If the six conditions are present, we expect that the self-structure will loosen, little by little, and people will move towards living in a way that takes account of their own first-hand experiences rather than according to rigid ideas of how they 'should' be. We call this the client's *process*.

SEVEN STAGES OF PROCESS

Individuals move, I began to see, not from fixity or homeostasis through change to a new fixity, though such a process is indeed possible. But much the more significant continuum is from fixity to changingness, from rigid structure to flow, from stasis to process. (Rogers, 1961: 131)

In Chapter 7 of *On Becoming a Person,* Rogers (1961) describes the characteristics of each of seven stages of personality change. These 'stages' are, in one sense, artificial – like signposts along a route. It is entirely arbitrary whether a highway engineer has chosen to put MANCHESTER 40 miles or MANCHESTER 50 miles. The car does not stop at each signpost: it is the overall direction that is important.

In many ways the car is a poor analogy because it implies a linear route, with the vehicle pressing on until it reaches its destination. People, of course, are very different. A client is unlikely to move through more than one or two 'stages' in the course of a counselling relationship, although many clients return to counselling if they have benefited from their first experience. Moreover, it is rare to find someone who shows signs of being in only one 'stage' at a time. At some points, a client might even seem to the counsellor to have 'gone backwards'. However, I have never known this to be the case when viewing the relationship as a whole. The overall movement always seems to be a positive one.

First stage

A person at the first stage has very little overlap between his organismic experience and his self-structure. He has little awareness of his own experiencing and does not accept that his feelings have any value. His view of the world is rigid and his beliefs are strong and unyielding.

Close relationships are dangerous for him, but he himself is not aware of this. He does not communicate about himself – only about external things. As far as he is concerned, he himself is fine. He does not need to change and has no desire to do so. He certainly does not need counselling.

This client might have problems, but they are not of his making. The world and other people create them. For example, he has continual 'bad luck'. Or other people always take what he says the wrong way.

Second stage

A person in the second stage is a little more communicative, but still about external things. He might acknowledge some problems, but they are still always to do with outside factors and other people. He himself is in no way responsible for his difficulties. He is frustrated and misunderstood.

His feelings do 'show' to others at times, but he himself does not recognise or acknowledge them.

His view of the world is still rigid. He believes his view to be factual and cannot understand or accept other perspectives. He might show frustration that he cannot get others to see the 'truth'. If he comes for counselling, he will expect to change the other people involved or to alter the circumstances he finds himself in.

People in these early stages of process can be frequent users of agency services of various kinds. They communicate their frustration and neediness, even though they are not themselves fully aware of it, and they can elicit a genuine wish in others to help them. However, the help offered or given is never quite right for them. They always need more. Eventually the helpers, drained of energy and goodwill, begin trying to avoid them. Doctors have a term – *heartsink patients* – which describes this feeling of hopelessness on the part of the helper.

Client-centred theory suggests that such people have an overwhelming need to be accepted, to be *received*. However, their self-structure is such that they cannot easily *experience* being received because the level of threat and anxiety would be too high. The nearest they can tolerate is receiving practical help, which only partially and temporarily relieves the need. And when they eventually experience rejection from the helper, their self-structure is confirmed.

It is unlikely that people in the early stages of process will seek counselling, because they do not see themselves as part of the problem. When they do begin counselling – often because someone else thinks it would be a good idea – they tend to react against the person-centred approach. Unconditional acceptance is a profound threat to a self-structure which holds the individual to be unlovable, worthless, stupid – and which holds the world to be a place in which no one is genuinely caring about another person. So in order to avoid the anxiety which arises when organismic experience (in this case a counsellor communicating congruent acceptance) conflicts with the self-structure, the client distorts the experience: 'She's only doing it because she gets paid', 'I haven't worked it out yet, but there must be a catch'. Often, the client will miss appointments and turn up late. This might be to prove that the counsellor is not as accepting as she seems, or it might simply be that the client cannot easily tolerate the core conditions – however much, at an organismic level, he longs for them.

The counsellor can easily become impatient with such a client. It is very hard to stay engaged with a client who keeps dipping a toe in the water and then running away. It is even harder if the counsellor is under pressure to show results within a limited time frame, or has a waiting list – or both.

Third stage

A person in the third stage is more communicative. He will talk about himself, but as though he views himself from the outside. How other people see him is one of his main concerns. He talks a lot about past events and things that are happening outside the counselling room.

This person is aware of some of his own (usually past) feelings, but he might be ashamed of them, seeing them as abnormal or unacceptable. He expresses them unwillingly, usually expecting that the counsellor will think less well of him as a result.

Fourth stage

This person is able to describe more intense feelings and is aware of some of his present feelings. He will often distance himself a little from the feelings, for example saying 'The anger was strong' rather than 'I was very angry'. There is less of a 'time delay' between his experiencing a feeling and being able to express it, but he is still frightened of feelings breaking through in the present.

He is beginning to discover his own point of view and to recognise that others might hold different views. The 'truth' becomes of less concern. He also begins to question himself and the validity of some of his views and to consider his own responsibility in his difficulties.

He is becoming aware of some of the incongruence between his experience and his self-structure and is more willing to risk a little of himself in relationships.

Fifth stage

Here, the person is becoming much more able to experience and accept his feelings and there is less likely to be a delay between the experience and the acknowledgement of feeling. More and more feelings are recognised in the present, even those which are more difficult to express, such as feelings about the counsellor and the therapy.

The person is more able to tolerate confusion and uncertainty – not knowing what he thinks or feels about something, or being able to recognise a feeling without knowing 'where it is coming from'. He still, however, finds it unpleasant and rather scary when feelings rise to the surface unexpectedly and may avoid them or cut them off.

At this stage, the person is able to face contradictions and incongruities in himself: *In my head, I know it's OK to cry, but I still feel embarrassed and inadequate when I do.*

He is making new discoveries about himself and the desire to learn about himself and become the 'real me' increases.

Sixth stage

At this stage, the person no longer sees the world in terms of 'problems'. His primary concern is to experience, to *be.* He is much less likely to fear or avoid the feelings that rise to the surface, wishing to know them and discover their origin. Along with the freeing of psychological experience comes a physiological loosening. The person's facial and bodily expressions become less tense and he might express experiences as, for example, a knotting in his gut or a lump in his chest.

He is able to accept responsibility for his own responses and reactions and does not confuse his own constructs and values with those of others. He is curious about himself and the world, not seeking to blame himself or others but to understand and accept.

Seventh stage

> The person experiences new feelings immediately, with richness and intensity, and he has a fundamental trust in himself and his own process. He does not deal with new experiences according to past patterns, but is able to meet them with openness and a willingness to learn in the present. He can use his past experiences in order to understand the present but, because he is not trapped by them, he can recognise the differences in his current experiencing and set them aside. He can hold constructs tentatively, changing them as his experiences change.

There is sometimes a misunderstanding about the outcomes of counselling – an assumption that the person will never feel bad again. This is far from the truth. On the contrary, a person at stages six and seven will feel more intense grief at a loss than someone at stages two or three. But he will not be frightened of the feeling, nor will he react according to a set pattern. He will express the grief in a way appropriate for him, neither distorting nor denying it. In day-to-day interactions, he will be angry or upset if, for example, a family member breaks a treasured object, and he will express that. But in expressing and acknowledging it, the feeling will pass. He will not hold grudges or nurse secret wounds so that stored-up feelings threaten to come out in the future in ways that might be damaging to himself or others.

EXERCISE

In a small group, choose a fictitious character from a television serial or a film or novel – one which is familiar to all of the group members. (It might be easier, if you are working in a large group which needs to divide, to choose some characters first and form groups around them.)

Consider the character in relation to the *Seven Stages of Process*. Can you apply the characteristics of a particular stage to the fictitious person you have chosen?

The *Stages of Process* can be a useful guide to the development of a client over time. It is noteworthy that Rogers and his colleagues had little success with clients who were at stages one and two. Given, in particular, the stage one client's fear of communicative relationships, it is easy to see that, however much the counsellor *offers* the core conditions, the client might not be able to *experience* them. If, for example, a client believes himself to be deeply unattractive, unworthy or unlovable, a counsellor's unconditional positive regard will be a strong and immediate threat to his self-structure and he will feel anxious.

Many clients in the early stages of process are ambivalent about counselling, finding it (organismically) attractive and (self-structurally) threatening. They waver, unwilling to end the relationship but fearing it at the same time. They cancel appointments, turn up late, 'forget' the time and so on, but insist that they get a lot out of the sessions.

Although the stages of process are useful in understanding the theory of person-centred therapy, I have found it unhelpful to try and place a particular client in a particular stage of process. It is the general *direction* that is important rather than any one signpost. Some features of this direction are shown below:

From:	**To:**
Rigidity	Fluidity
External	Internal
Blaming others	Accepting own responsibility
This is how the world is (facts)	This is how I perceive the world (constructs)
Believing in 'the truth'	Accepting others' opinions and constructs
Fearing feelings	Accepting feelings
Perceiving own feelings (if at all) as past	Experiencing feelings in the here-and-now
Not believing in own ability to change	Welcoming own capacity for change
Living according to others' judgements (external locus of evaluation)	Living according to own values and first-hand experience (internal locus of evaluation)
Fearful of the unforeseen	Unthreatened by changed circumstances
Wanting quick fixes	Working towards long-term solutions
Preferring rules	Preferring flexibility
Set ideas about meaning	Searching for meaning
Predictable and constrained	Spontaneous and creative
Judging success or failure	Believing in growth through experience
Hiding	Being visible
Judging others	Respecting others
Preferring distance	Wanting intimacy

EXERCISE

Thinking about the two extremes of the seven stages of process, how might someone *think, feel* or *act* in relation to the following:

(Continued)

(Continued)

At Stage 1: fixed, rigid, closed, unaccepting	At Stage 7: flexible, fluid, open, accepting
Parenting	
Religion	
Sexuality	
Helping others	
Work	
Other	

REVIEWING PROGRESS

This understanding of process is useful for the counsellor to identify development in our clients within the person-centred understanding of theory. We can then feed back to a client any changes we have noticed so that he can check them against his own perception.

EXAMPLE

A client is angry about an incident with his manager. He describes it in detail. Later in the session, he bemoans the fact that he is still feeling awful. The counsellor is accepting and empathic about his sense that he is still feeling bad after six sessions of counselling. She pays considerable attention to his frustration that he is not feeling happy and his impatience to 'move on'. Then she says:

Counsellor: Do you remember talking to me about your colleague criticising you? You told me that you just crumbled inside. [*She smiles*] This time, with your manager, you don't seem to have crumbled.

Client: [*looks surprised*] No, I didn't, did I.

Counsellor: I know it was unpleasant for you, though.

Client: Yes, it was awful. And I don't think I handled it very well. But I told her how I felt.

Counsellor: So even though you're not totally happy with the way you handled it, there's a difference … . Like trying out something new and not getting it quite right yet?

Client: No, that's not it. More like something just bursting out from inside me.

Counsellor: Ah ... so it felt a bit out of control.

Client: Yes. But I'm glad I said it [*Client becomes thoughtful*]. Actually, a friend of mine was badgering me to go to the match with him last week and I wouldn't. I just didn't want to.

> *Counsellor*: It sounds as if you're saying that's a new thing.
> *Client*: [*slowly*] Yes, it is. I usually go for the sake of peace – because I know he hasn't got anyone else. But this time I thought, 'Sod it. I've got a life too'.
> *Counsellor*: As though you realised 'I don't want to do this'.

In this example, the counsellor has noticed something different and decides to test out her perception against the client's. If he had not recognised the difference in his own responses and behaviour, she would certainly not have tried to persuade him that her perception was 'right'. She would have stayed with her client's frame of reference and accepted that, for him, nothing had changed – or even that any changes were for the worse.

In both incidents – with the manager and with the friend – she notices that her client is sufficiently aware of his own needs and feelings to express them there and then. She contrasts this with other things he has told her, where he only realised after the event that he did not want to do something, or felt paralysed by his perceived lack of power.

Drawing a client's attention in this way can, however, interrupt his process and caution is needed. It is important that the counsellor is sure that the client has 'finished' expressing his own feelings and that she is not negating them. Hopelessness and helplessness are valid emotions which need to be fully 'received'. In this, as in every other aspect of the relationship, the counsellor exercises judgement and sensitivity.

TRUST

Trust the process. This is a phrase you will often hear in person-centred circles and it is repeated as a reminder that the particular way in which the process unfolds for an individual is unpredictable. It is often only with hindsight that you can see the sense in what has happened.

CASE EXAMPLE: EMMA

Emma's presenting issue is agoraphobia. She suffers a degree of anxiety whenever she leaves her house and, on occasion, the anxiety is crippling. To begin with, this is the focus of the counselling, but in talking about visiting the supermarket she describes how important it is for her to have her 16-year-old daughter, Brenda, by her side. This leads her into remembering her own relationship with her mother.

Talking about her mother brings the realisation of how distressed and angry she still is that her mother never stood up for her, but left her to cope on her

(Continued)

(Continued)

own. She also realises that she has perhaps been over-protective of Brenda in the past and also that she has now come to rely on Brenda to help her when she is out of the house. Her daughter's presence somehow reduces the anxiety she feels.

Emma then begins to talk about an incident which she has alluded to several times, but never spoken about in detail. She was brutally assaulted when Brenda was a toddler. She went to her mother immediately afterwards for help and comfort, but her mother's instinct was to hush it up and pretend it hadn't happened. Emma realises that part of this was to do with avoiding the stigma of rape, but she still feels immensely let down by her mother.

In going over the rape for the first time since it happened, Emma remembers that the man threatened that he would harm her little girl if she ever told anyone.

With sudden clarity, Emma remembers that she thought she saw the man in her local town centre about two years ago. He did not, as far as she was aware, see her. In a rush of excited realisation, she puts the two events together. Her agoraphobia began just after she saw him. And it helps to have Brenda with her when she goes out because her anxiety has, in part, been about what the man might do to her daughter!

In this example, the counsellor trusted Emma's process enough not to try to 'steer' her back towards the agoraphobia. In fact, for several sessions, agoraphobia was barely mentioned. The therapist reassured Emma that if her relationship with her mother was uppermost in her mind, it was important in some way. Neither of them yet knew why, but that would probably become clear in time.

The strong feeling Emma had of being 'let down' by her mother was something that had been a feature of Emma's childhood. During several sessions she expressed distress and anger about childhood incidents with friends and teachers where her mother had assumed that Emma was at fault rather than hearing her grievance. The counsellor's acceptance and empathy enabled her eventually to re-address the trauma of the rape.

Neither Emma nor her therapist had any idea that the agoraphobia would have such a clear link with the rape. (In fact, they discovered that the matter was rather more complex and it took several more sessions before Emma was ready to conclude the counselling work.) In her feedback to the therapist, Emma said that she was surprised at how much difference the counselling had made in her life generally. In particular, she had repaired her relationship with her mother and was able to be much more tolerant of her mother's 'faults'.

CASE EXAMPLE: JULIAN

Julian is referred by a psychiatrist, who describes him as 'obsessive-compulsive'. Julian describes his own problem as being unable to commit himself. He has been living with his partner for seven years, but he cannot take the step of giving up his own flat.

He begins by talking about his relationship, disclosing the fact that he can no longer have sex and this is why he sought a referral. His partner insisted that he get help. His other key relationship is with his father, his only parent since the death of his mother when he was six.

Whatever Julian begins to talk about, he ends up talking about his father, who can do no wrong in Julian's eyes. Julian has had to have his approval for every decision he has ever made. He feels guilty at not telling his father that he is in counselling, but he strongly suspects that his father would see this as a waste of time.

In passing, Julian mentions that his mother died when he was a child. He shrugs off the counsellor's reaction, saying that his father was an excellent parent and all he ever needed.

Over a few weeks, Julian begins to realise how many of his decisions are made according to whether or not his father would approve. He begins to be a bit more daring and to do some (small) things which he supposes his father would not like. To his surprise, his father is perfectly accepting.

To the counsellor's own surprise, Julian discloses that he resumed his sex life with his partner three weeks previously, but wanted to keep coming to the counselling sessions. He says that the sessions have made a big difference, citing other changes of which the counsellor was unaware.

Here, the therapist was sorely tempted to focus on what seemed to her like an important event in the client's life: the death of his mother. However, she disciplined herself to follow Julian's lead and accept his perception that this event was unimportant. She had also assumed initially that Julian's father must be something of a tyrant, despite Julian's picture of him as a concerned and loving parent. Wisely, she also accepted Julian's perception in this.

Even as the relationship was ending, the counsellor was wondering whether it was Julian's childhood fear of losing his father as well as his mother which led to his anxiety to please and his compulsive behaviour, but she realised that it was not necessary to know that. Julian took what he needed from the therapeutic relationship. His self-structure loosened to allow him to trust more of his present experience, and he was able to make a number of small but significant changes in his life.

EXAMPLE

You learn, in passing almost, that your client's mother left the family home when he was seven. Your ears expand – you 'hear' this much more loudly than your client is telling you. 'That must have been terrible for you', you say spontaneously. He looks surprised. 'Not really', he replies, dismissing the matter. He is focused on something entirely different at the moment.

Are you 'right' to believe that this event will have had a profound impact upon the seven-year-old boy? You might be. But at the moment, to the man who is your client, it is not important. The main reason is likely to be that his present distress is centred on something different and this is what he needs to explore now.

It might also be the case that his mother's leaving was not so terrible to the seven-year-old. Although your first assumption is that the pain of her leaving was so great that he has locked it securely away, it might in fact be that the child's mother was abusive and her leaving was a relief, or that his contact with his mother was so nebulous that her final departure was really not a matter of great moment.

PUSHING THE RIVER

As you become more perceptive and knowledgeable, you begin to see the ways in which your client's self-structure might be hampering his organismic experiencing. At some stage in your learning, you will probably be tempted to try to short-cut the process in some way – to impart your perceptions to your client or show him what to do. This may be considered an appropriate challenge in some schools of counselling, but in person-centred work it is known as *pushing the river.*

The river is the natural, but sometimes slow, process of integrating organismic experiencing into the self-structure and there is nothing you can *do* to hurry it up. Like the plant, the person will develop in his own time. Your job is to provide as rich an environment as you can – the therapeutic conditions – and watch the blossoms unfold.

What happens if you try to hurry the process? Let us take a couple of examples of a client who finds it difficult to express feelings – who experiences them as a great lump in the chest or who is fearful of them. The counsellor gets caught up in the client's desire to 'get rid of the lump'; after all, it's 'good' to express your feelings, isn't it?

CASE EXAMPLE: RIFAT

Rifat is a successful lawyer who has come to see you following the death of her father. All her life she has striven to be a good daughter for him, but she has never been able to make him love her. Deep down, she feels worthless and believes that if her colleagues ever caught sight of the real Rifat, they would despise her.

After several sessions, she identifies a 'big lump' in her chest, like a physical pain, which she thinks is anger. If only she could get rid of this lump, she's sure she would feel better. What can she do?

Why not try punching a cushion? you suggest. It works for some people. She tries it and it provides a little temporary relief. But despite all her punching, the lump still sits there.

> Oh dear, she thinks, it must be her. She's useless. She can't even do counselling right. It proves again what a waste of space she is. She's tried so hard all her life to do her best, but it's never been good enough. And now she's let her counsellor down too. But her counsellor is such a nice person – the only one who's ever listened. She'll pretend it has made her feel better because otherwise, the counsellor might think it's her fault.

CASE EXAMPLE: BARTHOLOMEW

Bartholomew has been coming to see you for some months. He is still, at the age of 32, living with his mother and feels that he cannot leave her on her own. He has had a number of jobs but there has always been something wrong with them and he has now been unemployed for some months. He tells you that he feels as though he is raging inside – wanting to tear and destroy things – and this frightens him. He wants you to tell him how to deal with these rages so that he does not do any damage.

Why not try punching a cushion? you suggest. It works for some people.

The next time Bartholomew feels overwhelmed by rage, he does as you suggest. It doesn't work. And besides, he feels foolish doing it.

It just proves that counselling is a sham like everything else in this miserable world. There's no point in going on with it. These bloody counsellors. They pretend they've got the answers but they know no more than the rest of us.

If you are tempted to hurry the process, you might well be picking up a desire in your client for something he can *do*. He wants to feel better *now* and this longing can be distorted into dissatisfaction or even punitiveness toward you, the counsellor who is not giving him what he needs. Rather than reacting to his wish from your own self-structure (I *must give my client something now, or I'm not good enough*), stay with the conditions. Empathise with his frustration, despair and weariness at the length of time this seems to be taking. Empathise with his longing to *do* something so that he can feel better quickly. Disclose your own wish for a magic wand (which in a perfect world would be issued along with your diploma). But, above all, *accept* that there are no 'quick fixes'. If there were, every therapist in the land would be using them.

FRAGILE AND DISSOCIATED PROCESS

This chapter has been concerned with the more everyday manifestations of the process that we see when we provide the necessary and sufficient conditions in a therapeutic setting. Increasingly, however, person-centred therapists are working with clients whose emotional distress and relational sensitivity are more extreme. Margaret Warner (2000) has described two forms of process, *fragile process* and *dissociated process,* which are more common in such clients (often those with a psychiatric history), but which can be encountered in any client population. Although Warner's considerable experience is that the 'conditions of person-centred therapy are necessary and sufficient for work with these styles of process', there are aspects of work with such clients which can be very challenging for practitioners.

In Chapter 10, we look at what we mean by assessment in person-centred practice, and it is important for all therapists to be familiar with fragile and dissociated process in order to assess their capacity to work with clients whose process is likely to be more lengthy and challenging.

WHAT CAN THERAPY DO?

'Am I ever going to feel any better?'

Clients are entitled to answers to questions such as these. So how do we answer, when we are working with something as nebulous as an individual and his process? We cannot give a timescale, because each individual is different. We can only tell the client something about our experience and our expectations.

One aspect of the process which is a common feature of stages four and five is that painful material from the past comes to the fore. The self-structure has loosened enough so that previous distortions and denials are beginning to weaken. However, this means that a client is beginning fully to experience emotions which he has successfully kept at bay. In his terms, he might well 'feel worse' than before he began the counselling process. How can this be a good thing?

The first thing to say is that no one can close down all uncomfortable and painful feelings and, at the same time, let in all excited and joyful feelings. If that were the case, who would need – or want – therapy? So experiencing and expressing the pain also leads to experiencing more of the contented, happy feelings.

A common assumption made by clients and sometimes by beginner counsellors is that a successful therapeutic process will result in our never having 'bad' feelings again. This is far from the case. Being aware means that our feelings are experienced in all of their intensity, whether those feelings are welcome or unwelcome. The difference is that they can be acknowledged and expressed and thus, become past feelings. If someone does something to hurt us, we can shout or cry, we can communicate our hurt to them or to someone else. We do not have to suppress it, or worry about whether our feelings are justified or acceptable. We are able to make choices about when, and to whom, we express ourselves – not denying or distorting the experience, but managing it.

When clients ask questions such as, 'Do you think I need counselling?' or, 'How will I know when I have had enough counselling?' or, 'What will counselling do for me?' or, 'How can counselling help?' or, 'Why am I still feeling so awful?' we can respond in different ways, depending upon our own perception of what is going on in the relationship. These ways are not mutually exclusive, and the counsellor will probably use a mixture appropriate to the particular client.

The first way is to respond empathically to our client's sense of confusion, of 'not knowing'. Person-centred counselling can be a profound culture shock to clients used to a problem-solving approach.

- Are you wondering whether you're ever going to feel any better?

- Does it feel like this is taking forever?

The second is to answer the question in terms of the client's possible expectations:

- I don't think you 'need counselling' in the sense that I think there's something wrong with you. But it might help you to feel better in yourself.

- I would expect that, as we go on, you will begin to feel calmer and more set-tled in yourself – less churned up inside.

- If you're still turning things over and over in your mind, if things are still get-ting to you more than you want them to, then it might help to carry on seeing me. If you're feeling more at ease with yourself, then you probably don't need me any more at the moment.

- You've had a devastating experience. Nothing can change that. But at the moment it's raw and it hurts all the time. I would hope that counselling will lessen that, so it doesn't interfere with your life so much.

- Losing your partner is an awful experience. But at present it sounds like an endless ache that you carry around inside you all the time. With counselling, I would expect that it will turn into more of a gentle sadness. Something which will eventually be in the background of your life rather than something that hurts all the time.

The third way is to use an analogy:

- You've had a shock to your system – rather like, in physical terms, breaking your leg. The first thing which happens when you break your leg is that you keep it very still so that it doesn't hurt. But then you have to start exercising it or you'll lose the use of it – and that does hurt. That's the kind of thing you're doing with me – starting to use a part of yourself which you've kept immobi-lised for a long time. And it will be painful for a time.

- It's like moving house and you're in the middle of it all. You've taken all of your things out of their cupboards and they're in a right mess. You know that when you get settled in the new house it'll be better, but at the minute you're wish-ing you'd never decided to move.

- It's like you are a container of liquid and each time you've been hurt, or got angry and couldn't express it, a bubble has been trapped beneath the surface. Now you have a huge bubble which is threatening to burst out, so you have to move very carefully. Hopefully, we are letting out bits of that hurt in small manageable bubbles so that in a while you'll be able to slosh around and be yourself again without worrying.

The fourth way is to ask your client what he wants:

- Would you like me to tell you something about the theory? Do you want a technical explanation or do you want me to use more everyday language?

The fifth way is to notice what is happening in the relationship:

- Do you imagine that I have some kind of diagnosis in my head that I'm not telling you about?
- Are you upset with me because I'm not helping you as much as you hoped I would?
- You keep looking to me for reassurance. Are you saying that you don't think this is doing any good?
- Does it seem like it's my fault that you're not over it yet?

Even when the counsellor believes she can see evidence of the process, some clients seem unwilling to acknowledge any positive changes. The most common reasons for this seem to be fear that the counsellor will stop seeing them and fear that the counsellor will stop empathising with the awful, painful parts of their lives. The counsellor can invite the client to voice whatever is happening for him.

- I'm puzzled, Tariq. I'm getting all excited about this, but you seem to be very flat. As though it doesn't matter to you.
- I'm really impressed with the risk you took there. And I'm wondering why you don't seem to take any pleasure in what happened. If it were me, I'd be dead proud of myself.

UPS AND DOWNS

The most difficult times for clients and counsellors are when the client has been recognising progress and feeling pleased at the direction his life is taking. Then something happens that seems to plunge him back into gloom and distress. This can be an external event – or simply waking up one morning feeling bad once again.

When someone comes to counselling in pain or distress, there is rarely a smooth path to their feeling better. In fact, they may believe strongly that they will never feel better again, even as they hope that they are wrong. Counsellors, too, may despair – may worry that the person-centred approach is not good enough.

What does 'getting better' mean? It certainly does not mean that they will forget the dreadful thing or things that have happened. What it does mean is that the pain will gradually become less *raw* – that it will slowly intrude less into their ability to lead an everyday life. It does not mean that they will never again be touched by the sadness or distress of their experience.

Figure 9.1 represents a client's experience through the counselling process. To begin with, the pain is constant and deep. Then there are occasional and fleeting

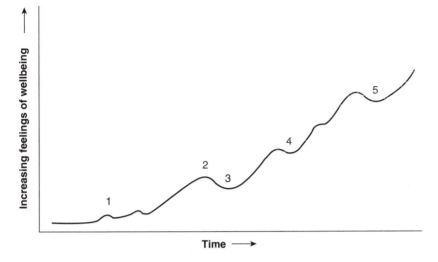

FIGURE 9.1   Example of a Client's Experience of the Process

times when it is not at the forefront – small windows of relief from the agony. Then there might be longer periods when it is less: *I bought a dress. It's lovely – dark green with some beautiful embroidery on the collar* (point 1 on the graph). The client is able to take pleasure in something at last. But the hope which comes with such times seems cruelly dashed when the pain returns and the belief that it will never get better returns with it. This pattern of long periods of distress and short times when the despair lifts is typical of the first weeks.

Then there might come a longer period when the client's pain seems less. The bad experience recedes a little. They find they can go about their daily business with the experience at the back rather than the front of their mind (2). Then the pain hits again (3). It is actually less than it was when they started, but in comparison with their recent joyful sense of being on the road to happiness, it feels awful. They are back to despair. They will never be truly happy again.

Each time, the pain is less raw and it lasts less long. Each time, the periods of relief are longer and lighter. But to someone who has been feeling that at last they have something of their energy back, any return to misery can feel as though they are right back at the beginning (4 and 5).

This general pattern seems to hold true for many different kinds of issue: bereavement, abuse, sudden trauma, depression . . . The depth of the pain and the length of the process overall vary considerably, though. If someone in an otherwise supportive and loving context has been mugged, the line will probably represent much less time overall than for someone who has suffered prolonged abuse or neglect in childhood.

CONCLUSION

In person-centred counselling, the process of the client is seen as something that can be trusted, which has its own internal wisdom. For all counsellors at the beginning of practice, however, this involves a 'leap of faith'. Until we have our own experience of the process working, we are reliant upon theory and the experience of others. And even when we do have experience, we can still doubt: Will it be true for *this* client? Trusting the process is perhaps the greatest of challenges for all counsellors.

FURTHER READING

Cooper, M., O'Hara, M., Schmid, P. and Wyatt, G. (eds) (2007) *The Handbook of Person-Centred Psychotherapy and Counselling.* Basingstoke: Palgrave Macmillan.

Embleton Tudor, L., Keemar, K., Tudor, K., Valentine, J. and Worrall. M. (2004) *The Person-Centred Approach: A Contemporary Introduction.* Basingstoke: Palgrave MacMillan.

Gaylin, N. (2001) 'Family therapy process', in, *Family, Self and Psychotherapy: A Person-Centred Perspective.* Ross-on-Wye: PCCS Books.

Haugh, S. and Paul, S. (2008) *The Therapeutic Relationship.* Ross on Wye: PCCS Books.

Hawkins, J. (2002) 'Paradoxical safety', *Person-Centred Practice*, 10(1).

Joseph, S. and Worsley, R. (eds) (2007) *Person-Centred Practice: Case Studies in Positive Psychology.* Ross-on-Wye: PCCS Books.

Levitt, B. (ed.) (2005) *Embracing Non-Directivity.* Ross-on-Wye: PCCS Books.

Mearns, D. (ed.) (1994) *Developing Person-Centred Counselling.* London: Sage. (Section IV.)

Mearns, D. and Cooper, M. (2005) *Working at Relational Depth in Counselling and Psychotherapy.* London: Sage.

Merry, T. (1999) *Learning and Being in Person-Centred Counselling.* Ross-on-Wye: PCCS Books.

Proctor, G. (2002) *The Dynamics of Power in Counselling and Psychotherapy: Ethics, Politics and Practice.* Ross-on-Wye: PCCS Books.

Sanders, P. (2006) *The Person-Centred Primer.* Ross on Wye: PCCS Books.

Tolan, J. and Wilkins, P. (eds) (2011) *Client Issues in Counselling and Psychotherapy.* London: Sage.

10

BEGINNINGS AND ENDINGS

STRUCTURING

All relationships have rules of some kind, although these are usually unwritten and unspoken. These 'rules' are usually experienced as *things we do or don't do* – except in times of emergency or crisis. Take, for example, one of your friends or a family member – is it ok to call at their home at any time? Do you ring first? Does one of you always initiate contact, or do you take it turn and turn about? How late in the evening could you ring them? Could you ring them at work? Can they ring you at work? Do you talk openly about your partners or families – or would this feel like disloyalty?

It is easy for the beginner counsellor to forget that there are two people in the counselling relationship, one of whom is the counsellor herself. As with all person-centred therapy, the counsellor seeks to make explicit the unspoken or hinted-at. This includes making explicit those aspects of the 'rules' which are laid down by the therapist or which are therapist preferences. Many beginners are reticent about acknowledging that they play a much larger part than the client in making the rules for the relationship. Somehow, it seems to run against the idea of person-centredness to impose their own needs and wishes on the client. It is easier to fudge the issue by pretending that the structure is there solely for the good of the client, or to hide behind 'professional practice'.

In fact, any good relationship balances the needs and wishes of both parties, and the counsellor needs a clear structure at least as much as the client. Counselling is an exhausting business if it is done well and, in part, the structure is there to guard against the therapist becoming too depleted.

Counsellors have many slight differences in the way that they work. For example, some work a '50-minute hour', with a 10-minute break between clients, and others work a full hour with a 15-minute break. Some counsellors keep very strictly to the set starting and ending times and others choose an ending time which seems appropriate within a five- or ten-minute 'band'. Few experienced therapists overrun the ending time frequently, but most will overrun occasionally in exceptional circumstances. Even this is likely to depend upon whether or not another client is waiting to see them.

The important thing for the client is that he has some clarity about what the counsellor's 'rules' are.

BEGINNINGS

The initial contract between a person-centred therapist and her client is a start point for a working relationship – a relationship between two people. One of those people – the counsellor – has considerably more power than the other. She knows how a counselling session is likely to unfold. She has a theoretical base – a framework for understanding what is happening for the client. She has a supervisor – someone to turn to for help and support.

The client is feeling vulnerable to a greater or lesser degree. It is he who will be taking the great risk of disclosing himself to the counsellor. He may not, initially, be able to voice his own needs and wishes very clearly – if at all.

For these reasons, the initial contract between a person-centred therapist and her client is not a set of absolute rules, set in stone, fixed for all time. Nor is it necessarily something that is discussed immediately the client sets foot across the threshold, particularly if a client is anxious to tell his story. If the client launches in, it may be better to go with him and then stop after he has told you what he needs to, say 15 or 20 minutes before the end of your time together. 'We have about 15 minutes left and there are some things we need to discuss before we finish today'.

Even a client who seems to be engaging with the business of contracting may not be fully taking in the details, so a short information sheet is always useful, giving a client time to read and digest and to prepare any questions he might have. In this, as in other aspects of client-centred work, the client gives the lead. For example, if confidentiality is important, he will ask about this and the counsellor will go into more detail than with the client who does not.

Above all, the counsellor in her first contact with a prospective client is *demonstrating*, not necessarily talking about, the core conditions.

There are two elements to initial contracting. One is the *business contract,* covering such aspects as length and frequency of sessions, payment, cancellations and so on. The other is the *therapeutic contract,* covering the needs and expectations of the client and the nature, limitations and possibilities of what the counsellor is able to offer.

The two are linked, in that even when the subject matter is the business contract, the therapist is empathic, congruent and accepting of the client. The client will also be *showing* the counsellor something of himself. He may be compliant, agreeing without question to everything the therapist suggests. He may be demanding, pushing against the framework offered by the therapist. Sometimes, the counsellor will have a strong reaction at this stage and voice it, thus raising something which has a bearing on the therapeutic contract.

EXAMPLE

This is an extract from a first meeting with a prospective client. The counsellor is in private practice but does not charge for the initial meeting. The counsellor gives the client her information sheet and highlights the main points, concluding as follows:

Counsellor: I usually see people weekly for 50 minutes.

Client: Oh, 50 minutes will be far too long. I was thinking of half an hour.

Counsellor: [*Counsellor considers*] I don't think I could work very effectively in half an hour. It would seem like we'd just got going and we'd have to stop.

Client: Well, we could carry on if we needed to.

Counsellor: Not if there were someone waiting to see me.

Client: Well, I can't afford an hour a week.

Counsellor: I sometimes work on a fortnightly basis, but it can feel like a long gap ...

Client: Oh no, I definitely need weekly.

Counsellor: Would you prefer to look for someone else? Or there might be a free service available to you.

Client: Oh, I've tried those. It's no good. My GP's given me a referral but there's a 12-week waiting list and I need to see someone now. Anyway, you've been recommended and it's you I want to see.

Counsellor: [*interested to discover her own reaction to all this*] I'm beginning to feel quite ... cornered. As though you're pushing at me to see whether I'll bend.

Client: Call yourself a counsellor! You obviously care more about money than people.

Counsellor: Wow, that's a strong accusation! I'm tempted to defend myself ... and I'm also wondering whether there are other people in your life who don't care about you. But that would be getting into the counselling, and we haven't come to a decision yet. Do you want some time to think about it?

Client: Are you hoping I'll go somewhere else?

Counsellor: [*Counsellor thinks, and then grins*] Perhaps part of me is. But that's mostly because I think that you might get resentful about paying my fees. Otherwise, no. I think we could do some useful work together. The question is, would the money side of it get in the way for you?

Client: [*grudgingly*] Well, you hit the nail on the head about other people not caring. How long would it take?

Counsellor: [*sighs*] I *wish* I could answer that question. The trouble is, we don't know what we'll discover when we start working together. I think we should reckon on at least six sessions to start with. And my sense is that it might take longer than that.

> *Client*: It seems like a lot of money.
> *Counsellor*: [*nods*] It *is* a lot of money. I think you should seriously consider going on the waiting list for free counselling.
> *Client*: No. I've decided. I want to see you.
> *Counsellor*: Ok, let's make an appointment. The only thing I would ask is that if you do change your mind, you ring me by the weekend. Oh, I'm forgetting. There are a couple of other things we need to discuss, like how can I get in touch with you if I'm ill or something. And my cancellation fees.

Congruence is an important aspect of the counsellor's input to the contracting. For the beginner person-centred counsellor, empathy and the establishing of herself as a trustworthy person can seem overriding. She is very sensitive to the client's pain and vulnerability and wants above all to alleviate it. This can sometimes lead her, without her being fully aware of it, into agreeing to something that actively gets in the way of the therapeutic process.

Take the example of the prospective client who is adamant that he does not want to talk about his childhood. The new therapist rushes to reassure him. Later in the relationship, he starts to talk about his mother. The therapist is seized by worry. Should she intervene? Will he blame her for letting him carry on? Has she agreed to be responsible for him not going into childhood events?

Having become aware that she had not thought through the initial agreement, and realised her own good reasons for this, she is able to revisit the contract:

> *Counsellor*: I'm aware that when you first came, you said you didn't want to talk about your childhood. But what you were saying about your mother seemed very important to me. Perhaps what happened to you as a child has a real bearing on what's happening now.

Clients are usually anxious to make counselling safe for themselves, and they often have preconceptions about what they want and don't want. These preconceptions may be based on other people's experience or something they have read. Sometimes, they result from a previous negative experience with a counsellor. There are three possibilities: one is that they are asking for something which you have no difficulty in agreeing to. The second is that they ask for something that, if you agreed, would not allow you to work in a person-centred way. The third is that they ask for something which seems, superficially, to be reasonable, but which you want to check a little further.

> *Client*: I definitely do not want to talk about my childhood.
> *Counsellor*: The person-centred approach is about following, not leading. I certainly won't ask intrusive questions, but if you do go into your childhood, I'll go with you.
> *Client*: But I want you to stop me if I start talking about it.

Counsellor: That's not the way I work. I believe that if you talk about *anything,* it's because it's important. *You* might stop yourself, but I won't.

Client: I want you to meet my wife before we start. Then you'll know who I'm talking about.

Counsellor: I'm struggling a bit with why that seems useful to you.

Client: Well, I don't want you to take my word for it. You have to make up your own mind.

Counsellor: Ah. I think you might have misunderstood what counselling is about. I'm not here to give you an opinion or make any judgements. My job is to help *you* to do that.

Client: But I need some advice.

Counsellor: Are you trying to make a difficult decision and feeling rather stuck?

Client: Yes, that's exactly it.

Counsellor: It sounds as though it's a decision which might affect the whole of your life. And you rather wish someone else would make it for you.

Client: Is that wrong?

Counsellor: Not at all. It would be wonderful, wouldn't it, if you could get a guarantee that you were doing the right thing? I'd love to have someone to make *my* decisions for me at times.

Client: But you don't do that?

Counsellor: I don't know of anyone who does. After all, you're the one who knows the situation best. If there were an easy solution, I'm sure you'd have thought of it.

Client: So if I came for counselling, what *would* you do?

Client: You won't keep any records on me, will you?

Counsellor: I do have to keep some brief notes and statistical information. It's part of my accountability to the agency. But I never put people's names in them, only a number or a letter.

Client: But if someone knew me, they might realise it was me.

Counsellor: [*doubtfully*] I suppose it's just about possible. [*Frowning*] Is there anyone in particular you're worried about?

Client: I had a neighbour who used to work here. That's why I thought of coming.

Counsellor: Ah! Ok. It wouldn't be ethical for *anyone* you know to see your notes. If we knew there was a connection, it just wouldn't happen. Does he or she still work here?

Client: Supervision! I thought this was confidential.

Counsellor: It is. Supervision is just as confidential as counselling. And supervision is about me rather than the people I'm seeing. It's so I can check that I'm doing the best for my clients and get help if I'm feeling stuck. Is that a problem for you? Would you like to know the name of my supervisor?

Client:	The last person I went to kept talking about feelings the whole time.
Counsellor:	And you don't see your feelings as important?
Client:	I've come for counselling because I want to *stop* feeling, not make it worse.
Counsellor:	In that case, I'm probably not the right counsellor for you either. The approach I use is based on the idea that feelings are telling you something. A bit like a physical discomfort or pain is telling you that you need to pay attention to the cause. But mine is not the only kind of counselling. You might be happier with someone who works in a cognitive way, concentrating much more on the way you *think* than the way you feel.
Client:	I think I need some anger management.
Counsellor:	Do you sometimes feel rather out of control?
Client:	Yes. It's like a volcano inside me, always waiting to erupt.
Counsellor:	OK. I want to be clear with you about the way I work. It would be a matter of exploring and coming to understand those angry feelings rather than me giving you techniques to deal with them. I would expect you to get better at handling them the more you understand them, but that might not be what you're looking for.
Client:	Oh. I don't really know. The thing is, it's taken quite a bit for me to come and see you ...
Counsellor:	Right. So it's been rather a risk for you to come in the first place, and the thought of starting again with someone else is a bit daunting.
Client:	Exactly.
Counsellor:	On the other hand, if my style of working is wrong for you ...
Client:	Mmmm.
Counsellor:	Do you need to have a think about it?
Client:	Can I tell you a bit more, first?
Counsellor:	Of course. That might also give you a sense of how I work.

TRUST

One of the phrases which is often used to characterise the beginning of a counselling relationship is *establishing trust*. As we have seen in previous chapters, though, this is not something the counsellor can *do*. A client's self-structure and experience might have taught him that people are *not* trustworthy and no therapist can overturn this in a session or two. For some clients, an inability to trust others might be at the heart of work lasting weeks or even months.

But the counsellor can *be trustworthy.* As the client allows more of his experiencing into awareness – in this instance his experience of your trustworthiness – his self-structure might loosen enough for him to begin to trust you.

Client:	How do I know you won't tell other people about me?
Counsellor:	You don't. It's a real risk for you at the moment, because you've been let down so often. *I* know I'll keep whatever you say in confidence, but that's not the same thing as *you* knowing it.

ASSESSMENT

The term 'assessment' raises many hackles in the person-centred world because of its connotations of expertness and diagnosis. But unless a therapist believes that she can work effectively with every person who comes through the door, some judgements must be made. Can I work with you? Can you work with me? What are you looking for? What am I offering? Are we making good psychological contact? Is person-centred therapy an appropriate approach for you? Are your expectations realistic? Am I experienced enough? Am I competent to work with you and your issues? Can I give the time and commitment you are likely to need?

Despite the wealth of experience and writing on the subject, there is still a perception that person-centred therapy is not 'enough' for people with psychiatric diagnoses, and an expectation that assessment will be used to rule out those with 'mental illness'. My own experience as a newly qualified counsellor (in a Community College) was that clients did not tell me of their psychiatric history until well into the counselling relationship. The first time this happened I was shocked and rather scared. I asked myself *why* this client had not been open with me at the start. My answer to myself was immediate and obvious. I would have treated the client differently. I would have been more fearful – more hesitant. I would have doubted my own competence. The last thing a client who is already stigmatised by a psychiatric label needs is a therapist's fears and prejudices. With the help of my supervisor, I realised that I had been working successfully with this client for more than three months and that nothing had changed except that he felt received enough as a person to let me know more about himself. The client's wisdom, again, was trustworthy. And so, in a way, was mine. I had not perceived anything in the first session which led me to believe I could not work with this client. Had I felt that our psychological contact was poor – perhaps as a result of medication, or his not being in contact with reality – I would have been cautious. But he was willing and able to engage in a therapeutic relationship, and did so very successfully.

In person-centred therapy, the client takes part in the assessment process but there may well be occasions when the counsellor makes the decision either that the person-centred approach will not lead to the outcomes that the client wants, or that she cannot work with this particular person.

EXAMPLES

'My feeling is that you really want someone who is able to show you relaxation techniques and help you to manage the problem. I'm not trained to do that. Your GP might be able to help, or I can give you some telephone numbers.'

'I don't feel as though we're making a good enough connection to be able to work together effectively. It's like any other relationship – sometimes people just don't "click".'

'Thank you for being straight with me. I'm going to be honest with you, too. The ideals of the British National Party are so alien to my way of thinking that I really don't think I'm the right counsellor for you. I'd want to have a debate with you when I should be concentrating on the therapy.'

'I haven't been able to follow you properly for the past half-hour. I don't have a problem with the drinking itself, but we wouldn't be able to do any work when you're like this. And I think you're saying that unless you're "out of it", you can't get through the day.'

'It sounds as though you have had a huge amount of pain in your life. The thing is, I have plans to move away from the area in a few months. Under other circumstances, I think we could work very well together, but I don't want us to start work and then find that I have to move before you're ready to finish. I think it would be better for you to see someone else.'

'You're saying you want someone who can help you with your daughter's murder, your own sexual abuse and the voices in your head. I simply don't have enough experience at present to feel I'm the right person to work with you.'

ENDING A SESSION

One anxiety that is often expressed by beginning therapists is that they might come to the end of the time and leave a client feeling awful. To some extent, there is no getting away from that. The process does not stop simply because a client leaves the counselling room. In fact, there is often significant movement between sessions – as though counselling provides a series of nudges to the process rather than containing the whole.

Looking back to the chapter on empathy, we saw that focusing on particular times, events and people helps clients to become more fully in touch with their experience – to feel their feelings as well as recollect the events. It follows, then, that moving away from the particular to the general might help someone to leave behind the rawness of their experience for the time being and prepare to go back into everyday life. When the end of the session approaches, the therapist will stop focusing upon 'opening up' or deepening areas of the client's experience, but will be mindful of the fact that the client will shortly be leaving the counselling room.

Moving from the specific to the general does not mean discounting the client's feelings, but, in contrast to the early part of the session, it does mean trying to avoid the sore spots. For example, if, early in a session, a client said, 'My manager just laid into me. I didn't know what to say', the counsellor, seeking to fully understand and hence to deepen the client's experience, might respond, 'As though you were paralysed by the force of his attack'. If the client said the same thing towards the end of a session, the counsellor might say, 'It's been a tough week for you, hasn't it?'

If the client introduces new material in this ending stage, the therapist might say something like: 'That sounds like a big area to explore and I'm aware that we only have ten minutes left', or, 'I really want to respond to that, but we're close to the end of our time. Could we come back to it next week?'

If the client seems to be overwhelmed with emotion, the counsellor might say, 'We're coming towards the end of the session, so we need to begin to leave that behind for now'. Usually, a client will respond to this kind of prompt without much further help from the counsellor, but, very occasionally, someone might be so deeply into their experience that the counsellor needs to be more proactive.

Throughout their expressions of grief and pain which are connected to past events, clients usually maintain an awareness of themselves in the present. Occasionally, however, this awareness seems to recede so far that a client is reliving the past in the therapy room. A client in this state will take on the mannerisms and characteristics of themselves at a previous, usually young, age. It is important that the counsellor allows enough time for the client to take leave of this place and fully re-enter the present. She might signal this by saying something like, '*We're going to leave little Chris behind for now, and find grown-up Chris again*'. This kind of thing would sound patronising if said to 'grown-up' Chris, but at this point the therapist is in contact with the child and not the adult. She might remind the client of present realities: '*We're in my counselling room and we have about 15 minutes left together*'. She might begin to prepare her client for leaving, '*Where will you be going to when you leave here today?*' – re-focusing him on his current life and concerns. She might even walk around the room with her client, engaging him in talking about the things in the room and outside the window. At some point, not necessarily there and then, the therapist will also refer to what has happened, so that the client can talk about the experience if he wishes.

ENDING A RELATIONSHIP

Sitting back and waiting for the client to make a decision to end the relationship is problematic in two ways. One is that this ignores the power imbalance within the relationship. A client may well be waiting for the counsellor to make the first move, or even expecting the counsellor to make a decision about his 'progress'. The second is that it ignores the fact that the therapist is a part of that relationship and that her perceptions and wishes can be taken into account.

EXERCISE

Why might a client be hesitant about raising the matter of ending with his or her counsellor? Make a list of all the possible reasons.

Waiting for the counsellor to give him permission to end, or worrying about offending her by the suggestion that she is no longer needed are just two of the many possibilities. Clients often approach the matter obliquely, 'I'm feeling a lot better now', or they may give clues such as beginning to miss sessions. If the therapist does not take the hint, they might just cease to turn up, leaving the therapist with numerous questions and feelings of her own.

Experience suggests that approximately a third of the total duration of the relationship constitutes the ending phase and the counsellor must be alert to the signals which might indicate that the client is ready to talk about drawing the work to a close. This is not, of course, the same as finishing immediately. Except in very short-term relationships, both client and counsellor will need time to make the ending a satisfactory one.

Many of the clues given by clients are in fact the same as the material which makes a good ending. As in other respects, the client's process is trustworthy. The therapist's job is to recognise the significance of these clues and, if the client is not doing so himself, raise the prospect of an ending. You may find that your client begins to:

- Reminisce about the relationship – 'Do you remember that time when …'.

- Review his progress – 'I'm feeling a lot more confident than when I first came'.

- Celebrate achievements – 'I wouldn't have been able to do that six months ago'.

- Give feedback – 'What I like about the way you work …'.

- Show appreciation – 'I wouldn't have got through it without you'.

- Pay attention to the external world as well as the internal. (This can sometimes be perceived by the counsellor as 'not working', 'just chatting', etc.) – 'Pat and I went to the pub yesterday …'.

- Look forward – 'I'm thinking of applying for a new job'.

The client is beginning to disengage from the relationship. Again, the key is in *hearing* the possible meanings in the client's communications and *responding* to them.

Client:	I'm feeling a lot better now. You've really helped me.
Counsellor:	I'll be here for you as long as you want me.
	[*This may be true (one year? six years?) but it cuts off exploration*]

Client:	I'm feeling a lot better now. You've really helped me.
Counsellor:	Thank you. That's very welcome feedback for me. Perhaps we should be thinking about bringing our work to an end?

Client:	I'm feeling a lot better now. You've really helped me.
Counsellor:	Are you saying you want us to think about ending?
Client:	I'm feeling a lot better now. You've really helped me.
Counsellor:	Oh! I'm really pleased, but also a bit surprised. When we started, the 'biggie' was you wanting to change jobs, but we seem hardly to have touched on that. Has it stopped being relevant?
Client:	I'm feeling a lot better now. You've really helped me.
Counsellor:	[*Counsellor is troubled*] And I was thinking how *little* this seemed to be helping you. I was going to say that today.
	[*Client looks uncomfortable*]
Counsellor:	I am wondering whether you're trying to let me off the hook gently. Are you really saying that you want to stop because we don't seem to be getting anywhere?
Client:	I'm feeling a lot better now. You've really helped me.
Counsellor:	I'm really pleased. Thank you for telling me. Are you saying you've achieved what you wanted from these sessions?
Client:	[*horrified*] Oh! Do you think I should stop coming?
Counsellor:	You seem quite shocked by that idea.

The therapist will have similar impulses to the client during the ending phase and may initiate her own reminiscing, celebrating the changes and acknowledging that the future will hold its own challenges for the client. Since it might be more difficult for the client to express sadness and regret, or to say the things he has *not* found helpful in the relationship, the counsellor might invite these kinds of disclosure.

Once each person knows that the counselling is coming to a conclusion, such thoughts occur and can be voiced. There seems to be a naturally occurring process of reviewing and considering the relationship and the work once the therapy is agreed to be coming to an end. This does not mean that all of the time is given to this ending process. Much of the therapeutic work still continues. However, as the agreed ending approaches, the balance of time shifts away from the inner world of the client to reviewing, reminiscing, consolidating and looking forward.

EXAMPLES — CLIENT

- 'When I first came, I was really in awe of you. I was afraid you'd say I was a hopeless case.'
- 'I didn't understand what counselling was about at all. If I'd known, I'm not sure I'd have had the courage to do it!.'
- 'I hated it when you went on holiday that time. I was so angry.'
- 'There were times when I would have topped myself if I hadn't had this to come to.'

EXAMPLES — COUNSELLOR

- 'I'm very aware that we have only two sessions left, and I'm feeling quite sad.'
- 'I'd really like some feedback from you. Perhaps next week, you could tell me about anything that was particularly helpful – and anything I did that wasn't helpful.'
- 'We had a bit of a rough ride last autumn. I wasn't at all sure at one point that you were going to come back.'
- 'Do you remember when you told me you'd applied for the job? I was stunned that you'd found that much confidence.'
- 'You seemed so timid and fearful when you first came.'
- 'You hardly said anything the first few sessions. I'm really appreciating how open you are now.'
- 'You were very generous to me when I cocked up your appointment that time.'
- 'It's going to seem odd to me, too, not to be seeing you on Tuesdays.'

THE LOSSES

It can seem a little like blowing your own trumpet to pay attention to the client's losses in ending a counselling relationship with you.

Self-deprecating statements like: 'Oh, I didn't do anything really', or 'But *you* did all the work', can be dismissive of both the client's experience and the energy you have devoted to offering the therapeutic conditions.

EXERCISE

A client has been coming to counselling every week for six months. He has a busy job and family responsibilities but has been committed to the process. Initially wary about therapy, he has come to trust you, and himself, and been able to look at some very painful aspects of his life. At one stage, he became very angry with you and you were able to stay with him. As a result, he realised that he was still deeply angry with his mother and was able to grieve for the first time. Despite the ups and downs, the relationship has been very productive for him.

- Take a sheet of paper and list the things the client will be losing in ending this relationship.
- Take a second sheet of paper and list the things you will be losing.

If you are able to be congruent, you will acknowledge your own pending losses. If you are not able to acknowledge them, or are not sufficiently aware of them, you will be less likely to play your part in bringing the relationship to an appropriate conclusion.

Some of your losses might be purely pragmatic. For example, if you are a student, your course might require you to 'clock up' a given number of counselling hours, or might require you to work long term with a certain number of clients. If you are in private practice, ending with a client might adversely affect your income – the more so if two or three clients seem to be coming to a conclusion at the same time. When such factors are out of your awareness, you might well fail to pick up on or respond to your client's indications that he is wishing to move to a conclusion. You will not *intend* to 'hang on' to him, but will by omission prevent him exploring whether or not he has met his need for counselling.

UNSATISFACTORY ENDINGS

We all have our own experiences of endings, some of which will be of endings which were mishandled. Without our necessarily being aware of it, these will affect the way we approach the closing stages of a therapeutic relationship. In particular, we are likely to want to prevent a client from feeling something awful which we ourselves experienced in our own partings.

EXERCISE

Think of a time in your life when you experienced a parting or an ending. Here are some examples to help you.

- Leaving school
- Family members or close friends going away
- Leaving home for the first time
- Leaving work for a new job
- Moving to a different part of the country
- A death of family member or close friend

What happened? How was the ending or parting managed?

Imagine yourself having to say goodbye to someone close, perhaps at a railway station or airport. Perhaps you find yourself doing one of the following:

- Rushing away with a cheerful farewell
- Looking on the bright side to blot out the sadness
- Hanging around awkwardly, not knowing what to say
- Trying to prolong the last moments, because the parting is so unbearable
- Saying goodbye by proxy – encouraging others (children, for example) to do the hugging and kissing while you hang back

How might you show this tendency when ending with clients?

If you ignore the indications that your client is moving towards an ending, you will be preventing exploration of the matter. In effect, you can be making a decision for your client by omission and keeping that power to yourself. Alternatively, your client might make the decision without discussion, leaving you feeling 'unfinished'.

EXAMPLE

After the third session, when you come to make the next appointment, your client says that he doesn't think he needs another. He thanks you and goes.

When you review the session in supervision, you realise that there were some indications that you could have picked up on. He seemed much more cheerful than in the first two sessions. He was telling you that he had made the decision to leave his wife, which was the issue he had brought in the first place. He was talking about practicalities rather than expressing strong feelings.

You admit to yourself and your supervisor that you were hoping he would continue. You had seen some 'meaty' issues, in passing, which you thought he could usefully work on: the fact that he could not ask for support from anyone else; the death of his father ... .

Reluctantly, you conclude that you were in part following *your* agenda, rather than his and you missed the opportunity to conclude the work satisfactorily.

DRIBBLING ON

One temptation for counsellors and clients alike is to stage or phase the ending. On the face of it, this makes sense. Moving to a session a fortnight, for example, allows a client to test out his ability to manage on his own for a longer period. A client might want to come back and see you in a couple of months, 'just in case'.

However, some caution is needed here. The client, the therapist, or both might be trying to make the ending less difficult or painful. Is this realistic? And what does it say about the validity of feelings? The conclusion of any relationship, good or bad, involves losses, and the longer the relationship the more intense are likely to be the feelings. These feelings cannot be reduced or ameliorated through the practicalities of when and how often the people meet. Moreover, sessions with greater and greater intervals between them can reduce the psychological contact between client and counsellor. They might take longer to 'get into' the work. They might be unclear about what the work is, and how much can be done. Most worrying, such 'staging' of an ending can be a substitute for paying attention to the wide range of feelings and emotions to which endings give rise.

> EXAMPLE
>
> *Client*:   Can I make an appointment in about three months? After Christmas, say.
>
> *Counsellor*:   [*considers*] I'm really tempted to say yes, because I'd love to know how you're going on. But it would feel rather odd – almost as though you were 'reporting back' to me. I'd rather we left it until you feel you want more counselling – if you ever do!
>
> *Client*:   But if I don't I might never see you again.
>
> *Counsellor*:   [*quietly*] It's an awfully sad thought, isn't it. We've been through so much together.

A similar phenomenon can sometimes be seen on counselling courses. Course members might avoid the reality of the course ending by arranging to continue meeting. In some cases, this means that the course dribbles to an end over time, with strong feelings avoided and few participants feeling satisfied.

Although moving to a session every two weeks can be appropriate for some clients, I have found that my client and I lose the thread if we meet less frequently than that. Typically, 'catching up' takes much of the session and we have struggled to engage in the therapeutic work.

In addition to the sadness of ending, clients are often worried about losing the safety net of counselling and managing on their own. Empathising with this, or even sharing the worry, can easily lead the therapist to agree to something within the session that she finds herself questioning once the client has left.

DEPENDENCY

The idea of a client clinging to you forever is a very scary one, but it can be hard to acknowledge our own fears. The label 'dependency' rather neatly shifts the focus onto the client. So let us re-focus on the relationship and look at what might be happening, for the client and for the counsellor.

The client

The client, possibly for the first time in his life, is experiencing warmth and acceptance. Someone is listening with deep respect to *him*. He does not want to lose his counsellor. Is this dependency?

The client's life is barren of warmth and care. He feels isolated. The counselling session is the only time in his week when he connects fully with another human being. He clings to this one hour in 168 as his only reason for living. Is this dependency?

The client is having some seriously painful memories of his childhood. The therapist is the only person he feels he can trust with these memories. Is this dependency?

The client's childhood abuser has begun appearing to him. 'He' is usually in the counselling room at some point during the session, and the client is visibly terrified of 'him' when he 'appears'. The therapist is not frightened, but she does take 'him' very seriously. The client believes that, without the therapist, he would not have the strength to withstand the abuser's commands to kill himself. Is this dependency?

The counsellor

The counsellor is feeling very weary. The client keeps returning to the same points over and over again. Nothing seems to be changing for him. He just cries and cries throughout the session. She is getting worried. Is he becoming dependent on her?

The counsellor is alarmed to discover how important she is to the client. It feels like a huge responsibility, which she doesn't want to carry. Perhaps she should suggest he enrol for a course or something?

The counsellor is anxious. The client is suffering such pain during the sessions and he keeps asking her whether she thinks it is doing any good. What if it isn't? What if the pain just carries on forever? It will be her fault for encouraging him to feel it.

The counsellor is frightened. She feels out of her depth. Perhaps her client needs medication. Perhaps she should refer him to someone more experienced.

The big problem with the 'dependency' label is that a counsellor may be panicked into making a premature ending, without taking into account the needs and wishes of her client. It is entirely natural that a client should feel dependent for a time during the therapeutic relationship. But the counsellor might need extra support and supervision for herself in order to 'carry' a client's pain for a prolonged period of time. If the client does need help which she cannot provide, she needs to consider carefully whether this might be an alternative to, or in addition to, her work with him. If she decides that working with this client is beyond her competence, the client still needs plenty of time to make an ending – probably more time than usual if the ending feels to him like an abandonment. Either way, the ending is likely to be a difficult and challenging one for the therapist.

And, rather neatly, we are back to beginnings and assessment, in particular the question *Can I give the time and commitment which this client is likely to need?* We cannot work with everyone and it is far better to be cautious at the beginning than find ourselves in over our heads.

FURTHER READING

Biermann-Ratjen, E. (1998) 'Incongruence and psychopathology', in B. Thorne and E. Lambers (eds), *Person-Centred Therapy, A European Perspective*. London: Sage.

Cooper, M., O'Hara, M., Schmid, P. and Wyatt, G. (eds) (2007) *The Handbook of Person-Centred Psychotherapy and Counselling.* Basingstoke: Palgrave Macmillan.

Haugh, S. and Paul, S. (2008) *The Therapeutic Relationship.* Ross on Wye: PCCS Books

Joseph, S. and Worsley, R. (eds) (2007) *Person-Centred Practice: Case Studies in Positive Psychology.* Ross-on-Wye: PCCS Books.

Lambers, E. (1994) 'Person-centred psychopathology', in D. Mearns (ed.), *Developing Person-Centred Counselling.* London: Sage.

Mearns, D. and Cooper, M. (2005) *Working at Relational Depth in Counselling and Psychotherapy.* London: Sage.

Mearns, D. (ed.) (1994) *Developing Person-Centred Counselling.* London: Sage. (Section III.)

Sanders, P. (2006) *The Person-Centred Primer.* Ross on Wye: PCCS Books.

Van Werde, D. (1998) '"Anchorage" as a core concept in working with psychotic people', in B. Thorne and E. Lambers (eds), *Person-Centred Therapy, A European Perspective.* London: Sage.

11

PROFESSIONAL
ISSUES

BOUNDARIES

Boundaries is the term given to the limits which we set for ourselves and our clients.
They provide safety and the security that comes with clarity.

Many boundaries are imposed at least in part for the benefit of the counsellor. We
have our working lives to organise, so we need time boundaries in order to offer set
appointments. We have our own lives to live, so we do not usually invite clients, no
matter how needy, to live in our homes.

If as a counsellor, my self-structure bids me to put others' needs before my own, I
need to remind myself of the issues around boundaries in order for me not to give
more than I can cope with.

For example, simple compassion pulls at me in such a way that I could easily give
material help to a client in poverty. It is so tempting to think of my (relative) wealth.
Selfish! cries my self-structure. And yet, what would I achieve if I gave money to my
client? And what damage might I do?

A gift of money might help someone in the short term, but looked at in the whole
context of a counselling relationship, what messages does it contain? The obvious
message *I have more than you* is easily confused with *I am more than you (more successful, more able to cope . . .)*.

Is giving money also a way of relieving the counsellor's feelings? Is it easier
for me to give you money than empathically to bear with you the burden of
poverty?

I must confess that I have in fact given a client money on occasion – and
lied about it, saying that it came from a college fund. At the time it seemed the
right thing to do. In retrospect? Wouldn't we all like to have an authority to
tell us that we did the right thing – or to warn us that we were about to do
the wrong thing? One of the continuing challenges of counselling is that just

as we refuse to make decisions for our clients, so our supervisors often refuse to make decisions for us!

EXERCISE

Consider the following vignettes and explore how they might pull at your boundaries.

'You know I told you about Alan. Well, it's getting worse. He never does it when anyone else can hear – always in a snide way when we're on our own. I just can't stand it anymore. Can you have a word with him? You are the counsellor for the whole organisation, aren't you, and no one is supposed to make sexist and racist comments.'

'Do you know, I always feel better for having talked to you. It's as though you understand everything before I even say it. You are on the same wavelength as me. You are the only person I ever talk to like this. That's because I trust you not to laugh at me or tell me to shut up. You really are very good at what you do. I'd actually like to see you more often, because in between times it's awful. No one else understands what's going on for me. I think that if I saw you twice or three times a week, I'd soon get myself sorted out – you're so good at counselling people. Or could I perhaps have your phone number – just for an emergency?'[1]

'Now that we're finishing the counselling, could we meet up for a coffee every so often?'

'I'm terrified of going into hospital. I know you don't normally do this, but would you come and visit me? Otherwise, I'll be stuck in there with no one.'

Someone once likened boundaries to a tree which might flex a little in the wind and, because it has some flexibility, will not break. There are times when you might wish to be flexible about a boundary, and this will always depend upon the particular client and the particular circumstances. The rule of thumb is to imagine yourself in the future. Are you likely to resent having committed yourself to something you don't usually do? Can you guard against this by putting limits on it?

For example, you might agree to – or even suggest – seeing someone twice a week if they are going through a particularly difficult time, while making it clear that this is a short-term measure only. As always, your supervisor will be there to help you to explore the issues.

---

[1] This vignette is taken from J. Tolan and S. Lendrum (1995) *Case Material and Role Play in Counselling Training*. London: Routledge.

CHALLENGE

The concept of challenge is an interesting one in person-centred counselling. Interesting in that it arises from the core conditions rather than being something different which the counsellor actively sets out to do.

Challenge can be seen as something that sets off a movement or change in the client. And in person-centred counselling, the important movements are towards the person's

- allowing more of his experience into awareness ('getting in touch with' himself);
- symbolising his experience more accurately, with less distortion (understanding and accepting what really happened/is happening for him);
- loosening his self-structure to accept and integrate more of his experience (changing the way he sees himself and the world);
- moving from an external to an internal locus of evaluation (becoming more accepting and trusting of his own experience and values).

Take, for example, the person who believes that crying is a sign of weakness. There has been a death in his family. The counsellor's *empathy* for his sadness will challenge his own distortions – the ways in which he hides his own tearfulness from himself. ('Everyone has to die some time', perhaps, or 'I'm just feeling tired at the moment with so much to organise'.) He might become more aware of his own sadness and more aware that he is choked up.

The counsellor's *acceptance* will challenge his belief that crying is weak. ('This person still respects me, even though I am struggling to suppress tears.')

The counsellor might go on to *empathise* with his sense of vulnerability and exposure: 'It seems to be a bit embarrassing for you to be emotional with me here'. Again, this is a possible challenge. The client might become more aware of his own discomfort. His self-structure might loosen a fraction as he acknowledges that not only is he sad, but it is hard for him to express it.

It is these small challenges that make person-centred counselling effective because the self-structure is not under threat and does not need to defend itself by becoming rigid. If the challenge is too great, the client will not acknowledge, or will deny the validity of, the counsellor's response. The counsellor in turn will accept that her client is the final arbiter – he is the only person who knows himself 'from the inside':

Client:	I'm not embarrassed.
Counsellor:	A little . . . uncomfortable? Is that nearer?
Client:	No. I'm not at all uncomfortable with you.
Counsellor:	Ah. Perhaps I misread what you were feeling.

However convinced the counsellor is that she saw embarrassment in her client, she will not impose her frame of reference on her client. His reality is at least as valid as hers. But if he goes on to check hers, she will be congruent.

Client:	Did I look embarrassed to you?
Counsellor:	Yes, you did for a moment.
Client:	Well I wasn't.

Now the counsellor is beginning to hear that the idea of being embarrassed is more of a challenge to his self-structure than being sad. He is certainly not ready to admit *this* experience into his self-structure and the counsellor is able to accept either that she has misread the signs or that he has no awareness of his own embarrassment. Even if she is *convinced* that what she saw was embarrassment, she knows that this is unimportant. The client's perception of himself is what matters.

She can, of course, try to 'show' her client his own embarrassment – or try to convince him that crying is a natural and healthy emotion. Theory predicts that this will result in the self-structure defending itself and becoming more rigid. Moreover, the client is likely to feel misunderstood or judged and this might result in him becoming more wary and self-conscious.

This last example illustrates another aspect of challenge in person-centred work. Particularly in the early stages of a relationship, the counsellor cannot predict with any certainty what the client will find challenging and what he will not. He might react violently against something that the counsellor has intended as a supportive, empathic response. The reason for the violent reaction will probably lie in his self-structure rather than in any misperception or clumsy wording on the part of the counsellor.

EXERCISE

A counsellor is meeting Pat for the first time. Pat is talking about work, particularly the sense that effort is not acknowledged, and that those higher up in the hierarchy 'take advantage of people's good nature'. The counsellor might offer the following responses:

- You sound very frustrated.
- You'd really like to give your boss an earful.
- You're not getting any recognition for all the work you're putting in.
- You sound angry with the whole of management at the moment.
- It's really upsetting for you that other people don't seem to give a toss.
- You're really fed up with putting in all this effort when others couldn't care less.

The counsellor does not yet know that Pat is a committed Christian, with an introjected belief that anger is wrong and shameful. Pat's perception of self is of not 'giving in' to anger.

Which of the counsellor's attempts at empathic understanding might be denied by this client because they present too much of a challenge to the self-structure?

So challenge is something that *happens* if a counsellor is offering the therapeutic conditions. It is not something that the counsellor *does*.

Having said that, a counsellor might have a strong sense that she is 'hearing' something that she believes that the client would not want her to voice. But the difficulty with assuming a knowledge of what any individual might or might not want to hear is twofold. First, it involves predicting the self-structure of the client. Second, it could be that the counsellor's own values and culture are getting in the way.

Say she believes that she is hearing her (male) client hinting at the fact that he is sexually attracted to his best friend, Winston. The counsellor might assume that her client is ashamed of such feelings. She might assume that such an attraction would seem as 'unnatural' to the client as it does to her. So she wonders whether or not to 'challenge' her client. By this, she means saying something which will be unwelcome to the client. But the real challenge here is to the counsellor, not the client. It is *her* self-structure which cannot accept his emerging feelings. She does not yet know whether acknowledging them will be challenging to his self-structure, nor the nature of that challenge.

Perhaps her client does *not* have any sense that homosexuality is 'wrong'. For him, it's just unknown – not an overt part of his culture or experience. In this case, an accepting, empathic response might be met with wonderment in the client: 'Is that so? Do I really fancy him? Perhaps I do!' This is one kind of person-centred challenge. In theoretical language, it enables the client to symbolise his experience more accurately: 'I thought I liked Winston a lot as a friend. But perhaps I'm in love with him. That would explain why I get so wound up when he goes out with Debbie instead of coming to the pub with me.'

He might, of course, feel ashamed of, even revolted by, his own sexual feelings towards another man. But it is not for the counsellor to make predictions about this. If he does have such feelings, it is her job to accept these, along with his other feelings. However, the counsellor who cannot offer unconditional positive regard is right to hesitate – not because voicing her perceptions would be a 'challenge' to the client, but because she is too caught up in her own values to accept him.

There might be a second reason for her hesitation – she fears that her client will be angry with her if she says something he does not want to hear. Again, she is making a prediction and, in effect making a decision *for her client*– the decision that he should not talk about this area of his experiencing. Instead of opening up the client's experience, she is closing it down.

Going back to our client, it might be, of course, that he knows that he is gay. Hinting about his friend Winston might be his way of testing out whether or not he can trust his counsellor with this part of himself. When she fails to acknowledge his hints, he has his answer.

The question for a counsellor is not, 'Should I challenge this client?', but, 'Why am I hesitating to say this?'. The hesitation is often an extremely useful pointer to the counsellor's own feelings, whether fear of the client's reaction or disapproval of his experience.

TOUCH

Physical touch between counsellor and client is potentially very powerful. It has a multiplicity of meanings and a counsellor's awareness of these meanings is essential if touch is to be therapeutic rather than disempowering or even abusive of the client.

Potentially, touching a client crosses an important boundary and muddies the clear waters between counselling and other relationships such as friendship. Some counsellors hug their clients regularly. What are they wishing to communicate? What are they actually communicating? Is it possible for a client to reject the hug? Is it possible for a counsellor not to hug a client once it has become part of the ritual of the session?

Assume that it is the end of a counselling session and the therapist and client are both getting to their feet. The counsellor has a strong impulse to put her arms around the client. What might she be wishing to express?

- I feel warmth towards you.

- Your communications today have affected me deeply.

- You are still distressed and although I have to finish now, I want to show you that I recognise your distress.

- You are still distressed and I feel a bit responsible, so I want to make it better for you.

- I wish I could carry on the session and I'm hugging you to bring it to a close.

- You wanted to carry on the session, so I'm hugging you to reassure you that I still care, even though we had to stop.

- I'm a warm and caring counsellor.

- I always hug my clients at the end of a session.

Although the example of a counsellor who regularly hugs clients is an extreme one, it illustrates some of the dangers of touch.

Should we touch our clients at all? There are numerous arguments for and against touching clients. But as with all such global arguments, they can be 'right' or 'wrong' depending upon the individual client and therapist.

- Counsellor A sees her client in pain and is finding it difficult to tolerate. She grabs her client in a bear hug to try to relieve the suffering. She is not sufficiently self-aware to realise that it is she who needs relief and not her client.

- Counsellor B has been taught never to touch a client. She mistrusts her own impulse to reach out and hides behind her training when her client asks to be held.

- Counsellor C is male and his client is female. He is, quite appropriately, aware of the potential miscommunications which touch might provoke.

Arguments against using touch with clients

- The emotional 'holding' of a therapeutic relationship is sufficient and physical touch is unnecessary.

- Many clients find touch intrusive or frightening or abusive.

- Clients in fragile process (see Chapter 9) are likely to be swamped by a counsellor's touching them.

- Clients who have had bad experiences of being touched might not be able to say so to the therapist.

- The counsellor can be meeting her or his own need for reassurance or to 'make things better' or to be seen as warm and caring through touching or hugging.

- Touch and holding can provide immediate comfort and so block a client's pain or distress or feelings of isolation.

- Touch might be misunderstood by a client and give rise to a complaint against the counsellor.

- A therapist's touch might blur the boundary for a client and raise erotic feelings or expectations of friendship.

- If a counsellor's touch is the only physical contact in a client's life, s/he might prolong the relationship beyond its therapeutic usefulness.

Arguments in favour of using touch with clients

- There is a natural healing power to touching someone, and it is a deprivation to deny this to a client if s/he wishes it.

- Some clients say that being touched or held enables them to feel safer in exploring distressing or painful material.

- The counsellor's touch can be an anchor to the here-and-now reality of the therapeutic relationship when clients are getting 'lost' in their past pain.

- A blanket prohibition might have more to do with counsellor fears – of their own sexuality or of misinterpretation by others, for example – than client needs or wishes.

- Many clients have been deprived of appropriate touch and the therapist's touch can help them to develop a congruent response when touched by others.

- For some clients, the counsellor's touch can be powerful evidence of their acceptability.

Clearly, this is an area which requires great sensitivity on the part of the therapist, and offering touch to a client is not something to be done lightly. When a counsellor experiences an impulse to touch, or even hold, a client, this impulse is worth attending to – but not necessarily acting upon. The counsellor who bypasses expression in favour of action is usually imposing something upon a client. The client might perceive it as a welcome imposition, particularly if the counsellor has sensed and responded to an unspoken desire, but it is an imposition nevertheless. The client-centred therapist tries to put words to her impulses – to communicate something of her own experience in the relationship:

- 'Just then, I felt very maternal towards you. As though you were a small child in need of a cuddle.'
- 'You seem very lonely. I wanted to reach out to you just then.'
- 'As you were talking then, I had a strong image of myself putting my arm around you.'
- 'Would you like a hand to hold?'

Any touch between counsellor and client needs to be contracted for very carefully and on every occasion. The fact is that touch can be very powerful. A client once told me at the end of our work together that it was my willingness to offer to put my hand on her arm that began to break down her sense of herself as contaminated and 'untouchable'. If we make touch, or even hugging clients, a routine, we probably lose the self-awareness that gives it its therapeutic value.

THERAPY OR MANAGEMENT

One of the commonly held misunderstandings of person-centred work is that the counsellor does whatever the client wants. Another is that the counsellor does whatever *she* wants. Neither of these is true. But the reverse, which is that the therapist pays *no* attention to what the client wants, is inimical to person-centred philosophy.

So to which client wants should counsellors respond? Or should the person-centred therapist solely empathise with the wanting?

At the heart of person-centred counselling is what we describe as 'the process' (see Chapter 9). By this we mean the gradual loosening of the self-structure and the opening up of the individual to more of his organismic experiencing. However, there are some occasions when the client may have immediate needs that the therapist wishes to help him meet. It is important, though, in order not to get side-tracked, to distinguish such immediate needs, which are often matters of information, education or management, from the therapeutic business of person-centred counselling.

The waters are not always easy to negotiate. There is often more than one 'layer' to a comment or question, and the therapist must make a judgement about which to respond to and when. For example, a client asks where to catch a bus for home. The counsellor can simply give the information which has been requested. This, though, might be to ignore something important in what the client is 'saying'.

Depending upon *when* in the session or the relationship the question has been asked and, to some extent, *how* it is asked, the client might be telling you something as well as asking you something. The question might come, for example, in the middle of a session.

Does he get very wound up or anxious about things like travelling? Is part of his mind disengaged from the counselling process? Is he protecting himself from difficult feelings by switching to more mundane matters? Is he asking the question to fill a silence?

If there is a hidden 'message' such as this, the counsellor can respond congruently or with tentative empathy. Either is an invitation to the client to explore the matter further:

'You seem quite anxious about how you're going to get home.'

[*Counsellor's tone is interested and enquiring*]: 'That felt like an abrupt switch.'

'I'm wondering whether we were touching on something a bit raw just then?'

[*Counsellor smiles*]: 'I got the impression then that you felt you had to say something. As though being quiet is somehow *not allowed*.'

When in the session the question is asked will probably make a difference to the response. If the question is asked at the end of a session, when the therapeutic work has come to a close, the therapist will probably just give the information. But what if the question is asked in the middle? Is it ever appropriate to withhold information which would reduce a client's anxiety? On the other hand, would giving the information have the effect of ignoring or belittling the anxiety? This is one instance in which the counsellor may separate the practical need from the therapeutic need:

'I'll give you directions at the end of the session. But the thought of how you're going to get home is obviously on your mind. It makes me realise what a big step you've taken to come here today.'

EXERCISE

Below are a number of client questions. First, identify any different 'layers' of communication. Then, discuss how you might respond to each 'layer', depending upon when in the session the question is asked.

- Do you have children?
- How many times will I need to come and see you?
- Do you ever get angry?
- Is flying really as safe as they say?
- What is this counselling supposed to be doing for me?
- What's this medication the doctor has given me?

THE COUNSELLOR'S EXPERTISE

Central to person-centred work is the notion that we as therapists are *not* the experts. By this, we mean that we cannot predict the client's process – we cannot know what is 'right' for a client at any given point in time. We trust that the actualising tendency will take our clients in a direction which will enhance their lives and so we do not seek to influence their thoughts, feelings or behaviour. We also try, as far as is possible, to redress the imbalance of power in the counselling relationship.

We must not, however, deny the expertise which we *do* possess, for that would be to withhold from our clients important information and, effectively, to *increase* the imbalance of power. A client who does not understand what is happening in counselling, and why, may feel unsure and unsafe.

Fundamentally, our task is to acknowledge our own authority where it exists and share our understanding and experience in the right way and at the right time for each client. Person-centred therapy is not mysterious. It has a clear and coherent theory and practice base that we learn through training and experience and which we can communicate to clients if they wish to know it.

Some clients only wish to reassure themselves that the counsellor knows what she is doing. Beyond that, they are not interested in the detail of person-centred work. Others are more nervous. It is a frightening business, experiencing painful emotions that may have been suppressed for years, and they want to be sure that it will do some good. Yet others are curious and interested in client-centred counselling because they are curious and interested.

There are, of course, limits. I cannot *guarantee* that person-centred therapy 'will work' for a particular client. In fact, accompanying each new client into their dark and dangerous places leads to moments of great trepidation for me, when staying in psychological contact seems to shake my faith in the process at that time. I *can* say, though, that in my belief *and* my experience, person-centred therapy has been effective for me and for my clients.

I can say what person-centred therapy will entail, in particular that it will entail feelings as well as thoughts, since my theory tells me that emotions promote and accompany change. If a client does not want to explore and express his feelings, he might be better advised to find a cognitive-behavioural practitioner.

I can also say what I expect to happen: that experiences which have been distorted or denied will come into awareness and that anxiety and other strong feelings may accompany this process. But how and when I might say this will depend considerably upon the client.

EXERCISE

You have a client, Henry, who wants to 'find the real me'. He has talked about how he was abused and neglected as a child, so that he became very quiet and compliant. Between you, you have come to talk about the *real me* as a little mouse, who expects to be jumped on if he shows his nose outside his hiding place.

Your client has begun to express some of his reactions at home and at work and is quite surprised and pleased with himself for 'not letting people walk all over me'. However, he often feels anxious and a bit panicky and he asks you, quite tearfully and in a bewildered voice, what is happening to him.

a How does the person-centred model explain what is happening to Henry?

b How might you communicate this to Henry, perhaps using the mouse metaphor if it seems appropriate?

CONCLUSION

Appropriate counsellor decisions arise always from the therapeutic conditions. From the very first moments with a client, the therapist's full awareness of her own part in the relationship is important. She has considerable power in those moments: she knows the rules because she has introduced them. She knows what counselling is about because she is the one with the training. If she is not aware of her power, she will not be able to share it or will give it away inappropriately and may end up resenting her client.

Throughout the relationship, the person-centred counsellor tries to hear the uncertainties and questions implicit in the client's communications and to voice the decisions that are being made, so that nothing is 'hidden'.

FURTHER READING

Bond, T. (2000) *Standards and Ethics for Counselling in Action* (2nd edn). London: Sage.

Keys, S. and Proctor, G. (2007) 'Ethics in practice in person-centred therapy', in M. Cooper, M. O'Hara, P. Schmid and G. Wyatt (eds), *The Handbook of Person-Centred Psychotherapy and Counselling*. Basingstoke: Palgrave Macmillan.

Lambers, E. (2007) 'A person-centred perspective on supervision', in M. Cooper, M. O'Hara, P. Schmid and G. Wyatt (eds), *The Handbook of Person-Centred Psychotherapy and Counselling*. Basingstoke: Palgrave Macmillan.

Mearns, D. (2003) *Developing Person-Centred Counselling in Action*. London: Sage.

Schmid, P. (2007) 'The anthropological and ethical foundations of person-centred therapy' in M. Cooper, M. O'Hara, P. Schmid and G. Wyatt (eds), *The Handbook of Person-Centred Psychotherapy and Counselling*. Basingstoke: Palgrave Macmillan.

Tolan, J. and Wilkins, P. (eds) (2012) *Client Issues in Counselling and Psychotherapy*. London: Sage.

Tudor, K. and Worrall, M. (eds) (2004) *Freedom to Practice: Person-Centred Approaches to Supervision*. Ross-on-Wye: PCCS Books.

Tudor, K. and Worrall, M. (eds) (2007) *Freedom to Practice II: Developing Person-Centred Approaches to Supervision*. Ross-on-Wye: PCCS Books.

Worsley, R. (2007) 'Setting up practice and the therapeutic framework', in M. Cooper, M. O'Hara, P. Schmid and G. Wyatt (eds), *The Handbook of Person-Centred Psychotherapy and Counselling*. Basingstoke: Palgrave Macmillan.

12

MANAGING THE WORK
IN AN ORGANISATION

RELATIONSHIP SKILLS

We have been focusing on the core conditions in the context of therapeutic work but they are, of course, the basis of all good relationships. If you feel intimidated in an unfamiliar situation, it is easy to forget that you have considerable expertise in relationships that you can use to very good effect.

Counsellors often work within settings where the work and purpose of the organisation is not therapeutic but to do with education, business, general practice and so on. The therapist is a specialist, holding a particular expertise as a resource for the organisation. In this respect, it is the organisation that is your client. You are paid to see individuals because this therapeutic work forwards the aims of the organisation and not because the organisation wants individuals to be contented or fulfilled *per se*. The educational organisation wants people to achieve good examination results, the commercial organisation wants to reduce stress and absenteeism and increase productivity, the general practice wants to increase the general health of patients.

In almost all cases, there is no conflict between the organisation's and the individual's wishes. A person who is moving towards being more contented or fulfilled in himself is more likely to achieve educationally or be more motivated at work.

NEGOTIATING WITH MANAGERS AND COLLEAGUES

Counsellors often perceive themselves to be in a 'piggy-in-the-middle' position within an organisation. On the one hand, they are deeply concerned about the needs of clients. On the other, they are aware of the limited resources of the organisation.

Beginning counsellors can feel themselves to be undervalued, or even under attack, within the organisation. This can affect their ability to offer the relationship conditions to colleagues and to managers (who might also be potential clients).

Colleague:	Do you really need that room all to yourself?
Counsellor:	Well, I couldn't work in a room where people could interrupt all the time.
Colleague:	No, I realise that. But there are lots of times when you don't use it.
Counsellor:	But it has to be available for emergencies. Sometimes people are in a state and they have to be seen straight away.
Colleague:	[*muttering*] There are other people who need a nice room too, you know.
Counsellor:	But counselling is different. Clients need a decent place and privacy or it doesn't work.

In this example, the therapist is feeling a bit threatened. She also 'hears' a criticism – that she is not seeing enough clients (because her room is not fully used). She tells the colleague what he already knows about counselling and comes across as rather precious. Because she is on the defensive, the conditions are absent. In the following example, the conversation turns out rather differently.

Colleague:	Do you really need that room all to yourself?
Counsellor:	It sounds as though you might have a use for it yourself.
Colleague:	Well, there are times I could do with some privacy to talk to the people I manage. It's impossible in my office – I share with Baldip.
Counsellor:	That does sound difficult, particularly if it's something personal.
Colleague:	Exactly. *And* I notice that you don't use the room all the time.
Counsellor:	No, that's true at the moment. But I haven't been here long, and that might change once people get to know I'm here. You're very welcome to use the room if I haven't got a client. The trouble is, I couldn't tell you in advance really, because people sometimes come at very short notice.
Colleague:	But I could give you a call if I needed some privacy?
Counsellor:	Absolutely. If I haven't got a client, you're welcome to use it. I can always find somewhere else to do my admin.

Let us take this example a little further and assume that whenever the colleague rings, the counsellor *does* have a client.

Counsellor:	I wanted a word with you about the room. I feel a bit bad because it's always booked when you ring. I was wondering whether it's worth making out a case for somewhere else to be used for private meetings. Do you think other people are in the same boat as you?
Colleague:	I should think so. This open plan set-up makes it very hard to have a confidential conversation. I know Denise in Planning has the same problem.

Counsellor:	What about the medical room? That doesn't seem to be used very much.
Colleague:	It's a bit … bare.
Counsellor:	Do you think it could be made more user-friendly? Some comfortable chairs or pot-plants or something?
Colleague:	I suppose it could.
Counsellor:	Anyway, we'd have to talk to the nurse. She might not like the idea. Why don't you have a think about it and let me know whether you believe it's worth pursuing?
Colleague:	OK. I'll get back to you.

In this example, the counsellor is recognising a possible difficulty for the organisation as a whole. She does not see her remit as solely working with individual clients. She is a part of this organisation and can help to facilitate the working of the whole organisation when it seems appropriate. The colleague might not think it worth taking this matter further, but he now knows that the counsellor will listen to his concerns and take them seriously.

This is an important message for a counsellor to be giving to all colleagues. Clearly, she will have to be careful about her boundaries, as with individual clients. In particular, she will need to make judgements about what she does herself, and what she supports others in doing. In the example above, she might become involved with the colleague in talking to the nurse, but after that, those involved would need to pass the matter on to the person formally responsible for decision-making about room usage.

RELATIONSHIP CONDITIONS

How do the relationship conditions work when applied to a whole organisation?

Psychological contact

This is often a matter of intent and attitude. The counsellor who works to understand the organisation, its structures and decision-making processes – and the part played by her service within it – is likely to be establishing appropriate contact. In some organisations, all colleagues may be potential referrers and potential clients, so there can be a complexity to the contact with individuals which therapists are uniquely trained to understand. However, there can be a temptation to avoid this muddiness. The counsellor who sets herself apart, rarely emerging from her room, is clearly not making psychological contact with the organisation as a whole.

Unconditional positive regard

This involves being non-judgemental about the organisation as a whole. Just as the individual is trying to negotiate his way in a difficult world, so is the organisation.

External demands, financial constraints and so on place real pressures upon the organisation. The person-centred counsellor does not pressure an individual client with her views about what he *should* do. She tries to approach the organisation with the same open-mindedness. She puts aside any prejudices she might have – managers have all the power and workers are downtrodden, for example – and seeks to understand the struggles of each individual to do their best in their own situation.

Empathy

As with the individual, empathy involves first perception and then communication. The counsellor might perceive a difficulty through talking with colleagues or through her work with a number of clients. She will not, of course, breach confidentiality, but there are sometimes general difficulties that can be addressed without risking the anonymity of clients.

The next question is how to communicate her perception. There are numerous ways of doing this, from a quiet word with an individual to a formal report. This can be seen as the equivalent of 'reflecting back' to an individual client.

Senior managers' energy is often focused upon day-to-day business matters and they can fail to pay attention to organisational difficulties that are obvious to a counsellor. If such difficulties are fed back in an accepting, rather than a blaming way, managers are generally appreciative.

EXAMPLE

Counsellor: I'm a bit hesitant to take up your time. I know how overloaded you are at the moment.

Manager: That's certainly true. I didn't get home until nearly ten last night. [*The counsellor gives an understanding look, but does not say anything. The manager is not her client*]

Counsellor: There's a lot of ill feeling around at the moment. I know that people are worried about the reorganisation, but it's not just that. It's like they feel that they're not important any more – that the senior team is so tied up with the reorganisation that you don't care about them.

Manager: As if I don't have enough to worry about! What on earth do they expect me to do?

Counsellor: I don't think you need to *do* very much. But I do think that some memos thanking people for holding the fort, or something in the newsletter, would help.

Manager: Point taken. Sometimes this job is like having dozens of kids.

Counsellor: [*smiling*] All wanting your attention now! And I'm adding to it. It's not fair I know, but I come to you because I know you'll listen. Will you drop a word in other senior ears?

Manager: First the flattery, then the punch, eh?

Counsellor: [*grinning*] I'll leave you to it.

Sometimes, the organisation cannot 'hear' what is being fed back. As with the individual, it is not the counsellor's job to *make* them hear. She has discharged her responsibility and must leave the matter to others in the organisation.

It helps to get permission before feeding something back to the organisation in a formal way, for example, 'I've been having some thoughts on the problem of absenteeism and I wondered whether you'd like me to put them on paper'. A formal report that can be read, circulated and discussed at others' convenience can be more powerful than a conversation with an individual.

Congruence

In an organisational context, counsellor congruence often revolves around boundary and other ethical issues. At one end of the spectrum the therapist might try to be everything to everybody. At the other, she might be unwilling to consider helping in any way other than seeing individuals for formally contracted counselling sessions.

The counsellor who is congruent is able to assess any requests made of her and communicate something of her own decision-making process without defensiveness.

EXAMPLE

HR Manager: I've got a tricky disciplinary matter on my hands and I'd like you to get involved.

Counsellor: Oh, I don't deal with disciplinary issues, I'm afraid.

Here, the counsellor has reacted to the word *disciplinary,* immediately seeing the potential boundary conflicts. She is so worried about being asked to do something inappropriate that she cuts off any exploration.

HR Manager: I've got a tricky disciplinary matter on my hands and I'd like you to get involved.

Counsellor: Perhaps we'd better go somewhere private.

The counsellor here is seeing the manager as her potential client. Is he asking her to help him to explore his own issues relating to the disciplinary process, possibly without being fully aware of it?

HR Manager: It's a harassment case. The thing is, the complainant has plenty of support, but the guy concerned is a bit on his own.

Counsellor: And you're feeling rather sorry for him.

HR Manager: Well, to be honest, no. He's one of those pompous idiots who gets up everyone's nose – this is confidential, isn't it? Personally, I think he had something like this coming.

Counsellor: So is it a question of being fair? Even though he's a pompous idiot, he still deserves some support.

HR Manager: Exactly. He hasn't a clue what he's done wrong, even.

Counsellor:	What were you thinking I might do?
HR Manager:	Well, I thought if you could see him, at least he'd have someone ...
Counsellor:	Someone to turn to.
HR Manager:	Yes.
Counsellor:	The difficulty is that he doesn't sound like the kind of man who would want counselling. And, as you know, you can't counsel someone against their will!
HR Manager:	But can I suggest it to him?
Counsellor:	Of course. The service is open to everyone.
HR Manager:	How about if I made him an appointment?
Counsellor:	[*takes a minute to consider this*] Now I'm feeling as though you're pushing me – and him! I suspect that you're feeling a bit at the end of your tether with this one ...?
HR Manager:	You're right there! I've done my best with him, but I don't know where else to go.
Counsellor:	OK. I'll make the appointment, but only if you stress to him that it's entirely voluntary.
HR Manager:	Great!
Counsellor:	And I do want to be clear with you about what I can and can't do. If he's feeling a bit anxious or vulnerable, coun-selling might be useful to him. But if he's adamant that he's done nothing wrong, neither of us is going to make a blind bit of difference. It might be that you have already done everything possible.

After this exchange, the therapist is aware of her own apprehensions, particularly as to whether she will be able to offer acceptance if the client attends the appointment. She reminds herself that if the client *does* attend, he might be very different with her from the way he has been when faced with a formal disciplinary hearing. This, however, is for the counsellor and her supervisor and not for discussion with the manager. She is congruent because all of this is available to her awareness, although she has chosen to maintain a professional boundary by not voicing some of it to the manager.

MEETINGS

Counsellors are frequently invited to meetings on a whole range of topics in order to bring their particular expertise to bear on the subject under discussion. Here again, though, relationship skills – expressed in meetings as facilitation skills – can also be used and valued. For example, our expertise in active listening might mean that we pick up immediately when someone has been misheard and misunderstood, or when someone's contribution has been completely overlooked. The counsellor can draw attention to this where the colleague themselves might be hampered by feeling angry or upset or simply not know how to respond, for example, 'Oh,

I thought Bernard was saying more that...' or 'I wonder whether Selma's point about funding comes into this'. A good meeting Chair might well be taking this role but, in practice, a Chair often has a strong interest in the outcome of a discussion and will welcome some additional help with facilitation.

TIME-LIMITED COUNSELLING

It is increasingly common for organisations to put limits on the number of sessions available to any individual client. How should we, as person-centred practitioners, respond? Is the whole idea of limiting time for clients antithetical to person-centredness? The questionnaire below might set you thinking about such issues.

EXERCISE

Complete the questionnaire shown in Table 12.1 on your own, then discuss with one or two other people and consider the implications for time-limited work.

TABLE 12.1

Beliefs about Counselling	Don't Agree						Agree Strongly
The client should be in control	0	1	2	3	4	5	6	7
Clients should have as much time as they need	0	1	2	3	4	5	6	7
It is the counsellor's responsibility to make sure the client is OK	0	1	2	3	4	5	6	7
Clients are better off having no time than limited time	0	1	2	3	4	5	6	7
If time is limited, a client may feel worse at the end of counselling than when they started	0	1	2	3	4	5	6	7
We should not 'open up' a client's pain if we cannot see them through to the end of it	0	1	2	3	4	5	6	7
Other:	0	1	2	3	4	5	6	7

If you make a decision that you *are* prepared to work within resourcing constraints, there are two areas which become highlighted, that is, managing the workload and managing the therapeutic work.

One complaint that is often heard from counsellors in various workplaces is that of pressure from referrers to take more clients than they can cope with. They are often trying to manage a substantial waiting list and feeling like 'piggy-in-the-middle', not able to meet client needs and having to fend off the dissatisfaction of colleagues or managers who want to refer someone *now*.

Somehow, the sense of mutual responsibility for the service has been lost. It is either all the referrer's fault for not understanding what counselling is about, or it is all the counsellor's fault for not seeing enough people.

Counsellors may well contribute to this kind of situation through their initial enthusiasm. Understandably, they want to emphasise the benefits of counselling and fail to warn employers of the limitations of a service which has finite resources. It is possible that they themselves have not thought through the implications.

EXERCISE

You are funded to provide 18 hours of counselling per week and you take six weeks' holiday a year. Each client is allowed a maximum of 10 sessions. The statistics collected by the previous counsellor show that the average number of sessions taken by each client is six.

On the basis of this information, how many referrals will you be able to deal with each week without an ever-increasing waiting list?

As a counsellor employed by an organisation or agency, you are co-responsible for how, and to what extent, the needs of clients are met. You have an expertise that others in the agency may not have and one of the main ways in which you take your part of the responsibility is in informing others of the options.

Counsellor:	There are 4000 people working for this organisation and it seems as though about 5 per cent want to use the counselling service in any year. That's 200 referrals a year. The average number of counselling sessions required is six, that's 1,200 counselling hours a year, or 26 a week. Now, we're only funded for 18 hours a week, which is why we're running a waiting list and why it's getting longer.
HR Manager:	Well the only way out seems to be to reduce the number of sessions.
Counsellor:	The six sessions is an average, don't forget. Many clients only come for one or two sessions and that's enough. But we also get people who need longer. It would be a bit daft, it seems to me, to stop the work in the middle for the sake of an extra three or four hours. We do make referrals to outside agencies whenever we can, but staff are often a bit reluctant to go to a psychologist or to their GP counsellor.
HR Manager:	Why should anyone need more than six hours with you? It seems like a lot.
Counsellor:	It tends to be the person who's stressed out with work, and then something happens on top, like a bereavement, or their relationship breaking down. They're really having to think about making some changes to their whole life. And if they don't get some help, they're prime candidates for going off long term with stress.

HR Manager:	Yes, I know absenteeism has gone down since the service started. We don't want that to get worse again.
Counsellor:	Mostly, we're doing shorter-term work which stops people getting to that stage, but we do see people who've let themselves get to the edge.
HR Manager:	Can you see any way through this?
Counsellor:	Well, there are some possibilities. The obvious one is to increase the budget for counselling, but I assume that's a non-starter?
HR Manager:	I'll put the case forward, but it's not going to be a high priority at the moment, I'm afraid. As you know, there has been talk of cutting the service.
Counsellor:	One option would be to see everyone for an initial interview of half an hour before they go on the waiting list. Then we could suggest alternatives for them if they wanted to see someone immediately. The drawback is that it would take an hour a week *out* of the service. But it would be worth it if we could make more outside referrals.
HR Manager:	But people would at least be seen straight away, so we might not get as many complaints. Sounds good. What is the other?
Counsellor:	The difficulty with making referrals once you've built up a relationship with someone is that they feel they'd be starting all over again. One way round this would be to make a charge after someone has had, say, six or eight sessions. The money would go into the counselling budget to provide more hours as needed, and it could be made cheaper than going to a private counsellor. They would still have the option of referral to an outside service if they wanted it, of course.
HR Manager:	Hmm. I don't like the idea of charging our own staff.
Counsellor:	To be honest, neither do I. I'm simply trying to come up with something which would help to keep the waiting list down without compromising the effectiveness of the service. If you have a strict time limit, you're denying the service to the people who most need it.

… and so on.

There are several ways of organising counselling within limited resources.

1   A strict limit on the number of hours' counselling per person.

2   A limit on the *average* number of hours per person.

3   A division of counsellor hours into short-term and long-term work (e.g. four clients out of 18 can be long term).

- Clients choose at the start whether they need short or long term.
- All clients begin as short term and move to a long-term 'slot' when available.

Different patterns will be more or less appropriate to different organisations and different client groups. However, (1) is the least efficient and effective for two main reasons. The first is obvious: that people are different and have different needs, so imposing the same rigid constraint upon everyone is counterproductive. The second is that if they are given a limit, clients tend to fill the time available in case they cannot get any more in the future, even when they would otherwise take fewer sessions.

Most organisations we hear of these days impose a time limit of between six and twelve sessions despite the fact that in the seventies and eighties, when no time limit was imposed, clients came for an *average* of between six and eight sessions (statistics gathered by many organisations showed remarkably consistent averages). Clearly, some came for more but this was balanced by those who only needed one or two sessions. When organisations came under financial pressure, we can only assume that managers who did not understand the way the averaging worked imposed a set number of sessions (ie the average number) on all. It is a little akin to surgeons being required to cease every operation after three hours in order to cut their waiting lists.

Training in person-centred counselling sometimes focuses on long-term work to the extent that students are not adequately prepared for the client who says, after two or three sessions 'Thank you very much. That was extremely useful. I've had enough'. In fact, the counsellor may believe that she has not been good enough if the client does not stay for longer.

Moreover, the training heightens perceptions to the extent that therapists might see the work that they believe the client *needs to do*. There is a real danger here that the counsellor will work against the process and draw things to the client's attention which are not current difficulties for the client.

It is clearly important that we be accountable to the organisation for the effectiveness and the efficiency of the counselling services we offer. We must be actively engaged in collecting and presenting statistical information and outcome data as part of discharging this responsibility. Irrespective of whether anyone else wishes to know, *we ourselves* need this information to monitor and make decisions about our work. It is then also less likely that we will have constraints placed upon us from outside and more likely that we will be able to negotiate with managers and funders to provide, if not the perfect service, one that meets more of our clients' needs more of the time.

COUNSELLOR SELF-CARE

Looking after ourselves, knowing when we are depleted, being able to provide self-nourishment, are important for all therapists but perhaps particularly so for the counsellor working in an organisation, since the organisation will place demands upon us additional to those we place upon ourselves.

In order to have the emotional and physical energy to work with our clients, we need to make sure we look after ourselves.

EXERCISE

1 How do you recoup your physical energy?

2 How do you recoup your emotional energy?

3 How do you make sure you have contact with colleagues to talk about work, counselling in general, developments in the field and so on?

4 How do you make sure you keep in touch with the wider world of counselling?

5 What other needs might you have?

There are two main sources of support for counsellors in our therapeutic work. The first is an individual supervisor, with the addition, if possible, of a supervision group. Supervision is the place where we can take our worries and concerns and offload our stresses and strains. If we have the bonus of a supervision group, it can be heartening to hear that others are having similar experiences. Out of this process are likely to come new insights and ways forward with our clients, but it is just as important to receive appreciation for the things we are doing well. This is the restorative function of supervision – venting our difficulties and stresses and being valued for our good work (Inskipp and Proctor, 1995).

The second support for our therapeutic work, as well as for ourselves, is our own counselling. As person-centred practitioners we are not expected to be 'in therapy' continuously (although many are), but to act in a mature way by accessing our own counselling when we are troubled, or when a supervisor or colleague perceives something out of our awareness that may be affecting our client work.

Achieving a qualification after three or four years of hard work is something to be celebrated, but it can also involve great loss – of the support and colleagueship of a training course and the sense of being in touch with developments in the field of therapy. Workshops, training days, conferences and other forms of professional development such as reading books and professional journals become ever more important.

The nature of our work means that we are 'giving out' for a large part of the day. Supervision, therapy and all forms of professional development are ways of 'taking in' – of laying aside other people's concerns and focusing on our own needs. However, it is equally important to be playful, to have activities that are not worthy or even meaningful beyond the simple pleasure they give us. Walking in the country, dancing, playing football, listening to music, swimming, playing computer games or card games, readings trashy novels, slobbing out in front of the telly … .

CONCLUSION

Person-centred therapy is a demanding activity which draws upon our intellect, emotions and physical energy. We are not using equipment or techniques to do our job, but ourselves and the relationships we form. It can be exciting, frustrating, depleting and rewarding – but it is never dull.

FURTHER READING

Braaten, L. (1998) 'A person-centred perspective on leadership and team-building', in B. Thorne and E. Lambers (eds), *Person-Centred Therapy: A European Perspective*. London: Sage.

British Association for Counselling and Psychotherapy (2002) *Ethical Framework for Good Practice in Counselling and Psychotherapy*. Rugby: BACP Publications.

Henderson, V.L., O'Hara, M., Barfield, G. L. and Rogers, N. (2007) 'Applications beyond the therapeutic context', in M. Cooper, M. O'Hara, P. Schmid and Wyatt, G. (eds), *The Handbook of Person-Centred Psychotherapy and Counselling*. Basingstoke: Palgrave Macmillan.

Mearns, D. (ed.) (1994) *Developing Person-Centred Counselling*. London: Sage. (Section II.)

Merry, T. (1999) *Learning and Being in Person-Centred Counselling*. Ross-on-Wye: PCCS Books. (Time-limited work, Chapter 6.)

Rogers, C. R. (1977) *On Personal Power*. New York: Delacorte Press. (Chapter 5.)

Sanders, P. (2006) 'Applications of person-centred counselling', in, *The Person-Centred Counselling Primer*. Ross-on-Wye: PCCS Books.

WEBSITES

Center for the Studies of the Person: www.centerfortheperson.org/approaches.html

World Association for Person-Centred and Experiential Psychotherapy and Counselling (WAPCEPC): www.pce-world.org

British Association for the Person-Centred Approach (BAPCA): www.bacpa.org.uk

Association for the Development of the Person-Centred Approach (ADPCA): www.adpca.org

PCCS Books and links to relevant and related sites: www.pccs-books.co.uk

13

EDGY AND ETHICAL ISSUES

BY JANET TOLAN AND ROSE CAMERON[1]

[Humankind's] moral sense is not a strong beacon light, radiating outward to illuminate in sharp outline all that it touches. It is, rather, a small candle flame, casting vague and multiple shadows, flickering and sputtering in the strong winds of power and passion, greed and ideology. But brought close to the heart and cupped in one's hands, it dispels the darkness and warms the soul. (James Q Wilson)

Perhaps the first thing to say is that having good intentions is not a sound indicator of ethical practice. Nor is doing something (or not doing something) because the client wants you to. In practice, ethics usually involves thinking through the 'what ifs' – and the 'what ifs' might be far from obvious until you have experience of what can go wrong. This sort of experience does not necessarily equate with having been in practice for a long time – even therapists who have many years' experience are not immune from making bad ethical choices. The benefits and limitations of experience will be a theme in this chapter as we argue that it is both essential and not sufficient to listen to the voice of experience. Ethical codes, frameworks and guidelines are invaluable in mapping out potholes, quagmires and unstable volcanoes, but they are maps, not the terrain. Real life practice is complicated, and we offer some of our more cringe worthy, heart-sink and tricky experiences in illustration of this.

---

[1] The 'I' voice in this chapter is sometimes Rose and sometimes Janet. We thought it interrupted the narrative to keep identifying which of us was writing – so those of you who know us might realise which 'I' is which, and those of you who don't can guess!

As person-centred practitioners we are, of course, strongly in favour of experiential learning, but ethical practice is an area in which learning from someone else's mistakes is a very good alternative to the anguish suffered by counsellor and/or client when a bad ethical choice is made. The history of therapy has numerous examples of therapists doing things that are now considered to be unethical. It is easy (and tempting) to be judgemental after the event – especially if the event happened to someone else – but salutary to remember that future generations of therapists will probably be as horrified by our mistakes as we are by those who have gone before us.

The mistakes that were recognised in the early days of counselling led to codes of ethics and practice such as those of the British Association for Counselling and Psychotherapy (BACP) so that they did not have to be repeated. However, learning from someone else's mistakes involves more than obediently following a set of rules. Understanding the issues is essential for (at least) two reasons:

a   The guidelines you are following may not take account of all the ethical issues that need to be considered in any particular instance. Overly defensive practice is often ineffectual practice. Playing safe may stop you from doing any harm, but may also stop you from doing much good. Approaching a therapeutic relationship with an attitude of fear-driven obedience to rules is not conducive to being relaxed, fully present, non-defensive and transparent. Understanding the issues and being able to make an informed and considered professional decision is.

b   Ethical practice is sometimes a simple case of doing the right thing (maintaining confidentiality, for example), or not doing the wrong thing (not having sex with a client), but sometimes there is no clear right and wrong. Ethical dilemmas that pull us in different – and often irreconcilable – directions are a part of professional life. Dilemmas occur when our obligations to one person or principle are at odds with our obligations to another. With a true dilemma there is probably no right answer, yet we still need to decide what to do or not do and commit ourselves to our decision. The discomfort of never quite knowing if you did the right thing, or living with the knowledge that in being loyal to one interest you betrayed another, is one of the inherent challenges of professional life.

It is important to understand the reasoning behind ethical principles and to consider them in context. Every practitioner is responsible for the decisions they make – it is not enough to just do what your supervisor, colleague, or even your professional body suggests. The two big mistakes I have made in the process of working with clients, and they are mistakes I will always regret, were the result of following what was simply bad supervision. Supervision – or consulting colleagues in any other (confidential) context – may be invaluable, but it is important to remember that nobody is infallible, and it is the practitioner's responsibility to take colleagues' opinions into account, but make their own decision.

In recognition of the complexity of many ethical issues, BACP changed from its codes of ethics and practice (which contained dos and don'ts) to an ethical framework (moral and ethical principles to be considered). The United Kingdom Council for

Psychotherapy (UKCP) and the Coalition of Scottish Counselling Associations (COSCA) have ethical codes. There are advantages and disadvantages to both systems, so regardless of which organisation you belong to, it is useful to go through their ethical requirements and make sure that you are familiar with and *understand* them.

EXERCISE

Look up UKCP's ethical code at www.psychotherapy.org.uk and COSCA's code of practice at www.cosca.org.uk. Go through each point carefully and make a list of any that seem unnecessary, over the top, or that you do not truly understand.

Look up BACP's ethical framework at www.bacp.co.uk. Go through each of the principles putting them into your own words. Make a list of any that you do not understand.

Now, find a colleague, trainer or supervisor with whom you can discuss the points you have made a note of, but read the paragraph below first.

Although the need for a non-judgemental relationship in which ethical issues can be explored is obvious, it may not be so easy to find. Ethics involve questions of right and wrong and so stir up fears of being judged and shamed – colleagues or supervisors may become unusually rigid at the very time that genuine questioning and exploration is most needed. It is important that practitioners look after themselves and their clients by striving to find someone who is likely to provide a safe space in which they can be honest about what they do not understand, or do not agree with.

Other therapists' experience and opinions are invaluable in giving us access to a pool of wisdom, but each therapeutic relationship is the creation of two individuals in a particular time and place. It needs to be taken care of in a way that recognises its particularity. Moral and ethical dilemmas are dilemmas because there is no easy answer. However, we seem to have arrived at a situation where individual therapists and their supervisors are almost discouraged from weighing up the issues and coming to the best decision for all concerned. Many workplaces, with the best of intentions, have taken to setting lists of rules to be followed. These rules may serve to protect the organisation and the counsellor but can work against thinking through the ethical challenges and might even damage the therapeutic process. In the rest of this chapter, we focus on general ethical issues, giving examples of actual situations which point to the importance of embracing the spirit of ethical practice rather than hiding behind the letter of the law.

Ethical complexities generally arise in two main areas. The first is in creating and protecting the therapeutic space. In order to carry out effective therapeutic work the counsellor must create and protect a physical and emotional environment in which client and counsellor can focus solely on the therapy. In this environment, the client can do no wrong – by which we mean that whichever parts of themselves the client brings to the relationship with the therapist will be received and responded to

constructively. The second area of ethical complexity is where the therapeutic relationship and the outside world connect. The counsellor might become aware of
something within the relationship that has implications beyond it. Or, vice versa, she
might learn something in her life outside the therapy room that has implications for
her client. We will begin by discussing issues that may arise in the creation and maintenance of the therapeutic space.

CREATING AND PROTECTING THE THERAPEUTIC SPACE

Contracting, or setting up an agreement about what counsellor and client are going
to do, how they are going to do it, how long it will take and how much it will cost
is the first stage in creating the therapeutic space. Negotiating a contract before work
begins is an opportunity for counsellor and client to set up the therapeutic space
together. Unfortunately, this opportunity to begin collaboratively seems to have commonly degenerated into a defensive convention in which therapists issue clients with
a written contract that might be important to the therapist if s/he were defending
themselves against a complaint, but does not involve the client further than reading
and signing it. Something in writing is useful given that a client is likely to be preoc-
cupied and unlikely to retain information, but a written agreement need not replace
discussion and negotiation. It is, of course, important to inform a client of aspects of
the working agreement that may be non-negotiable, such as when you are legally or
ethically obliged to break confidentiality, but there may also be aspects that are nego-
tiable, such as whether you and/or your client would want you to break confidentiality if she were suicidal and whom your client might want you to tell.

We will return to the question of confidentiality with regard to suicide shortly, but
first ask you to consider that maintaining confidentiality may not be as simple as just
not discussing clients with anyone other than your supervisor.

It did not cross my mind, when setting up a private practice from home, that there
was any need to deceive my neighbours as to what it is I did for a living until someone who was coming to see me (thankfully a supervisee rather than a client) was
accompanied to my front door by a neighbour's child who demanded to know if he
was coming to see me because he 'had problems'. I tried hiring a room, but there
were still issues of confidentiality. The walls were (just) sound-proof enough for a
normal speaking tone, but not all therapy happens at the pitch of normal conversation. Not only did the receptionists constantly have to stop people in neighbouring
offices coming to rescue me, but clients who had screamed, shouted or wailed were
understandably embarrassed at having to pass the receptionist as they left. I have
resolved both problems for the time being by moving to somewhere so remote that
I don't have neighbours. The downside is that anyone who wants to work with me
not only has to have the time and means to travel a good distance, but also a sense
of direction equal to that of a homing pigeon.

When BACP had specific Codes of Ethics and Practice one of the interesting
translations often made was of 'Counsellors *may* break confidentiality if …' to the
inaccurate 'Counsellors *must* break confidentiality if …'. I am still hearing that students

are taught that they *must* break confidentiality if there is a danger of harm to self or others, even though the Codes have now been replaced by the Ethical Framework which, by its nature, suggests that therapists have ethical choices to make. The idea that there might be rules that we can all follow to keep us out of trouble continues to be a seductive one.

Reassuringly, at a training session run by BACP for accredited course representatives, the senior BACP staff member, Alan Jamieson, and Professor Tim Bond, who were presenting the session, pointed out that the Ethical Framework does not require practitioners to obey the law. This, they said, had been the subject of much debate, with the conclusion that there might in some rare instances be a conflict between acting legally and acting ethically. (One has only to think of laws changed relatively recently such as those governing homosexuality and rape within marriage.) Although there would not usually be a conflict, BACP wanted to preserve the option of supporting members whose actions might be subject to legal challenge provided that they met the test of being ethically and morally sound.

Confidentiality and sexual abuse

What I write about this is inevitably coloured by my own experience. At the time I started, counselling in the UK was in its infancy and training courses were of variable standard. It had not even been generally established that supervision should be a necessary and regular adjunct to practice. My introduction to counselling skills was through my joining a group of women to set up the first Rape Crisis line in the region. In the group were other professionals who shared their skills as we set about training ourselves to offer a telephone service.

I was then appointed as a counsellor in a community college and one of my first clients was a young woman (girl) under school leaving age. I will call her Lily. After a couple of sessions Lily asked for complete confidentiality, which I naively agreed to. She told me that her stepfather had been raping her since she was about eight years old and begged me again not to tell anyone. I weighed up in my mind the consequences of maintaining confidentiality as against disclosure to the authorities. Disclosure would feel to my client like a betrayal and, more importantly, would be a further loss of control for her. She would be removed from her family against her wishes and placed into care. On the other hand, I would probably lose my job if it came out that I had not reported this. Sigh. I decided not to tell.

After about six months' work, Lily came in with a new determination in her step and asked whether I would go with her to the police station. Of course I agreed, but one of my reactions was a sinking feeling in my stomach that now I would be found out and sacked – and possibly even prosecuted. (I was not sure for what – aiding and abetting by withholding information?)

We spent a lengthy and tedious time at the police station with Lily being interviewed and re-interviewed and pages and pages of statements being written. It became abundantly clear that I had known about this for many months and I was mentally preparing my defence during the times when someone else was supporting my client.

Eventually, when Lily was reading over her statements and we were drinking some unrecognisable Police Station brew, one of the officers commented that I had done a good job. Taken aback, I blurted out that I was expecting to be in trouble for not disclosing this earlier. The police officer looked at me with surprise. 'Oh, no', he reassured me. 'She'll make a good witness now. If you had made her come before she was ready, she might not have been able to stand up in court and testify against him. Now we'll get a conviction'. And they did.

It could easily have been argued that I was acting unethically by allowing Lily to stay in an environment where she was open to abuse, whatever her own wishes. But she opted for the therapeutic process and my choice was to respect that. Over time, the therapeutic conditions allowed her to give weight to her organismic experience. Her stepfather had told her that she was special, that she was the one who wanted sex and that it was a loving act. Now – at a gut level – she knew that this was a harmful and coercive act and not a loving one and that she was not inviting it and did not want it. She found her own locus of evaluation rather than being told what to think by others. Had the authorities been informed, she would have been removed against her will from her family and – in keeping with her previous experience of the world – been told that it was for her own good.

Confidentiality and suicide

Because the actualising tendency is central to person-centred theory, explaining why people commit suicide can be problematic. There are two basic theoretical stances. The first assumes an after-life and therefore sees death as a transition rather than an ending. In this explanation, the actualising tendency is still moving the person forward and sometimes propels them through the barrier of death into the next phase, whatever that is believed to be.

The second goes back to the analogy of plants growing in a nurturing environment. A plant can be deprived of water, sunlight and nutrients for a long time and still cling to life but there will come a point when putting it on the windowsill and starting again to water it will not revive it. Similarly, it is believed, there might come a point where a person has been deprived of the necessary conditions for so long that it is too late for any therapy to pull them back into life.

In practice, I have found that the paradox of working with people contemplating suicide is this: Once I have truly understood someone's world and their experience and fully appreciated their longing not to have to continue a dreary or painful existence; when I have stayed with their despair and their loneliness and felt it deeply in my own being; when I have been able to hear their plans to end their life and know how vital is having the means to end an intolerable existence; when I have been able to communicate all of this in such a way that they know that I would never blame them; then my clients have begun to turn towards life rather than away from it.

This is not to say that I would not have grieved any of my clients who decided to end their lives – far from it. In fact, because it has never happened, I do not know how I would react in such a case and rather dread ever having to find out. But I was ready to let go those of my clients who were close to that edge – with sorrow but with complete understanding.

Has my experience shaped my theory or did my theory shape my experience? Both are true, of course. Theoretically, I knew that placing any conditions on my clients would lessen the therapeutic effect. So overt conditions such as 'I will break confidentiality …' or, as appears in some organisations' contracts, 'You must agree not to take your own life while we are working together …', would severely hamper the process. Equally, covert conditions such as my own anxiety or my not listening to clients' hints would be unhelpful.

Client:	I was thinking all weekend about the car crashing into a tree or something.
Therapist:	With you driving?
Client:	Yes.
Therapist:	And would you be dead or alive?
Client:	[*with astonishment*] Dead, of course!
Therapist:	Sounds like that would be a huge relief …

So the more I could maintain the therapeutic conditions, I told myself, the less likely my client would be to commit suicide. Without such theoretical backing, I would have been much more likely either to ignore my client's wishes for complete confidentiality or to pay more empathic attention to her reasons for living than her reasons for wanting to die.

Did my clients not commit suicide because I put my faith in the theory? Did I put faith in the theory because my clients did not commit suicide? Yes!

Dual or multiple relationships

Avoiding dual or even multiple relationships with someone who is a client is important in terms of protecting the therapeutic space. If a counsellor and client have a work, social or even another kind of helping relationship that is additional to the therapeutic relationship, whatever happens in the other relationship is likely to impinge upon the therapy.

EXERCISE

Case vignette 1

Your client, a lovely woman who you know to be conscientious and hardworking, is desperate for a job to help support herself and her children – and you need a cleaner. However, a little bell rings in your mind and you decide to think it through before following your impulse to offer the work to your client.

Make a list of the things that might happen in your dealings with your new cleaner that might damage the therapeutic space for your client.

CASE EXAMPLE

It is not unusual for a client to invite their counsellor to a significant event such as a wedding or to suggest some other kind of contact outside the therapy room. Such invitations are likely to be very meaningful to the client, and a blunt refusal on the grounds that it would be unethical or an infringement of boundaries may be incomprehensible and hurtful, so it is important that both the request and refusal are discussed and understood. In the following scenario a client I had been seeing for a long time asked me to trust her with something that was precious to me, and I said no. I was at pains to not only resist an offer that would have suited me very well, but to also make it clear that, for me, the issue was not whether I could trust her. My priority was to ensure that I did not agree to something that could potentially damage the therapeutic space and therefore interfere with her trust in me.

I was due to go abroad for several weeks and had two worries. One was how a particular client would cope with my absence and the other was finding someone to look after my cherished cats. I had a private practice at home; it was obvious to my client that someone would have to look after the cats whilst I was away, and she asked if she could do it. She would, she argued, find it helpful to be in the room we worked in even if I wasn't there and I was already aware that being with my cats helped regulate her acute anxiety. I also knew she would be generous with her time and affection and I couldn't think of anyone I would be happier to leave the cats with. She begged me to agree to it as much for her sake as that of the cats. I affirmed my trust in her ability to look after the cats very well indeed, and I acknowledged that the arrangement also seemed like something that would be useful to her, but asked her to let me think about it. I thought through the 'what ifs' between sessions, and then asked her how she would cope if one of the cats became ill, or how she thought it would affect our relationship if one of them died. She took my point immediately and we were able to mutually agree that the risk was far too high.

EXERCISE

Case vignette 2

You are working with someone who has had such a deprived and neglected life that he regularly takes 'bits and pieces' from others to try and fill the void. One day, the manager of the Centre where you meet this client calls you in. One of your youth worker colleagues left two rings on her desk while she was doing some artwork and they disappeared at the time when your client was in the building. Do you think that your client might be the thief?

How do you see your responsibilities to:

- Your client?
- Your colleague?
- The Centre manager?
- Society and the rule of law?

The erotic in the therapy room

It is occasionally argued that clients are grown-ups who can make up their own minds about who to have a sexual relationship with. But counsellor and client are not just two adults, they occupy particular roles. The roles make the potentials of sexual attraction more likely. How can anyone not want a lover who is empathic, genuine and full of unconditional regard towards them? Whenever I start working with a new therapist, supervisor, trainer or anyone else whose job it is to support or help me in some way, I ask myself whether I find that person sexually attractive. If the answer is no, I resolve to remember that in six months' time because I know that by then I'll probably find them utterly irresistible.

The role of therapist confers power, and the client is necessarily in a vulnerable position. There is a strong possibility that the client will project all sorts of idealisations onto the counsellor, increasing the counsellor's power and the client's own vulnerability. I recently had the opportunity to observe this process at work as I watched myself become besotted with my dog's vet. He was not someone I had previously found remotely attractive, or even someone I imagined I would get along with socially, but once my dog was ill I wanted him to like me. I wanted him to approve of me. I wanted to impress him. I wanted him to notice me.

Of course, what I really wanted was for him to make my dog immortal. It is significant that my feelings and the unrealistic heroism I projected onto him were child-like. All helping relationships tend to activate very young configurations of self in the person who is being helped. A more adult part of me knew that what the vet could do was limited, but even this more adult part made him into a hero for helping to make the end of my dog's life as good as possible. Yet another part of me looked on, aware that I was experiencing what psychodynamic colleagues call transference[2].

Had I, rather than my dog, been the object of this man's attention, and if he had treated me with the intense interest that therapists take in clients, if he had been fully present, warm and understood me at least as well as I understand myself, I would have been in the vulnerable position our clients are in. Had my 'witness' configuration not been so strong, I might have found myself acting on my need to be close to someone who can make bad things better. Peter Rutter, in *Sex in the Forbidden Zone* describes a therapy client behaving seductively towards him and affirms that his client

---

[2] This phenomenon – of responding to another person according to our previous experience of people in our lives – is a common one in therapy and there are other examples in this book. However, we tend not to use the term 'transference' because the connotations implicit in the term are not always compatible with person-centred theory.

'had just done exactly what patients are supposed to do … : she was bringing me her … self destructive pattern, in the only way she knew how – by repeating it with me, right there in the room' (1989: 5).

I decided to break the spell by telling my partner that I had suddenly started to fancy the vet. My partner was aghast at my lapse in taste, but said he was aware that he too craved this man's approval. Those who have the kind of power we both conferred on this mere human being are often unaware of it. This means that it is easy to abuse a client's vulnerability and trust without recognising that this is what we are doing. How can anyone not want a lover whom they know in intimate depth and who is full of adoration for them? Especially if you can convince yourself you'd be doing them a favour? If you have not already done so, we recommend that you that decide that you will NEVER seek, or accept, sexual gratification with a client, supervisee or trainee.

When counsellors satisfy their sexual needs at the expense of a client's implicit trust they exploit everything about the client, including their 'inner child'. A client may not look or behave like a child – quite the opposite, but they may well be acting from a child-like state. A client cannot be presumed to be able to consent to sex in the context of the therapeutic relationship. All counsellors have the opportunity to sexually exploit a client. Practise safely. Tell your supervisor. Break the spell of secrecy before it pulls you and your client under.

ENGAGING WITH THE OUTSIDE WORLD – THIRD-PARTY INTERESTS

A client's interests may be in conflict with a group of people such as the wider community in general, or the organisation we work for. The organisation might have a set of rules about how the counsellor should behave and this will often include rules about when to break clients' confidentiality. The first thing to find out is, *If I were to disclose this, what would happen?*

If, for example, the organisation's rules state that 'suicidal ideation' must be reported, it can be useful to find out more. Talk it through with your manager or the person responsible for the counselling service. First, whom should I report this to? Second, what kind of circumstances would warrant my breaking the client's confidence? Presumably that person would not want to be notified of *everyone* who mentions suicide. Third, if I am to break confidentiality against my client's wishes, what should I tell my client about what will happen to them? What action would be taken? Who would be informed? Fourth, if the organisation wants me to use my judgement, what would happen to me if I made a wrong call and failed to spot an impending suicide?

Sometimes, broaching with a client the issue of telling others can end with a client being very happy to receive the additional support and help that other parts of the organisation and other agencies can provide. It can come as a surprise to the client that he matters enough to others for them to want to help. One client, for example, who agreed to meet up with her GP once a week just to check how things were going, was amazed to find that such an important person (in her eyes) was concerned about her. So, as with all ethical issues, there is no 'one size fits all'.

Most organisations will want to work *with* their therapist in the best interests of clients. Suicide is notoriously difficult to predict and almost impossible to prevent if the person is determined. Theoretically speaking, it is the therapeutic conditions that bring about change. So, paradoxically, provided that the client is able to stay in psychological contact, the more empathy and unconditional positive regard the counsellor has for the client and his wish to end his life, the less likely he is to do it. The therapeutic route can be far more effective in suicide prevention than any transmission of therapist or organisational anxiety – and definitely more effective than coercion.

Therapists in private practice have such decisions to make without the benefit of an organisational framework to support them. In recent years I have worked with many people, often senior in their organisations, who are private clients because they believe (probably with good cause) that any hint of 'mental problems' on their health record would hinder their career prospects. Here, the issue of disclosure becomes even more complex and difficult.

Fitness to practise

Acknowledging that you are temporarily (or perhaps even permanently) not emotionally robust enough to see clients is tough. This is most obviously true for the many counsellors who are self employed. We would like to say that any organisation that employs counsellors should understand and accommodate a counsellor who needs take time out, but we know that in reality this may not be the case.

Given that we all experience life's inevitable challenges – illness, bereavement and getting older to name but a few – it is likely that at some point we need to look after ourselves and our clients by changing our work/life balance or taking time out. It can be difficult to cancel or postpone clients who are very needy or who are in the middle of important work, but if we see clients when we are under par, we risk letting them down by not practising well enough. Letting clients down through bad practice is potentially damaging. Helping them to deal with one of life's inevitable frustrations is not. Moreover, demonstrating that we are imperfect and able to care for ourselves when necessary can be useful modelling. The client is likely to feel disappointment, frustration or be otherwise stirred up. This is grist to the mill on the counsellor's return, but only as long as the counsellor has enough emotional energy to help the client to process their response – and to have worked through any feelings of guilt sufficiently for them not to intrude on the client's process! Fitness to practise involves more than having enough internal calm to attend to someone else; it also requires emotional resilience. If you are not up to dealing with whatever your client might bring, do not try to do it.

There are different ways in which we may be 'not up to it'. I currently have a close relation who is ill. As luck would have it, I am not financially reliant on seeing clients at the moment, but if I were, I would have to ask myself if I had enough emotional energy for myself, my family *and* a full-time practice. The honest answer would be no. If I were still in full-time private practice I would be in a situation that challenged my commitment to ethical practice and my ability to otherwise generate an income.

Chronic pain has also given me cause to question my fitness to practise. I tested my own assessment of my fitness to work by asking for feedback from my supervisors, my peers and my clients. My main concern was that the painkillers I was taking would blunt my ability to be fully present and emotionally responsive. If I had taken a painkiller I would tell my client that I had done so, that I felt able to work, and ask them to please tell me if they thought otherwise. I also took the opportunity to do some 'gold-fish bowl'[3] work in a supervision group, after I had taken a pain-killer.

Had anyone questioned my fitness to practise I would have had to either stop working and explore the intricacies of the benefits system or take up work in which being a little bit 'out of it' is an advantage.

Challenges that are this tough warrant plain old advice – on the grounds that learning the hard way damages the client as well as the counsellor. Our advice is:

Listen to those who express concern about your life/work balance or your state of being.

Have a very good look at the small print of any insurance policy you're tempted to take out – it may only cover your psychological state if you're actually sectionable.

Build up some savings to see you through the crises that happen in every life.

When you feel bad about 'letting clients down' remember that bad therapy is worse than no therapy.

Endings

The majority of complaints against counsellors, even those that are ostensibly about something else, arise as a result of therapeutic relationships that have not ended as well as they might have done. It is therefore important for both parties that endings are managed as well as possible. The simple, straightforward ethical guideline is that an ending date should be set, issues around endings and loss worked through, and then therapist and client have no further contact (see Chapter 10).

In context, this formula can be simplistic and endings should be managed with regard to the difference in power that exists between therapist and client. A mutually agreed ending point, for instance, is an ideal that may not be realistic. In reality the ending point may be dictated by either the therapist or the organisation they work for. The effect of the power difference in endings that are not mutually agreed became apparent to me as a therapist as I became more experienced. In the early days of my practice, I often thought that I would miss my long-term clients when they stopped coming to see me. In the event, I didn't. I certainly felt poignancy at our parting, but I also had a sense of 'closure'. I felt that our relationship had come to its natural end and on the rare occasions that I think of those clients now, it is with nothing more than fondness. However, this is generally only true of clients with

---

[3]A training exercise in which one does live therapy in front of an audience of peers, who then give feedback.

whom I had had a genuinely mutually agreed ending; it was (and is) different with clients who just stopped coming. I wonder about why they stopped, and in some instances, worry about what became of them. There is no sense of completeness, just a nagging concern. I feel disempowered because (ethically) there is nothing I can do if they don't respond to a letter inviting them back.

Clients just stop coming for many reasons, and one of those reasons is in order to end it before the therapist does. When a therapeutic relationship is brought to a unilateral end by a client, I, as a therapist, have to live with always wondering. That is just one of the features of this kind of work, and I can always take it to supervision if necessary. The client who is disempowered by an ending imposed by the therapist may well be left feeling rejected, abandoned, hurt and doubtful that the therapist ever really cared about them in the first place. They don't have a supervisor to go to, and may well feel reluctant to trust another therapist. Much good work can be undone at this point. The therapist may protest that the client knew well in advance that their relationship was going to end, which would hopefully be true, but this does not take into account that clients often invest a huge amount not only in the therapeutic process, but also in the therapist. The other kind of relationships that are routinely emotionally intense and end absolutely are romantic relationships in which one partner 'dumps' the other. It is not unusual for clients to feel dumped when an ending is not in their control or because it is so absolute.

I think there are many good reasons to have no further contact with a client after they have finished therapy. It is unambiguous. The therapeutic relationship is asymmetric: I know a great deal about my ex-client's secrets and vulnerabilities; they know nothing of mine. They know I can help them hold distress and fear. I do not know whether they could do the same for me, and in some instances am very sure they could not. No matter how much we like each other, it is unlikely that we could ever establish a friendship that felt equal enough to both of us. An absolute ending also allows the client to work through feeling about other absolute endings, like death.

Paradoxically, it has been death that has prompted me to make my absolute endings less absolute. In recent years a couple of clients from many years ago re-contacted me to say that they were dying. Neither of them contacted me as a therapist who might help them through the process of dying, but simply as someone who had been important in their lives and to whom they wished to say goodbye. I felt that they were acknowledging my humanity in their process of preparing for death, and was grateful for the opportunity to say goodbye. Both had regularly sent me Christmas cards over the years just to let me know how they were doing. When I read the cards I felt I was being addressed as a fellow human being rather than as a therapist.

As a therapist who has worked mainly in private practice, I have rarely had to impose an absolute ending – I have had the freedom to say, 'you know where I am if you ever want to come back'. However, I recently decided to move to another part of the country and was obliged to impose an absolute ending with every one of my clients. We did end absolutely as therapist and client, but I decided to keep open a space for us as two people who had been significant to each other. Whilst making it very clear that we would never work together again, I said that I would be very happy to hear from them if they wanted to be in touch occasionally to let me know how were doing, or just to say 'hi' (and that it was also fine with me if they didn't).

This felt particularly risky, and a particularly important thing to do with the client who was the most distressed by my departure. It felt risky because this client was having a very difficult time accepting that we really were going to stop. I could see an argument for absolute, unambiguous clarity for both our sakes. But although that argument satisfied my mind, it did not satisfy my heart. Whilst I could see that she was starting to accept the fact that we were not going to continue, or ever resume, working together, something she said make me realise that the thought that she could never again have contact with me under any circumstances threw her into real existential terror.

Deciding to keep open the possibility of occasional contact was risky, but, I believe, helped her let go of me as her counsellor. She and I discussed it very thoroughly before we decided that this is what we would do. She now sends me the odd email or text. Sometimes, they are funny or about something she knows I will be interested in, and sometimes they are about her. I reply. Sometimes we have a little flurry of texts. But I do not feel obliged to respond. She knows that her issues are her new therapist's business, not mine. All she needs from me is an acknowledgement that we both still exist and we both think of each other sometimes. This arrangement, and it is likely to be a very long-term one, is only ethical in context. My own feelings were part of that context, and had I not been genuinely welcoming of occasional contact, I would have been very wrong to suggest it. I would have risked allowing myself to feel hounded and my client rejected. I would have created a monumental ethical conflict between her needs and my own.

A mutually agreed ending can be important in not skewing the power balance at the eleventh hour, but such an ending is not always possible.

Neither therapist nor client can predict the attachment issues that may arise in the course of time-limited therapy and a client may feel abandoned despite knowing that they only ever had a set number of sessions. It is difficult to know what to do when therapy has to end before the client has had a chance to work through whatever has been stirred up. On the occasions I have been in this position, I have, with the approval of the organisation, offered the client a number of self-referral options that include seeing me in private practice. I have been aware that offering a service for which the client pays in replacement of a free service makes me vulnerable to an accusation of financial exploitation, and so have been careful also to suggest as many free services as I know of. However I was also aware that if the client and I had a good relationship, or if our relationship was an issue we had worked with, it was possible that they might feel compelled to see me privately rather than see someone else for free.

I have, in the past, offered to see such clients without charging. One client, whom I knew to be in great need financially as well as psychologically did decide to continue seeing me, but insisted on paying. I knew that she needed what she paid me more than I did, and initially felt uncomfortable accepting it, but came to understand that paying me something enabled her to take the time that she needed. She worked with me for several more years, and in doing so taught me to be more careful in what I offered. The fact that she paid something made a positive difference to me too as the years went by. Had she taken me up on my offer to see her for free I am sure one of us would have felt the need to end prematurely.

Sorry may be the hardest word…

…but it is often all that a hurt client needs to hear. The only certain thing to be said about the process of a formal complaint is that it is painful for everybody. It is better avoided if at all possible. Clients make complaints because they feel aggrieved. Hurt easily becomes anger, and anger can become vindictiveness. Fear, shame and legal advice can make a defendant overly defensive. Empathic understanding is probably the only hope for a clean resolution. Understanding the client's point of view enables the counsellor to take responsibility and apologise for any mistakes ('I'm sorry I acted that way'), or empathically understand how the client feels.

But beware the words, 'I'm sorry you feel like that'. They are easily heard as the apologetic equivalent of 'damning with faint praise'. An apology needs to be sincere, and so you need to understand what you are apologising for – this means staying (or getting back to being) empathic and understanding what has happened from your client's point of view. Extending empathic understanding towards someone who is being accusatory, or even making, or threatening to make a complaint against you is about as challenging as it gets, especially if you think you haven't done anything wrong. Even if you *know* you haven't done anything wrong it is important to understand why the client feels wounded and to acknowledge the client's reality. Only then might you get away with, 'I'm sorry you feel like that'.

FURTHER READING

Bond, T. (2000) *Standards and Ethics for Counselling in Action* (2nd edn). London: Sage.

Gabriel, L. (2009) *Relational Ethics in Practice*. London: Routledge.

Jenkins, P. (1997) *Counselling, Psychotherapy and the Law*. London: Sage.

Rutter, P. (1989) *Sex in the Forbidden Zone: When Men in Power – Therapists, Doctors, Clergy, Teachers, and Others – Betray Women's Trust*. London: Mandala.

WEBSITES

www.bacp.co.uk/ethical_framework/
www.cosca.org.uk
www.psychotherapy.org.uk

14

DEBATES AND DEVELOPMENTS IN PRACTICE

BY ROSE CAMERON

This book begins and ends with an emphasis on the importance of theory. The skills we practise, the way we practise them, and whether we even think of ourselves as practising 'skills', are all determined by what we are aiming to do – or, in other words, by theory. As you have read this book, you may have noticed points of difference between what we say and what other writers or trainers say – these are due to theoretical differences. Theory is interpreted and understood in different ways. It is also subject to changes and developments. The purpose of these debates and developments is to enhance practice. Understanding and following them may be thought of as professional self-awareness and as an important aspect of practice.

This chapter, which is intended to give an overview of debates and developments rather than discuss them in depth, will begin with a brief introduction to the schools of theory and practice that consider themselves to be person-centred. As with all influential thinkers, Rogers's work has been examined, discussed, developed and, to some degree, challenged. There have been inevitable disagreements as to what is and is not essential in preserving the spirit of the original work. Pete Sanders (2004) uses the term 'turf wars' to describe the continuing debate as to what and who is or isn't person-centred. 'Turf wars' captures something of the passion – and heat – of the debate. There are also hands that reach out across the hotly debated turf. Margaret Warner (1998/1999) coined the metaphor of 'tribes' in the 'person-centred nation' to unite those who considered themselves to be person-centred within an external environment which was increasingly hostile to all humanistic therapies. The first section is a brief introduction to these 'tribes'. The last 'tribe' I will introduce is the 'classical'. This tribe has been the most influential in Britain and so the second section looks at some of the debates, developments and applications within 'classical' PCT. I will conclude with a discussion of some potentials that have, so far, been under-developed. Each section is necessarily brief and does not do justice to its subject, but I will suggest further reading that does.

TRIBES OF THE PERSON-CENTRED NATION

Warner's metaphor of 'tribes' in a person-centred 'nation' is apt in many ways – there is certainly historical and present-day conflict between these tribes, and some threat from political forces outside the nation. However, the metaphor of tribes suggests a clarity of distinction that does not exist. Pete Sanders's book *The Tribes of the Person-centred Nation* identifies five tribes – the 'classical', 'focusing-orientated', 'experiential', 'existential' and 'integrative' tribes. Sanders acknowledges that in reality there is considerable overlap between tribes, and acknowledges that the distinctions, inclusions and exclusions he makes are open to debate. I will use his distinctions, but add 'expressive arts therapies' and 'pre-therapy', which Sanders acknowledges, but does not include as tribes.

One fundamental debate within the person-centred nation is over non-directivity. Practitioners and theorists who identify as classical or are identified as 'literalist', argue that non-directivity arises out of an authentic attitude of unconditional acceptance and is an essential feature of the approach. Focusing-oriented, experiential and some integrative therapists, on the other hand, have a particular interest in the process of change within the client, and vary in the degree to which they are directive in working with this process.

FURTHER READING ABOUT THE DEBATE OVER NON-DIRECTIVITY

Bowen, M.V.-B. (1996) 'The myth of non-directiveness in the case of Jill', in B.A. Faber, D.C. Brink and P.M. Raskin (eds), *The Psychotherapy of Carl Rogers: Cases and Commentaries*. New York: Guilford Press. pp. 84–94.

Bozarth, J.D. (1998) *Person-Centred Therapy: A Revolutionary Paradigm*. Ross-on-Wye: PCCS Books. pp. 56–7.

Brodley, B. (1999) 'Reasons for responses expressing the therapist's frame of reference in client-centred therapy', *The Person-Centred Journal*, 6(1): 4–27.

Brodley, B.T. (1999) 'About the non-directive attitude', *Person-Centred Practice*, 7(2): 79–82.

(Continued)

(Continued)

Henricks, M.N. (2001) 'An experiential version of unconditional positive regard', in J.D. Bozarth and P. Wilkins, *Rogers Therapeutic Conditions: Evolution, Theory and Practice. Vol. 3: Unconditional Positive Regard*. Ross-on-Wye: PCCS Books. pp. 126–55.

Levitt, B.E. (ed.) (2005) *Embracing Non-Directivity: Reassessing Person-Centered Theory and Practice in the 21st Century*. Ross-on-Wye: PCCS Books.

Lietaer, G. (1998) 'From non-directive to experiential: A paradigm unfolding', in B. Thorne and E. Lambers (eds), *Person-Centred Therapy: A European Perspective*. London: Sage. pp. 62–73.

Mearns, D. and Thorne, B. (2000) *Person-Centred Therapy Today: New Frontiers in Theory and Practice*. London: Sage. pp. 190–1.

Rogers, C. (1942) 'The directive versus the non-directive approach', in, *Counselling and Psychotherapy*. Boston: Houghton Mifflin. Reprinted in H. Kirschenbaum and V.I. Henderson (eds) (1990) *The Carl Rogers Reader*. London: Constable. pp. 77–87.

Wilkins, P. (2003) 'Non-directivity: a fiction and an irresponsible denial of power?', in, *Person-Centred Therapy in Focus*. London: Sage. pp. 85–99.

FOCUSING-ORIENTED THERAPY

In 1957 Rogers and a team of colleagues undertook a research project with clients who had a diagnosis of schizophrenia ('the Wisconsin project') and Rogers invited Eugene Gendlin, a PhD student with a particular interest in existential philosophy, to join the team. Once the project had reached its unsatisfactory end, Rogers turned his attention to activities other than individual therapy while Gendlin continued to explore the process of change as experienced by individual clients. Gendlin researched the process in which personal meaning arises as the client struggles to find the words to express the 'partly unformed stream of feeling that we have in every moment' (1962). His formulation of this process into a series of steps ('focusing') split was what then known as the 'non-directive client-centred therapy' community. Some followed Gendlin in facilitating this process within clients while others objected to it on the grounds that it generalises individual processes and is directed by the therapist. Michael McMillan provides a useful comparison between Gendlin's and Rogers's work with process in Chapter 5 of *The Person-Centred Approach to Therapeutic Change* (see below).

Focusing-oriented therapy is more commonly practised in North America than Britain, and is more widely accepted there as part of the person-centred nation. However, there are practitioners in Britain, and two of these, Campbell Purton and Nick Baker give an excellent introduction to focusing-oriented therapy and where it sits in relation to Rogers's work in Sanders's (2004) *The Tribes of the Person-centred Nation*. Gendlin's (1998) *Focusing-oriented Psychotherapy: A Manual of the Experiential*

Method (Practising Professionals) and Campbell Purton's (2007) *The Focusing-Oriented Counselling Primer* are excellent basic textbooks on the practice. Gendlin's (2003) *Focusing: How to Open Up Your Deeper Feelings and Intuition* is a recent update on focusing as self-help. There have been developments within focusing-oriented therapy: Elfie Hinterkopf's (2008) *Integrating Spirituality in Counselling: A Manual for Using the Experiential Focusing Method* and Marta Stapert and Erik Verliefde's (2008) *Focusing with Children: The Art of Communicating with Children at School and at Home* are recent examples.

FURTHER READING

Baker, N. (2004) 'Experiential person-centred therapy', in P. Sanders (ed.), *The Tribes of the Person-Centred Approach.* Ross-on Wye: PCCS Books. pp. 67–94.

Gendlin, E.T. (1998) *Focusing-Oriented Psychotherapy: A Manual of the Experiential Method (Practising Professional).* New York: Guilford Press.

Gendlin, E.T. (2003) *Focusing: How to Open Up Your Deeper Feelings and Intuition.* London: Rider & Co.

Hinterkopf, E. (2008) *Integrating Spirituality in Counseling: A Manual for using the Experiential Focusing Method.* Ross-on Wye: PCCS Books.

McMillan, M. (2004) *The Person-Centred Approach to Therapeutic Change.* London: Sage.

Purton, C. (2004) 'Focussing-oriented therapy' in P. Sanders (ed.), *The Tribes of the Person-Centred Approach.* Ross-on Wye: PCCS Books.

Purton, C. (2007) *The Focusing-Oriented Counselling Primer.* Ross-on Wye: PCCS Books.

Stapert, M. and Verliefde, E. (2008) *Focusing with Children: The Art of Communicating with Children at School and at Home.* Ross-on Wye: PCCS Books.

EXPERIENTIAL

Gendlin's focus (no pun intended!) on the experience of the client inspired others to find other ways of helping clients gain fuller access to their stream of experience. The experiential tribe has a fuzzy boundary with the focusing-oriented tribe. It includes Gendlin's work, but also includes the work of Germain Lietaer in Belgium, David Rennie in Canada, Laura Rice, Leslie Greenberg, Jeanne Watson in North America and Robert Elliott in North America and Britain. The characteristic that unites these theorists and distinguishes them from the classical tribe is that they consider themselves as having expertise on process. They are as interested in *how* a client tells their story as in the story itself. Some experiential therapists understand psychological disturbance as arising from problems in symbolising or putting words to emotional and psychological experience. Baker (2004) identifies further differences as experiential therapists having the goal of helping the client connect more fully with their unverbalised stream of experience, and sometimes being willing to be slightly ahead of the client (as was Rogers when guided by his intuition – see Rogers, c.1986). Some forms of experiential therapies integrate theory and practice from other therapies – Emotion Focussed Therapy (developed by Leslie Greenberg, Robert Elliott and Jeanne Watson, drawing heavily on the work of Laura Rice), for instance, integrates material from Cognitive–Behavioural Therapy and Gestalt. However experiential therapists are deeply influenced by Rogers and see the therapeutic relationship as essential in creating sufficient trust to make the client's experience available to be worked with.

FURTHER READING

Cooper, M., Watson, J. and Hölldampf, D. (eds) (2010) *Person-Centered and Experiential Therapies Work: A Review of the Research on Counseling, Psychotherapy and Related Practices*. Ross-on-Wye: PCCS Books.

Greenberg, L., Rice, L. and Elliott, R. (1993) *Facilitating Emotional Change*. New York: Guilford Press.

Greenberg, L., Watson, J. and Lietaer, G. (eds) (1999) *Handbook of Experiential Psychotherapy*. New York: Guilford.

Henricks, M.N. (2001) 'An experiential version of unconditional positive regard', in J.D. Bozarth and P. Wilkins, *Rogers Therapeutic Conditions: Evolution, Theory and Practice. Vol. 3: Unconditional Positive Regard*. Ross-on-Wye: PCCS Books. pp. 126–55.

Rennie, D.L. (1998) *Person-Centred Counselling: An Experiential Approach*. London: Sage.

Watson, J.C., Goldman, R.N. and Warner, M.S. (2002) *Client-Centered and Experiential Psychotherapy in the 21st Century: Advances in Theory Research and Practice*. Ross-on Wye: PCCS Books.

INTEGRATIVE

Integrative work that combines person-centred therapy with another approach is common. Some training courses teach an integrative approach, and some practitioners construct their own. Integrative therapy is usually distinguished from eclectic therapy in that it uses a *meta-theory* to unite two theories whereas eclectic therapy – for instance Traux and Carkhuff's (2008) skills based model – tends to be more pragmatic. Most classical person-centred therapists take the view that to add or integrate any other practices to person-centred work is to destroy its essence – anything else *is* something else. Rogers advocated his therapeutic conditions for any helping relationship – the uniqueness of (classical) PCT is that those conditions are considered sufficient.

Richard Worsley, who wrote the chapter on the integrative tribe in Sanders' *The Tribes of the Person-Centred Nation*, makes a distinction between integrative work that theoretically integrates *practices* and his own approach of integrating knowledge (rather than practices) from psychology, philosophy and sometimes other therapies into non-directive practice.[1] Worsley makes it clear that he is happy to refer to his work as 'integrative' in so far as he seeks to integrate his life experience into his client work in order to be as fully present as possible. He suggests that most practitioners in effect do the same, but does not claim to write on behalf of them or on behalf of a tribe. His intention is to integrate other ideas in order to enhance his non-directive practice[2] and in order to discipline this integration, Worsley asks himself a number of questions about these ideas:

- What does it point to in the world or in the client's awareness?
- How do I empathise better if I hold this meaning-structure within me?
- Do I ever point openly to it?
- How might it be misleading me or narrowing my awareness? (Rennie, 1998)

FURTHER READING

Kriz, J. (2008) *Self-Actualization: Person-Centred Approach and Systems Theory.* Ross-on-Wye: PCCS Books.

Levitt, B.E. (ed.) (2008) *Reflections on Human Potential: Bridging the Person-Centred Approach and Positive Psychology.* Ross-on Wye: PCCS Books.

Worsley, R. (2004) 'Integrating with integrity', in P. Sanders, *The Tribes of the Person-Centred Nation: A Guide to the Schools of Therapy Related to the Person-Centred Approach.* Ross-on-Wye: PCCS Books. pp. 125–48.

Worsley, R. (2009) *Process Work in Person-Centred Therapy* (2nd edn). Basingstoke: Palgrave Macmillan.

PRE-THERAPY

As we saw in Chapter 7, pre-therapy was developed as a way of working with clients who seem to be unavailable for psychological contact. I include it as a distinct tribe rather than a way of working with a specific client group because it has developed into what its founder, Garry Prouty, called 'a theory and practice of psychotherapy' (2008) and also because Prouty acknowledged influences other than Rogers. The work of Rogers and also Fritz Perls, the founder of Gestalt therapy, 'inspired' pre-therapy, but Prouty makes it clear that it developed under Gendlin's mentorship. Pre-therapy clearly has a strong relationship to the experiential tribe and might also be considered an integrative therapy. However Prouty also has a home within the classical tribe and he makes it clear that Rogers thought his work important. He also

---

[1] Integrating aspects of theory from elsewhere is actually something that those who are considered 'classical' do as well. Warner, for instance, integrates theory from developmental psychology into her work on fragile process.

[2] Tony Merry (2002) takes issue with whether Worsley's practice is actually non-directive.

recounts how Rogers, after hearing him present his work told him that he had 'killed the Buddha', presumably referring to himself, and, anticipating that this would result in resistance to Prouty's work, advised him to not 'let the bastards get you down'!

Prouty's work has been well received in Europe, and a number of European therapists have developed it in relation to specific client groups. Dion Van Werde, who uses pre-therapy principles with clients with a diagnosis of acute schizophrenia, has introduced pre-therapy in Belgium, the Netherlands, France and Germany. The therapeutic environment he has created at St Camillus hospital in Ghent has become a model for other hospitals in Belgium and the Netherlands. Ton Coffeng uses pre-therapy principles in working with trauma, dissociation and dissociative identity disorder (previously known as Multiple Personality Disorder) in Belgium. Lisbeth Sommerbeck uses pre-therapy with psychotic and near psychotic clients in Denmark. Marlis Pörtner promotes pre-therapy with clients with special needs in Switzerland, Austria and Germany. There is currently a wave of interest in using pre-therapy with the elderly. Penny Dodds and Dave Deady are promoting this in Britain and Marlis Pörtner and Dion Van Werde in continental Europe.

FURTHER READING

Coffeng, T. (2005) 'The therapy of dissociation: Its phases and problems', *Person-Centred and Experiential Psychotherapies*, 4(2): 90–105.

Pörtner, M. (2007) *Trust and Understanding: The Person-Centred Approach to Everyday Care for People with Special Needs* (2nd edn). Ross-on Wye: PCCS Books.

Prouty, G. (ed.) (2008) *Emerging Developments in Pre-Therapy: A Pre-Therapy Reader*. Ross-on-Wye: PCCS Books.

Prouty, G., Van Werde, D. and Pörtner, M. (2002) *Pre-Therapy: Reaching Contact-Impaired Clients*. Ross-on-Wye: PCCS Books.

Sanders, P. (2007) *The Contact Work Primer: An Introduction to Pre-Therapy and the Work of Garry Prouty*. Ross-on-Wye: PCCS Books.

Sommerbeck, L. (2003) *The Client-Centred Therapist in Psychiatric Contexts: A Therapists' Guide to the Psychiatric Landscape and its Inhabitants*. Ross-on-Wye: PCCS Books.

EXISTENTIAL

While Worsley perhaps feels somewhat excluded in being asked to write a chapter as an integrative therapist when he thought he was 'just being himself' as fully as possible, Mick Cooper seems surprised to be included as an existential therapist. Cooper is at pains to point out that of all the tribes, existential approaches to therapy probably have the most tenuous links to classical person-centred therapy, both theoretically and in practice. Existential therapy, like PCT, has roots in Phenomenology (a philosophical movement which, amongst other things, puts great emphasis on experience) and was developed in continental Europe at the same time as PCT was being developed in the USA. It is widely accepted as a tribe in the person-centred nation in continental Europe.

Although both PCT and experiential therapies are philosophically grounded in phenomenology, the two approaches developed relatively independently of each other. The two schools of thought are distinct from each other, but did, and do, talk. They do not necessarily agree about their similarities and differences. In a dialogue between Rogers and Martin Buber, Rogers is insistent that he and Buber are talking about the same kind of connection or meeting between individuals – and Buber is having none of it! Rogers was influenced by Paul Tillich, another existential philosopher and by the existential therapists Rollo May and R.D. Laing. Rogers contributed a chapter to May's *Existential Psychology* (1961), which perhaps begs the question of whether PCT might be considered a tribe in the (much more diverse) existential nation rather than the other way round.

FURTHER READING

Arnett, R.C. (2002) 'Dialogic communication? Friedman's contribution and clarification', in D. Cain (ed.), *Classics in the Person-Centered Approach: The Best of the* Person-Centered Review. Ross-on-Wye: PCCS Books.

Cooper, M. (2003) *Existential Psychotherapies*. London: Sage.

Friedman, M. (2002) 'Carl Rogers and Martin Buber: Self-actualisation and dialogue classics', in D. Cain (ed.), *Classics in the Person-Centered Approach: The Best of the* Person-Centered Review. Ross-on-Wye: PCCS Books.

Laing, R.D. (1969) *Self and Others* (2nd edn). London: Penguin.

Spinelli, E. (1997) *Tales of Un-Knowing: Therapeutic Encounters from an Existential Perspective*. London: Duckworth.

Van Deurzen, E. (2002) *Existential Counselling and Psychotherapy in Practice* (2nd edn). London: Sage.

Yalom, I. (1998) *Love's Executioner and Other Tales of Psychotherapy*. London: Penguin Books.

PERSON–CENTRED EXPRESSIVE ARTS THERAPIES

Creative arts therapies – art, dance, writing etc. – have been increasingly used in the context of person-centred work in the last 20 years. The classical tribe has questioned whether the expressive arts can be used in therapy in a way that is truly non-directive, and whether their use implies that the therapeutic conditions need to be supplemented. The counter arguments are:

- that expressive arts are just another means of symbolising in awareness that which would otherwise be verbalised;

- expressive arts are a means of enriching that which is also expressed verbally;

- that non-verbal means of expression are a better way of accessing and symbolising experience at the edge of the client's awareness.

Some expressive arts therapists claim that we cannot profess to be working with the whole person unless we offer a range of expressive possibilities.[3] Natalie Rogers, Carl Rogers's daughter, for example, who developed Expressive Therapy in the 1980s uses a succession of different modes of expression to explore the same material in different ways because she believes that non-verbal forms of expression are better at accessing experience that is out of awareness. She regards creativity as a feature of the actualising tendency and the unleashing of creativity as the path to personal development. Expressive therapists do make process suggestions and so there is some argument between this tribe and the classical over non-directivity. Liesl Silverstone emphasises the non-directive nature of her form of person-centred art therapy (she is contrasting it with interpretative psychodynamic art therapy rather than expressive therapy). Silverstone sees the use of visual communication as balancing western cultures' propensity towards the verbal, and seeks to integrate the verbal and non-verbal.

FURTHER READING

Rogers, N. (1993) *The Creative Connection: Expressive Arts as Healing.* Palo Alto, CA: Science & Behavior Books.
Silverstone, L. (1997) *Art Therapy the Person-Centred Way – Art and the Development of the Person.* London: Jessica Kingsley.
Silverstone, L. (2009) *Art Therapy Exercises: Inspirational and Practical Ideas to Stimulate the Imagination.* London: Jessica Kingsley.

CLASSICAL

As mentioned in the introduction to this chapter, those practitioners who regard themselves as 'classically' person-centred are sometimes referred to by the somewhat pejorative term 'literalist', implying that they do not question the Word of Carl. In fact, the classical tribe has questioned and debated every tenet of Rogers's thinking from the concept of the self to whether the therapeutic conditions are necessary and sufficient; necessary but not sufficient; or sufficient, but not necessarily necessary. This chapter is not long enough to do any more than provide pointers to *some* of these debates – there are more!

The myth of the 'core' conditions

As mentioned in Chapter 1, it was commonplace, in the 1980s and 1990s to hear about the 'core conditions' being necessary and sufficient. Rogers specified six conditions as being necessary and sufficient. The term 'core conditions' was first used by

---

[3]Arnie Mindel's idea that different individuals operate particularly strongly or weakly in verbal, visual, kinaesthetic 'channels' and that good therapy encourages the use of weaker channels, might add to this debate.

Carkhuff, the eclectic theorist, who was trying to identify what common denominators various different approaches might share (1969). Some client-centred practitioners (although not Rogers) began to use the term '*the* core conditions' in relation to empathic understanding, congruence and unconditional positive regard. In 2000 Keith Tudor wrote a spoof on Sherlock Holmes, called 'The Case of the Missing Conditions'. Unfortunately the playful part was not published, but the rest of the article seems to have led to more widespread acknowledgement that there always were six conditions. Tudor (2000) argues that all six conditions 'develop through and with the therapeutic/helping relationship', the degree of psychological contact in any given moment affecting, and being affected, by the verbal and non-verbal dialogue. Similarly, the changing nature of the client's state of incongruence affects the therapist's ability to offer congruent empathy and UPR and congruence, and the client's ability to receive these conditions. The conditions – and the nature of PCT theory – are 'dialogic and, therefore, co-created'. The argument that the therapeutic relationship in PCT therapy is *dialogical* or created by the ways in which we affect each other, is a theme that has also been developed by Peter Schmid.

FURTHER READING

Schmid, P. (2007) 'The anthropological and ethical foundations of person-centred therapy', in M. Cooper, M. O'Hara, P. Schmid and G. Wyatt (eds), *The Handbook of Person-Centred Psychotherapy and Counselling.* Basingstoke: Palgrave Macmillan.

Tudor, K. (2000) 'The case of the missing conditions', *Counselling*, 11(1).

Tudor, K. (2011) 'Rogers' therapeutic conditions: A relational conceptualisation', *Person-Centred and Experiential Psychotherapies*, 10(3).

Tudor, K. and Worral, M. (2006) *Person-Centred Therapy: A Critical Philosophy.* Hove: Routledge.

The 'missing' conditions

Five of the six conditions are considered by various writers in a series published by PCCS Books (Bozarth and Wilkins, 2001; Haugh and Merry, 2001; Wyatt, 2001; Wyatt and Sanders 2002), the details of which are in the 'further reading' section below. Interestingly, only three of the conditions have a volume each dedicated to them (you can guess which ones those are). Conditions one (psychological contact) and six (that the client perceives the therapist's congruent empathy and UPR) share a volume. Condition two, that the client is in a state of incongruence, does not have its own volume and is only addressed in some of the chapters in the volume on contact and perception. Ivan Ellingham's chapter discusses distorted perception (2002). Chapters by Shaké Toukmanian (2002) and by William Whelton and Leslie Greenberg (2002) also relate to perception and incongruence. As Wyatt and Sanders say in their introduction 'Client/person-centred theory, has some way to go to elaborate the detail of client incongruence'.

The current partnership between developmental psychologists and neuroscientists has brought forth knowledge that can nuance our understanding of client incongruence. It shows, for instance, that we are not born with minds and bodies that work in synch, and that if a distressed baby is habitually left to cry instead of being soothed by someone who loves it, the baby's brain will not make the neurological connections that enable us to calm a racing heart once the emergency is over. It has long been recognised that some people have great difficulty in soothing themselves – Margaret Warner calls this 'high intensity fragile process' (see below). The neurological information can help us appreciate that such clients find it *impossible* rather than difficult, and that they may be experiencing an internal incongruence that the therapist is unfamiliar with. I 'got' this when, after working with a client for some time on something that had been causing her huge anxiety, I remarked that she no longer sounded worried. 'I'm not', she replied, 'It is really unlikely to happen, but if it does I know what I'll do'. She paused, looked at me, then said, 'but my heart is still racing'. It was the first time that *either* of us had really appreciated that her body did not settle once her mind was at rest (Cameron, 2012).

Condition one, that the therapist and client experience themselves as being in psychological contact, has had more attention than conditions two and six, especially in recent years. As I have already discussed, above, and in Chapter 7, Garry Prouty has developed a means of working with clients who do not seem to be available for contact. I have also suggested in Chapters 7 and 8 of this book that there are different degrees or kinds of (hopefully simultaneous) contact, including what I have called 'subtle contact'. Mearns (1997) too asserts that there are different degrees of contact. Tudor and Worrall (2006) refute this and also question Wyatt and Sanders' (2002) claim that contact needs to be symbolised in awareness. There has also been discussion of the significance of Rogers using the term 'psychological contact' in one paper, and just 'contact' in the other. Interestingly, in a late, and little known reformulation of the therapeutic conditions he completely omits contact as a condition (Rogers and Sanforth in Kaplan and Sadock, 1984).

FURTHER READING

Bozarth, J. and Wilkins, P. (2001) *Rogers' Therapeutic Conditions: Evolution, Theory and Practice. Vol. 3: Unconditional Positive Regard*. Ross-on-Wye: PCCS Books.

Haugh, S. and Merry, T. (eds) (2001) *Rogers' Therapeutic Conditions: Evolution, Theory and Practice. Vol. 2: Empathy*. Ross-on-Wye: PCCS Books.

Tudor, K. (2011) 'Rogers' therapeutic conditions: A relational conceptualisation', *Person-Centred and Experimental Psychotherapies*, 10(13): 165–80.

Wyatt. G. (ed.) (2001) *Rogers' Therapeutic Conditions: Evolution, Theory and Practice. Vol. 1: Congruence.* Ross-on-Wye: PCCS Books.

Wyatt, G. and Sanders, P. (eds) (2002) *Rogers' Therapeutic Conditions: Evolution, Theory and Practice. Vol. 1: Congruence.* Ross-on-Wye: PCCS Books.

Wyatt, G. and Sanders, P. (eds) (2002) *Rogers' Therapeutic Conditions: Evolution, Theory and Practice. Vol. 4: Contact and Perception.* Ross-on-Wye: PCCS Books.

To be — or to speak? The debate about congruence

One of the most long-standing and unresolved debates within the classical tribe is whether congruence should be implicit – the therapist being aware of her own flow of experience – or explicit – the therapist communicating some of this experience to the client (Tudor and Worrall, 2006). It is certainly the case that Rogers gave more prominence to the concept of congruence towards the end of his working life. Tudor and Worrall (2006) argue that he did so in relation to the person-centred approach rather than person–centred therapy. In arguing the case for implicit rather than explicit congruence, they point out that it would have been easy for Rogers to advocate explicit congruence when he set forth the necessary and sufficient conditions, and that he did not do so. It is certainly the case that Rogers did not do so in the papers in which he originally formulated the conditions for necessary and sufficient therapeutic change.[4] However, Wyatt and Sanders (2002) cite a little known paper, written with Sanford in 1984, in which Rogers reformulates the therapeutic conditions, and does advocate the communication of the therapist's experience. He also adds the client perceiving therapist's 'realness' as well as empathic understanding and UPR in condition six.

Rogers did suggest much earlier than this that it was helpful for the therapist to communicate their own experience, but only in instances in which their experience was interfering with their ability to be empathic and/or unconditionally accepting. This formulation of the therapist verbally communicating their experience if it needs to be acknowledged in order to clear the way to fuller acceptance and empathy is advocated by many PCT theorists – but a more liberal application may often be heard in practice! Tudor and Worrall make a helpful distinction between congruence that is 'self-involving' or comes from the therapist's experience of being in relationship with the client and that which is 'self-disclosing' and introduces information from the therapist's own life outside the therapeutic relationship.

---

[4]The paper published in 1959 was actually written prior to the 1957 paper.

FURTHER READING

Frankel, M. and Sommerbeck, L. (2005) 'Two Rogers and congruence: The emergence of therapist-centered therapy and the demise of client-centered therapy', in B. Levitt, *Embracing Non-Directivity*. Ross-on-Wye: PCCS Books.

Rogers, C.R and Sanford, R.C (1984) 'Client-centered psychotherapy', in H.I. Kaplan and B.J. Sadock (eds), *Comprehensive Textbook of Psychiatry, IV*. Baltimore, MD: Williams and Wilkins Co. pp. 1374–88.

Wyatt. G. (ed.) (2001) *Rogers' Therapeutic Conditions: Evolution, Theory and Practice. Vol. 1: Congruence*. Ross-on-Wye: PCCS Books.

Wyatt, G. and Sanders, P. (eds) (2002) *Rogers' Therapeutic Conditions: Evolution, Theory and Practice. Vol. 4: Contact and Perception*. Ross-on-Wye: PCCS Books.

Necessary and sufficient?

The larger debates as to whether Rogers's six therapeutic conditions (as he formulated them in 1959 and 1957) are necessary and sufficient for therapeutic change are between therapists and researchers from other orientations, and, within the tribe, between the classical and the experiential, existential and integrative tribes. I have already given pointers to the inter-tribe debate, and so the further reading suggested below gives pointers to the debate within the classical tribe.

FURTHER READING

Bozarth, J.D. (1998) *Person-Centered Therapy: A Revolutionary Paradigm*. Ross-on-Wye: PCCS Books.

Bozarth, J.D. (1993) 'Not necessarily necessary but always sufficient', in D. Brazier (ed.), *Beyond Carl Rogers*. London: Constable.

Brazier, D. (1993) 'The necessary condition is love', in D. Brazier (ed.), *Beyond Carl Rogers*. London: Constable. pp. 72–91.

Patterson, C.H. (1982) 'Empathy, warmth and genuiness in psychotherapy: A review of reviews', *Psychotherapy*, 21(4): 431–8.

Purton, C. (2002) 'Person-centred therapy without the core conditions', *CPJ Counselling and Psychotherapy Journal*, 13(2): 6–9.

Quinn, R. (1998) 'Confronting Carl Rogers: A developmental-interactional approach to person-centered therapy', *Journal of Humanistic Psychology*, 33(1): 6–23.

Schmid, P. (2002) 'The necessary and sufficient conditions of being person-centered: On identity, integrity, integration and differentiation of the paradigm', in J.C. Watson, R.N. Goldman and M.S. Warner (eds), *Client-Centered and Experiential Psychotherapy in the 21st Century: Advances in Theory, Research and Practice*. Ross-on-Wye: PCCS Books. pp. 36–51.

Watson, N. (1984) 'The empirical status of Rogers's hypothesis of the necessary and sufficient conditions for effective psychotherapy', in R.F. Levant and J.M. Shlien (eds), *Client-Centered Psychotherapy and the Person-Centered Approach*. New York: Praeger.

Is there another condition? Presence and relational depth

Rogers turned away from his early training in theology in favour of science, and devoted the first part of his career to trying to put PCT on a firm scientific footing. However, experiences that he had at the time of his wife's death left him interested in 'all types of paranormal phenomena' (Rogers, 1980), ready to consider that 'each of us is a continuing spiritual essence lasting over time, and occasionally incarnated in a human body' and 'compelled to believe that I, like many others, have underestimated the importance of this mystical, spiritual dimension'. One particular passage from his later work has attracted particular attention in recent years:

> When I am at my best, as a group facilitator or as a therapist, I discover another characteristic. I find that when I am closest to my inner, intuitive self, when I am somehow in touch with the unknown in me, when perhaps I am in a slightly altered state of consciousness, then whatever I do seems to be full of healing. Then, simply my 'presence' is releasing and helpful to the other. There is nothing I can do to force this experience, but when I can relax and be close to the transcendental core of me, then I may behave in strange and impulsive ways in the relationship, ways which I cannot justify rationally, which have nothing to do with my thought processes. But these strange behaviours turn out to be right, in some odd way: it seems that my spirit has reached out and touched the inner spirit of the other. Our relationship transcends itself and becomes a part of something larger. Profound growth and healing and energy are present. (Rogers, 1980: 129)

This passage has inspired the theorisation of two 'new' therapeutic conditions, Geller and Greenberg's 'presence' (2002) and Mearns and Cooper's 'relational depth' (2005). Geller and Greenberg and Mearns and Cooper arrive at the same conclusion – that 'presence' and 'relational depth' happen as a result of the client perceiving the therapist's congruence, empathy and UPR. However, the two different conceptualisations are indicative of a tension in the PCT community, that (at least in print) has not been fully debated since Van Belle's opening gambit (1990), which argued against Rogers's turn from scientific rationality towards mysticism. Van Belle is not alone in being uncomfortable with Rogers's interest in spirituality and mysticism. Although they refer to the above passage, Mearns and Cooper do not discuss it in relation to the context of Rogers's appreciation of the mystical. The categories that arise from Cooper's research into relational depth fit solidly into the rational materialist humanist tradition. Geller and Greenberg, on the other hand, and McMillan (2004), discuss presence in the context of the practitioners' spiritual practices, and I have offered an understanding using the concept of the 'subtle body' (Cameron, 2002) which I am currently reworking and developing.

FURTHER READING

Cooper, M. (2005) 'Therapists' experiences of relational depth: A qualitative interview study', *Counselling and Psychotherapy Research*, 5(2): 87–95.
Geller, S. and Greenberg, L. (2002) 'Therapeutic presence: Therapists' experience of presence in the psychotherapy encounter', *Person-Centered and Experiential Psychotherapies,* 1(1 & 2): 71–86.
Greenberg, L.S. and Geller, S.M. (2001) 'Congruence and therapeutic presence', in G. Wyatt, *Rogers' Therapeutic Conditions: Evolution, Theory and Practice. Vol. 1: Congruence.* Ross-on-Wye: PCCS Books.
Mearns, D. (1996) 'Working at relational depth with clients in person-centred therapy', *Counselling,* 7(4): 306–11.
Mearns, D. and Cooper, M. (2005) *Working at Relational Depth in Counselling and Psychotherapy.* London: Sage.
Schmid, P. (2002) 'Presence: Im-media-te co-experiencing and co-responding. Phenomenological, dialogical and ethical perspectives on contact and perception in person-centred therapy and beyond', in G. Wyatt and P. Sanders (eds), *Rogers' Therapeutic Conditions: Evolution, Theory and Practice. Vol. 4: Contact and Perception.* Ross-on-Wye: PCCS Books. pp. 182–203.

Configurations of self

Mearns and Thorne (2000a and b) suggest that the PCT theory can be usefully updated by replacing the idea of a unitary or single self with an inherently pluralistic or multiple self. This is, perhaps, the most radical revision of person-centred theory to date. They propose a model of many different 'configurations of self' that respond to different situations. Some of these configurations arise from the self-structure, and may be 'not for growth'. They present their concept of 'not for growth' configurations in the context of objecting to Rogers's promotion, from 1969 onwards, of the actualising tendency at the expense of the self-structure ('self-structure', 'self-concept' and 'self' tend to be used synonymously in PCT literature), and encourage therapists to value and empathise with these 'not for growth' parts.

Tolan (2002) also argues that the self-structure has a protective function and she too warns against imposing the spirit of 1969 on clients who have to live in a world that is usually not unconditionally accepting. However, Tolan conceptualises social adaptation and the self-structure as a manifestation of the *actualising tendency* towards self-preservation, as do Tudor and Worrall (2006) who challenge the popular misconception of a 'real' self that may be at odds with the self-structure, and instead emphasise the organismic process. The ramifications of Mearns and Thorne's proposal that PCT exchange a model of a single self for a model of multiple selves has not been much debated, and is perhaps a discussion that will emerge more fully in the future.

FURTHER READING

Cooper, M., Mearns, D., Stiles, W.B., Warner, M. and Elliott, R. (2004) 'Developing self-pluralistic perspectives within the person-centered and experiential approaches: A round table dialogue', *Person-Centered and Experiential Psychotherapies*, 3(3): 176–91.

Mearns, D. (2002a) 'Theoretical propositions in regard to self theory within person-centred therapy', *Person-Centered and Experiential Psychotherapies*, 1(1 & 2): 14–27.

Mearns, D. and Thorne, B. (2000b) *Person-Centred Therapy Today: New Frontiers in Theory and Practice.* London: Sage.

APPLICATIONS

This section briefly introduces some applications of PCT with particular client groups.

Psychopathology

The talking therapies have been increasingly drawn into medical culture over some time. The health service is a major employer of counsellors and sometimes there is pressure to describe clients, and counselling, in medicalised terms. This is a dilemma since one of the distinctive features of PCT is that it does not pathologise psychological difficulties. The titles of two papers (in the same book!) succinctly express the dilemma. One is Pete Sanders's, 'Principles and strategic opposition to the medicalisation of distress and all its apparatus' (2005) the other is Stephen Joseph and Richard Worsley's 'Psychopathology and the person–centred approach: building bridges between disciplines' (2005). Joseph and Worsley's *Person-Centred Psychopathology* contains 23 papers on PCT and psychopathology. David Cain's *Classics in the Person-Centered Approach: The best of the 'Person-Centered Review'* contains a further five. The issue is also addressed by Elke Lambers and Dion Van Werde in the second edition of Mearns's *Developing Person-Centred Counselling* (2003).

Some practitioners recognise the features of particular mental 'illnesses', but conceptualise them as a response to circumstances rather than an illness. Margaret Warner is particularly well known for her work with clients who experience what she calls 'difficult processes'. Although Warner's work on 'dissociated process' may seem very similar to Mearns' and Thorne's configurations of self in that both work with 'parts' of the self, the two concepts are very different. Warner is not proposing a fundamental change in the way PCT conceptualises the self, and is clear that dissociative process comes about as the result of trauma, rather than being 'normal' development that Mearns and Thorne are concerned with. One of the distinguishing features of Warner's dissociated process is that some 'parts' do not know about other 'parts' and the client experiences extended lapses in memory when certain 'parts' are in control. Ross's article (1999), further explores the differences between the two concepts. In terms of practice, it is the similarities between the two concepts that are perhaps the most important in that Warner, and Mearns and Thorne all emphasise the importance of offering the therapeutic conditions to *all* dissociated parts or configurations of self.

Warner also writes about work with clients who are unable to moderate the intensity of their feelings. Given that the therapeutic task for so many clients (and trainees!) is to allow themselves to experience their feelings fully, the idea that we ought to moderate or 'regulate' the intensity of our feelings may seem strange. It would also be inaccurate since the kind of emotional regulation Warner writes about is an essential ability rather than a response to a demand. The ability to regulate our emotions enables us to soothe ourselves after we have been upset, to calm down after the emergency is over, or maximise pleasant feelings. Warner draws on work by developmental psychologists that shows this ability to be something that we develop (or not) depending on how we are responded to as children. Warner writes about working with clients who have not developed this ability, and describes those who cannot turn the volume of their feelings down as being in 'high intensity' fragile process, and those who cannot turn it up as being in 'low intensity' fragile process.

Warner also writes about clients who experience hallucinations, as does Van Werde (2002a, 2002b, 2005). Van Werde's work in making contact with people who seem to be out of touch with consensus reality is embedded in Prouty's pre-therapy work (which is discussed in some detail in Chapter 7). As I mentioned earlier, some theorists consider the pre-therapy a tribe, and the fact that Van Werde and others are developing the theory and practice of pre-therapy may indeed lead to it being more widely regarded a tribe in its own right.

FURTHER READING

Cain, D. (2002) *Classics in the Person-Centered Approach: The Best of the Person-Centered Review.* Ross-on-Wye: PCCS Books.
Joseph, S. and Worsley, R. (eds) (2005) *Person-Centred Psychopathology: A Positive Psychology of Mental Health.* Ross-on-Wye: PCCS Books.
Joseph, S. and Worsley, R. (eds) (2007) *Person-Centred Practice: Case Studies in Positive Psychology.* Ross-on-Wye: PCCS Books.

Mearns, D. (2003) *Developing Person-Centred Counselling.* London: Sage.

Prouty, G. (2001) 'Humanistic psychotherapy for people with schizophrenia', in D.J. Cain and J. Seeman (eds), *Humanistic Therapies: Handbook of Research and Practice.* Washington, DC: American Psychological Association.

Prouty, G. (2002) 'The practice of pre-therapy', in G. Wyatt and P. Sanders (eds), *Rogers' Therapeutic Conditions: Evolution, Theory and Practice. Vol. 4: Contact and Perception.* Ross-on-Wye: PCCS Books. pp. 63–75.

Prouty, G. (2002) 'Pre-therapy as a theoretical system', in G. Wyatt and P. Sanders (eds), *Rogers' Therapeutic Conditions: Evolution, Theory and Practice. Vol. 4: Contact and Perception.* Ross-on-Wye: PCCS Books. pp. 54–62.

Prouty, G. (ed.) (2008) *Emerging Developments in Pre-Therapy: A Pre-Therapy Reader.* Ross-on-Wye: PCCS Books.

Prouty, G., Van Werde, D. and Pörtner, M. (2002) *Pre-therapy.* Ross-on-Wye: PCCS Books.

Ross, C.A. (1999) 'Sub-personalities and multiple personalities: A dissociative continuum?', in J. Rowan and M. Cooper (eds), *The Plural Self.* London: Sage.

Sanders, P. (2007) *The Contact Work Primer: An Introduction to Pre-Therapy and the Work of Garry Prouty.* Ross-on-Wye: PCCS Books.

Schmid, P. F. (2005) 'Authenticity and alienation: Towards an understanding of the person beyond the categories of order and disorder', in S. Joseph and R. Worsley (eds), *Person-Centred Psychopathology: A Positive Psychology of Mental Health.* Ross-on-Wye: PCCS Books. pp. 75–90.

Sommerbeck, L. (2003) *The Client-Centred Therapist in Psychiatric Contexts: A Therapists' Guide to the Psychiatric Landscape and its Inhabitants.* Ross-on-Wye: PCCS Books.

Warner, M. (2000) 'Client-centered therapy at the difficult edge: Work with fragile and dissociated process', in D. Mearns and B. Thorne (eds), *Person-Centered Therapy Today: New Frontiers in Theory and Practice.* Thousand Oaks: Sage.

Warner, M. (2007) 'Lukes's process: A positive view of schizophrenic thought disorder', in S. Joseph and R. Worsley (eds), *Person-Centred Practice: Case Studies in Positive Psychology.* Ross-on-Wye: PCCS Books.

Children and young people

Those who work with children and young people have a particular experience of the tensions and debates which are current in PCT. Behr and Cornelius-White (2008) take up the question of whether therapists working with children should create a safe environment and then stay out of their client's way (see Axline, 1964/1967) or create a more dialogical relationship in which the therapist is more engaged. The toys, crayons, glitter, and other expressive materials offered by many therapists who work with children are open to the same questions as the expressive materials used by Natalie Rogers. The underlying question in becoming more actively engaged or offering non-verbal ways of working concerns the power balance between the two individuals working together. The question of how children and young people are affected by the power that adults and systems have over them is particularly acute when responding to the fact that children's behaviour is becoming increasingly pathologised. PCT theory seems to be particularly well placed to resist the view of children and young people who live with emotionally difficult circumstances as either 'delinquent' or 'disordered'.

FURTHER READING

Keys, S.E. and Walshaw, T. (eds) (2008) *Person-Centred Work with Children and Young People: UK Practitioner Perspectives*. Ross-on-Wye: PCCS Books.
Prever, M. (2010) *Counselling and Supporting Children and Young People: A Person-Centred Approach*. London: Sage.
Romm, M. and Escher, S. (2010) *Children Hearing Voices: What You Need To Know and What You Can Do*. Ross-on-Wye: PCCS Books.

CONCLUSION

There will, of course, be further debates and developments in the future. It is impossible to know what those will be, but I offer one prediction and one hope. My prediction is that more will be written about PCT in the context of the recent partnership between developmental psychologists and neuroscientists. This body of work shows that much of our brain develops after birth. How – and whether – our brain develops is very much dependent on how we are responded to during vital windows of growth. There is much in this body of evidence that confirms PC theory. I discuss the implications of some of this work in a chapter on the person-centred approach to self-injury (Tolan and Wilkins, 2012) and Michael Lux (2010) suggests PCT is confirmed to such a degree that it might be regarded as a meta-theory for integrating neuroscientific findings into psychotherapy.

My hope for future developments is that we begin to distinguish between the elements of PCT that might be thought of as universally applicable, and those that are specific to North American culture from the 1950s onwards. My view is that although I believe congruent unconditional acceptance and empathic understanding to be something that all humans respond positively to regardless of culture, these attitudes are symbolised very differently in different places and at different times. Abstaining from advice-giving, for example, may be understood by one client as an expression of respect, an acknowledgement of their capacity and right to make their own decisions, but may be experienced by another as a lack of care for them, and even a withholding of something they have a right to expect. Given that Rogers lived, worked and thought in a culture that values independence and autonomy very highly it is unsurprising that PCT practitioners also value independence and autonomy and promote these values. Respect, commitment, empathy and love are expressed differently in cultures that value the inter-dependence of hierarchical structures. That there may be a mismatch between what a therapist intends to convey and what the clients understands is of concern in our multi-cultural society. It is also of concern as PCT, albeit often in a very diluted form, is exported to countries that think about human relationships in a very different way.

There has been much creative development within all the tribes of the person-centred nation, but relatively little dialogue between them. This has begun to change. More books are being published that bring together contributions from different tribes, and the World Association for Person-Centred and Experiential Psychotherapy and Counseling, established in 1997, publishes a journal that 'seeks to create a dialogue among different parts of the person-centred tradition, to support, inform and challenge each other and to stimulate their creativity and impact in a broader professional, scientific and political context' (see www.pce-world. org). However, the attitude still held by many (but not all) person-centred practitioners towards colleagues in other therapeutic modalities is an area that still needs to be worked upon. This attitude – and it seems to me to be in many cases a true prejudice in that it arises from ignorance – has been depressingly apparent as I've been re-reading some of the literature referred to in this chapter. I have, for example, come across prominent writers in widely respected training literature promoting the idea that psychodynamic practitioners must be motivated by a need for power. On the contrary, psychodynamic colleagues are also concerned to not abuse their power, and many would argue that PCT's reluctance to recognise transference when it arises (see p. 169 for an example) puts person-centred practitioners at risk of not fully recognising clients' vulnerability.

Stereotyping and taking the high moral ground in relation to those who have a different set of beliefs is not congruent with the ethical values of PCT. It is, of course, important to recognise our differences, but unnecessary to make ill-informed judgements on the basis of these differences. Rogers developed many of his ideas and attitudes in reaction against his early psychoanalytic training and the approach developed alongside – and in competition with – cognitive-behavioural therapy. All emerging groups establishing their identities initially define themselves in terms of how they differ from other groups, and so it is not surprising that early practitioners put emphasis on the ways in which PCT is different from other approaches. Person-centred therapy is no longer newly emerging, and our maturity is evident in the debates contained in this chapter. We have reached a stage in which we are able to consider theory and practice in terms of its coherence, consistency and its philosophy and to develop the positions held by Rogers and his colleagues. We are increasingly able to recognise areas of similarity with others and respect difference, or sometimes even recognise that the most glaring differences are usually different expressions of a broad similarity. It is time for us to fully let go of the tendency to define ourselves in terms of what we do not do rather than what we do and to appreciate rather than react against other perspectives.

Political and economic forces are threatening to augment divisions and competition amongst the many different kinds of therapy that exist today. It is heartening that, against such a threatening and prejudice-inducing background an article promoting 'pluralism' has been extremely well received. Mick Cooper and John McLeod (2010) (members of the 'nation') make a distinction between pluralism as a *practice* and pluralism as a *perspective*. Pluralism as a practice draws upon a range of therapeutic methods and concepts. Pluralism as a *perspective* enables us to appreciate and work alongside other therapeutic approaches without compromising our own.

Developing an empathic understanding for other therapeutic approaches, and being able to speak about them knowledgeably and respectfully is, I believe, having a positive effect on how others see us as well as upon how we see them. It enables us to take up Cooper and McLeod's call for a recognition that clients may be best served if the therapeutic community as a whole were more able to recognise the validity of different strokes for different folks, and different strokes for the same folks at different times. I began this chapter giving a brief account of how the person-centred approach became fractured: I end with the suggestion that it is time to extend genuine empathic understanding and unconditional acceptance to our colleagues within and outside the approach.

ACKNOWLEDGEMENT

Thanks to Jo Hilton for her reading and feedback.

REFERENCES

Axline, V. (1964/1997) *Dibs: In Search of Self*. New York: Galantine.

Baker, N. (2004) 'Experiential person-centred therapy', in P. Sanders (ed.), *The Tribes of the Person-Centred Nation: A Guide to Schools of Therapy Related to the Person-Centred Approach*. Ross-on-Wye: PCCS Books.

Behr, M. and Cornelius-White, J. (eds) (2008) *Facilitating Young Peoples Development – International Perspectives on Person-centred Theory and Practice*. Ross-on-Wye: PCCS Books.

Cain, D. (2002) *Classics in the Person-Centered Approach: The Best of the* Person-Centered Review. Ross-on-Wye: PCCS Books.

Cameron, R. (2002) 'In the space between', in G. Wyatt and P. Sanders, *Rogers' Therapeutic Conditions: Evolution, Theory and Practice. Vol. 4: Contact and Perception*. Ross-on-Wye: PCCS Books.

Cameron, R. (2012) 'A person-centred perspective on self-injury', in J. Tolan and P. Wilkins (eds), *Client Issues in Counselling and Psychotherapy: Person-Centred Practice*. London: Sage.

Carkhuff, R.R. (1969) *Helping and Human Relations. Vol. II: Practice and Research*. New York: Holt, Rinehart and Winston.

Cooper, M. and McLeod, J. (2010) 'Pluralism', *Therapy Today*, 21(9).

Ellingham, I. (2002) 'Madness and mysticism in perceiving the other: Towards a radical organismic, person-centred interpretation', in G. Wyatt and P. Sanders, *Rogers' Therapeutic Conditions: Evolution, Theory and Practice. Vol. 4: Contact and Perception*. Ross-on-Wye: PCCS Books.

Geller, S. and Greenberg, L. (2002) 'Therapeutic "presence": Therapists' experience of "presence" in the psychotherapy encounter', *Person Centred and Experiential Psychotherapies*, 1(1&2): 71–86.

Gendlin, E.T. (1962) *Experiencing and the Creation of Meaning*. New York: Free Press.

Gendlin, E.T. (1998) *Focusing-Oriented Psychotherapy: A Manual of the Experiential Method (Practising Professional)*. New York: Guilford Press.

Gendlin, E.T. (2003) *Focusing: How to Open Up Your Deeper Feelings and Intuition*. London: Rider & Co.

Hinterkopf, E. (2008) *Integrating Spirituality in Counseling: A Manual for using the Experiential Focusing Method*. Ross-on Wye: PCCS Books.

Inskipp, F. and Proctor, B. (1995) *The Art, Craft and Tasks of Supervision*. London: Cascade.

Joseph, S. and Worsley, R. (eds) (2005) *Person-Centred Psychopathology: A Positive Psychology of Mental Health*. Ross-on-Wye: PCCS Books.

Kaplan, H.I. and Sadock, B.J. (eds) (1984) *Comprehensive Textbook of Psychiatry, IV*. Baltimore: Williams and Wilkins Co.

Lux, M. (2010) 'The magic of encounter: The person-centered approach and the neurosciences', *Person-Centered and Experiential Psychotherapies*, 9(4): 274–89.

May, R. (1961) *Existential Psychology*. New York: Random House.

McMillan, M. (2004) *The Person-Centred Approach to Therapeutic Change*. London: Sage.

Mearns, D. (1996) 'Working at relational depth with clients in person centred therapy', *Counselling*, 7(4): 306–11.

Mearns, D. (1997) *Person-Centred Counselling Training*. London: Sage.

Mearns, D. (2003) *Developing Person-Centred Counselling*. London: Sage.

Mearns, D. and Cooper, M. (2005) *Working at Relational Depth in Counselling and Psychotherapy*. London: Sage.

Mearns, D. and Thorne, B. (2000a) *Person-Centred Therapy Today. New Frontiers in Theory and Practice*. London: Sage.

Mearns, D. and Thorne, B. (2000b) 'The nature of configurations within self', in D. Mearns and B. Thorne (eds), *Person-Centred Therapy Today*. London: Sage.

Merry, T. (2002) '*Process Work in Person-Centred Therapy* by Richard Worsley – A review article', *Person-Centred Practice*, 10(1): 49–55.

Proust, M. (1996) *Swann's Way. Vol. 1: In Search of Lost Time*. London: Vintage.

Prouty, G.F. (1990) 'Pre-therapy: A theoretical evolution in the person-centered/experiential psychotherapy of schizophrenia and retardation', in G. Lietaer, J. Rombauts and R. Van Balen (eds), *Client-Centered and Experiential Psychotherapy in the Nineties*. Leuven: Leuven University Press. pp. 645–58.

Prouty, G. (ed.) (2008) *Emerging Developments in Pre-Therapy: A Pre-Therapy Reader*. Ross-on-Wye: PCCS.

Purton, C. (2007) *The Focusing Orientated Counselling Primer*. Ross-on-Wye: PCCS Books.

Rennie, D. (1998) *Person-Centred Counselling: An Experiential Approach*. London: Sage.

Rogers, C.R. (1951) *Client-Centered Therapy*. London: Constable.

Rogers, C.R. (1957) 'The necessary and sufficient conditions for therapeutic personality change', *Journal of Consulting Psychology*, 21: 95–103.

Rogers, C.R. (1959) 'A theory of therapy, personality, and interpersonal relations as developed in the client-centered framework', in S. Koch (ed.), *Psychology: A Study of Science. Vol. III*. New York: McGraw-Hill. pp. 184–256.

Rogers, C. (1961) *On Becoming a Person*. London: Constable.

Rogers, C. (1978) *Carl Rogers on Personal Power*. London: Constable.

Rogers, C. (1980) *A Way of Being*. New York: Houghton Mifflin.

Rogers, C. (c. 1986) 'A client-centered/person-centered approach to therapy' in I. Kutash and A. Wolf (eds), *Psychotherapist's Casebook*. San Francisco: Jossey-Bass. pp. 197–208.

Rogers, C.R. and Sanford, R.C. (1984) 'Client-centered psychotherapy', in H.I. Kaplan and B.J. Sadock (eds), *Comprehensive Textbook of Psychiatry, IV*. Baltimore: Williams and Wilkins Co. pp. 137–88; cited by G. Wyatt in 'Introduction to the series' in G. Wyatt and P. Sanders (2002) *Rogers' Therapeutic Conditions:*

Evolution, Theory and Practice. Vol. 4: Contact and Perception. Ross-on-Wye: PCCS Books.

Ross, C.A. (1999) 'Sub-personalities and multiple personalities: A dissociative continuum?', in J. Rowan and M. Cooper (eds), *The Plural Self.* London: Sage.

Rutter, P. (1989) *Sex in the Forbidden Zone.* London: Mandala.

Sanders, P. (ed.) (2004) *The Tribes of the Person-Centred Nation: An Introduction to the Schools of Therapy Associated with the Person-Centred Approach.* Ross-on-Wye: PCCS Books.

Sanders, P. (2005) 'Principles and strategic opposition to the medicalisation of distress and all its apparatus', in S. Joseph and R. Worsley (eds), *Person-Centred Psychopathology: A Positive Psychology of Mental Health.* Ross-on-Wye: PCCS Books. pp. 21–42.

Stapert, M. and Verliefde, E. (2008) *Focusing with Children: The Art of Communicating with Children at School and at Home.* Ross-on Wye: PCCS Books.

Tannen, D. (1992) *You Just Don't Understand.* London: Virago.

Tolan, J. (2002) 'The fallacy of the "real" self', in J. Watson, R. Goldman and M. Warner (eds), *Client-Centred and Experiential Psychotherapy in the 21st Century.* Ross-on-Wye: PCCS Books.

Tolan, J. and Wilkins, P. (2012) *Client Issues in Counselling and Psychotherapy: Person-Centred Practice.* London: Sage.

Toukmanian, S. (2002) 'Perception in person-centered and experiential psychotherapies', in G. Wyatt and P. Sanders, *Rogers' Therapeutic Conditions: Evolution, Theory and Practice. Vol. 4: Contact and Perception.* Ross-on-Wye: PCCS Books.

Truax, C.B. and Carkhuff, R. (2008) *Toward Effective Counseling and Psychotherapy: Training and Practice.* Chicago: Aldine.

Tudor, K. (2000) 'The case of the missing conditions', *Counselling,* 11(1).

Tudor, K. and Worrall, M. (2006) *Person-Centred Therapy: A Clinical Philosophy.* London: Routledge.

Van Belle, H.A. (1990) 'Rogers' later move towards mysticism: Implications for client centred therapy', in G. Lietaer, J. Rombauts and R. Van Balen (eds), *Client Centred and Experiential Psychotherapy in the Nineties.* Leuven: Leuven University Press.

Van Ekeren, G. (1988) *The Speaker's Sourcebook.* London: Longman.

Van Werde, D. (2002a) 'Prouty's pre-therapy and contact-work with a broad range of persons' pre-expressive functioning', in G. Wyatt and P. Sanders (eds), *Rogers' Therapeutic Conditions: Evolution, Theory and Practice. Vol. 4: Contact and Perception.* Ross-on-Wye: PCCS Books. pp. 168–81.

Van Werde, D. (2002b) 'The falling man: Pre-therapy applied to somatic hallucinating', *Person-Centred Practice,* 10(2): 101–7.

Van Werde, D. (2005) 'Facing psychotic functioning: Person-centred contact work in residential care', in S. Joseph and R. Worsley (eds), *Person-Centred Psychopathology: A Positive Psychology of Mental Health.* Ross-on-Wye: PCCS Books. pp. 158–68.

Warner, M.S. (1998/1999) 'Person-centered psychotherapy: One nation, many tribes', in C. Wolter-Gustafson (ed.), *A Person-Centered Reader: Personal Selections by our Members.* Boston Association for the Development of the

Person-Centered Approach. Reprinted in Warner, M. (2000) 'Person-centered psychotherapy: One nation, many tribes', *The Person-Centered Journal*, 7(1): 28–39.

Warner, M. (2000) 'Person-centred therapy at the difficult edge', in D. Mearns and B. Thorne (eds), *Person-Centred Therapy Today*. London: Sage. pp. 144–71.

Warner, M. (2002) 'Pychological contact, meaningful process and human nature', in G. Wyatt and P. Sanders (eds), *Rogers' Therapeutic Conditions: Evolution, Theory and Practice. Vol. 4: Contact and Perception*. Ross-on-Wye: PCCS Books.

Whelton, W. and Greenberg, L. (2002) 'Psychological contact as dialogical construction', in G. Wyatt and P. Sanders, *Rogers' Therapeutic Conditions: Evolution, Theory and Practice. Vol. 4: Contact and Perception*. Ross-on-Wye: PCCS Books.

Wilson, J.Q. (1998) *The Moral Sense*. New York: Free Press.

Worsley, R. (2004) 'Integrating with integrity', in P. Sanders, *The Tribes of the Person-Centred Nation: A Guide to the Schools of Therapy Related to the Person-Centred Approach*. Ross-on-Wye: PCCS Books. pp. 125–48.

Wyatt, G. and Sanders, P. (2002) *Rogers' Therapeutic Conditions: Evolution, Theory and Practice. Vol. 4: Contact and Perception*. Ross-on-Wye: PCCS Books.

INDEX